THE
PRINCE
AND THE
KING

Also by Michael Gurian

As the Swans Gather
The Odyssey of Telemachus

THE PRINCE AND THE KING

Healing the Father-Son Wound
A Guided Journey of Initiation

MICHAEL GURIAN

Foreword by
DOUGLAS GILLETTE AND ROBERT MOORE

Jeremy P. Tarcher/Putnam
a member of
Penguin Putnam Inc.
New York

For my parents,
Jay P. and Julia M. Gurian,
and for
The Herzog Family

"Poem for My Father at 85 after Cross-Country Skiing with My Nephew, Marlon, Age 7" by Michael Blumenthal is copyright Michael Blumenthal, 1992. From *The Wages of Goodness* (University of Missouri Press, 1992). First published in *The Nation*, 1990.

Jeremy P. Tarcher/Putnam
a member of
Penguin Putnam Inc.
375 Hudson Street
New York, NY 10014
www.penguinputnam.com

Jeremy P. Tarcher, Inc.
5858 Wilshire Blvd., Suite 200
Los Angeles, CA 90036

Library of Congress Cataloging-in-Publication Data

Gurian, Michael.
    The prince and the king : healing the father-son wound, a guided journey of initiation / Michael Gurian.
        p.   cm.
    Includes bibliographical references.
    ISBN 0-87477-742-9
    1. Fathers—Psychology.   2. Fathers and sons.   3. Archetype (Psychology)   4. Masculinity (Psychology)   I. Title.
HQ756.G87   1992   92-4430   CIP
306.874′2—dc20

Design by Lee Fukui
Cover design by Eric Handel
Cover illustration © by Thom Sevalrud

Printed in the United States of America
    2   3   4   5   6   7   8   9   10

This book is printed on acid-free paper.
                ∞

Contents

Acknowledgments

This book could not have been written without the support of Michael B. Herzog, Rod Stackelberg, Leonard Butters, Linda Whittenberg, Allen Peery, Julia Bjordahl and Sandy Hank, Henriette Klauser, William H. Houff, Aykut Misirligil, Sally Green, Jim Connor, Chris Harding, Terry Trueman, Alan Rinzler (my editor, who helped me more than I can really say to make this book into something of which I am very proud), Gabrielle, and Gail, my beautiful and constant companion.

Special thanks to Robert Moore and Douglas Gillette, whose work has been essential as I developed my own theory and practice, especially with the King archetype. Their *King, Warrior, Magician, Lover*, as well as Robert Moore's individual tapes, *Rediscovering Masculine Potentials*, provided me with research and metaphor that greatly enriched my book.

My teachers, especially those who have helped me understand men as mythic heroes, have been crucial to my own growth and the growth of my work. In ways I cannot ever adequately trace, pieces of their work appear in my own. Chief among them are Shepherd Bliss, Robert Bly, Joseph Campbell, James Hillman, Robert Johnson, Sam Keen, John Lee, Michael Meade, George Taylor, and Doug Von Koss. My thanks to all these men.

Thanks to my Native American teachers, Red Cloud for his oral teaching and Hyemeyohsts Storm for his written teaching; to practitioners of Shamanic traditions Jim McNeill and Steve Koffman. My special thanks to the Southern Ute tribe and to my father for first introducing me as a young boy to Native American tradition.

This book was deeply influenced by the work of John Bradshaw, Alice Miller, Jean Shinoda Bolen, Anne Wilson-Schaef,

Daniel Wakefield, Joseph Palmour, Linda Schierse Leonard, Sam Osherson, Steven Foster, and Jim Sniechowski. My thanks for all your good work.

Special thanks are due David Feinstein and Stanley Krippner, whose ground-breaking *Personal Mythology* has helped men and women look inward for wisdom and growth. Two of their guided meditations have influenced forms I've used in Part 2 of this book.

In the end, all written and oral efforts to seek the father would be impossible without the courage of individual men (and the families and friends who stand by them), men who discover and embrace their father-son wound, explore it, deny it, find it again, live it, grieve it; men who write letters home to father, now aged; men who call their father on the phone and try to set up camping trips with him, who still face his fear and rejection ("Son, can't you just let the past be?") and hate him and love him and hate him again and then, finally, after months and years and decades, make a journey of deep forgiveness toward him—forgiveness even as he resists, even as he is indifferent; forgiveness even after he is dead.

To these men, many of whom have allowed me to help them make the journey of initiation, my deepest thanks.

Foreword

Men are gradually awakening to their ancient heritage. All over the United States, Europe, Australia, and other parts of the world, men are moving to reclaim the realms of feeling, of the instinctual male animal at their cores, and of a uniquely masculine spirituality. The centuries-long abdication of masculine fullness of being is gradually coming to an end as men begin to take up their swords and scepters, their magician's staves, and reaffirm their phallic joy, first in their inner worlds of archetypal potentials and resources, and then in the public sphere.

The "men's work" many men are now doing—from New Warrior Training to mythopoetic insight and expression, from psychotherapeutic process to a reappropriation of initiatory rites and symbols from traditional cultures, from the grieving of father-wounds to the re-fathering and re-brothering that major men's events and grassroots ritual/support/therapy groups offer—is shifting the center of gravity of ManSoul, and offering our societies, and even our planet, a real chance for survival.

Erik Erikson's Generative Man concept, a contemporary formulation of the ancient sacred kingship mythologies and traditions, is lifting up for men today an old/new vision of the wholeness, the fullness, the depth and richness that every man can embody in his own life. The decoding of the dynamics and structures of the male Self, of the core of the male psyche, which those kingship traditions have expressed, is becoming normative throughout the so-called "men's movement" through the bio-psychological terms of King, Warrior, Magician, and Lover. We have delineated these terms in our five-book series, and our theories in large part form a basis for this book.

The Warrior, the Magician, and the Lover can be found in their most primitive forms in the deepest layers of the human brain—the reptilian brain and in the limbic system. Even the archetypal program for the King seems to have its origins in these ancient structures. In the human brain, these rich potentials for full masculine living and being become elaborated in the cerebral cortex. At the heart of the male Soul, thus engendered, lives the King—imaged as Father-Moon, Father-Sun, Father-Earth, Father-Ocean, Father-God throughout the mythic heritages of virtually all peoples in all places and times.

Michael Gurian, in *The Prince and the King*, has used our research on the four foundational archetypes of the mature masculine—all centered around the King in his fullness—and made it more practical and immediate for every man to access his inner King. He has brilliantly combined one of the driving forces that powers men's work—the wound at the hand of the fathers, whether through abuse or absence—with the quest, conscious or unconscious, for the true inner King. He has also lifted up the intermediary archetype which lies in a developmental line between the archetypes of the Divine Child and the fully manifested King, and shown the relationship between the Prince and the King, which is so much a part of every teenage boy's life.

Michael's understanding of this relationship is interwoven with and grounded in the real-life pains and triumphs of contemporary men, who are struggling to consolidate a uniquely male sense of Self, who are searching for a sense of meaning in their lives, and who are hungering for an ultimately spiritual vision of generativity which can enable them to lead lives of empowered benevolence. Along the way, he rightly lifts up the much neglected truth that men do not need to become more like women; instead, they need to become more like men—men in the fullness of their being!

Michael's work is a deepening of the contemporary application of the King potential in every man. As such, it is a blessing for every man who reads it and who walks through the exercises presented throughout.

The wounds we have suffered, including the father-wound, are healable. No man needs to walk alone. No man needs to feel cut off from his own realistic greatness. No man needs to live exiled from the King!

Douglas M. Gillette
Robert L. Moore
Chicago, Illinois
May, 1992

Introduction

*I've heard one statement over and over from American
males, which has been phrased in a hundred different ways:
"There is not enough father."*

ROBERT BLY

Many men in our culture, like bewildered orphans, struggle
in search of their fathers—those men who seem to float around
us, yet never quite embrace us. They lead our cities and coun-
tries with awesome vigor, yet sit at home in silent, half-hidden
spaces. These men need their sons and their sons need them,
and neither knows the other's true language. Our fathers have
done what their fathers taught them to do—touch their sons in
punishment, see their sons from a distance, teach their sons to
feel as little as possible.

As it may have been for many of you, it was surprising to
me when almost a decade ago I realized I had within me a
wound, a source of weakness, shame, codependence, and grief,
that I had received at the hands of my father. I was also surprised to find that, in order to move forward into a fulfilling life,
I had to recover from that wound.

In my boyhood I was like the biblical Isaac. At times that I
no longer remembered, I had lain under my father's knife. My
father, my Abraham, had actually cut me, and cut me in my
deep heart's core. My father was a man of his generation. He
provided for his children's upbringing, but it was difficult for
him to be emotionally close. His shaming and distance left me
with a wound that affected my relationships with girlfriends,
male friends, then my wife and new family. Like most men, I
came to resign myself to these effects. In some deep place inside

myself, I came to have a profound distrust of the world, of people who come close to me, of other men, and of myself.

I resigned myself to a distrust that was, at root, a distrust of manhood. Therefore I had never been able to say with confidence and with authenticity that I was a man, a man who owned a place in any circle of men. Grown-up for almost twenty years, in my secret heart's core I knew myself as a male adult, but not yet a loving, wise, and powerful *man*. It was not until I realized my father had also lived his life with this feeling that I knew where to begin my journey.

The father-son wound is not the only source of troubles in a man's life, but it is one of the most profound. When we realize that wound, we realize to what extent fulfilling love and rich solitude depend on a sense of personal manhood defined from deep within our strengths, not from our wounds and the external stereotypes we use to fill the wounds. We must also realize that our healthy manhood depends on making genuine peace with the wounded and disengaged father inside us. Only upon realizing this can we begin to lick the wound, and no longer press at it daily till we wail. Only then can we begin to seek profound recovery and a new self-confidence.

The healing is a long process and a long journey. The book you are holding invites you to make that journey. *The Prince and the King* assumes that most of our fathers tried their best to raise us well, but that they were overworked, overtired, and not trained in intimacy. This book acknowledges that much of what we went through with our fathers our sisters also went through. While this book focuses on the father-son relationship, it is offered to women as well as men. I believe women will gain from it information, insight, and process that they will recognize and find beneficial. I also acknowledge that many of us may not even have lived with our fathers, that many of us lived with substitute fathers who could not supply us with the intimacy we needed. And this book assumes that many of our fathers are now dead or disengaged men who cannot really help us do the deep work of exploring our relationships with them.

The journey we'll take together in this book is based on the knowledge that to grow into self-confidence and the next healthy stage of our lives, we must confront whatever version of the disengaged father we had, and that we can do the bulk of that confrontation within ourselves. Most of us have no choice but to do so. We also assume that we men can engage in this confrontation with our own wounds as our need and inspiration, certain techniques and rituals as our tools, and ancient myths and stories as our guides. These wounds, rituals, and stories can be the basis of a journey of initiation.

The process of healing that I have facilitated with men, the process presented in this book, is a heroic visionquest. It is based on elements combined from the Hero's Journey of European lineage and the Vision Quest of Native American lineage. In combining elements of these journeys of initiation, it seeks to create an appropriate heroic quest for men of our age who seek to know themselves, to heal their wounds, and to strengthen their emotional lives. If we look closely at our ancestral mythology and at the rituals of Native Americans still available to us, we find that when a boy, man, or hero went off on a quest, he did so to know himself, heal his wounds, and strengthen his future.

THE VISION QUEST AND
THE HERO'S JOURNEY

A Vision Quest is a Native American ceremony in which a boy seeking initiation into full manhood or a man seeking deep connection with his world and his inner being—initiation into deeper manhood—makes a spiritual journey into a potentially dangerous wilderness. He faces ordeals that challenge his defenses and fears. After a few days he slows his life down, learning the rhythm of the wilderness. Undistracted by others, he seeks visions—experiences and projections of his hidden inner life. His fearful incipient goal, just to survive and tell the tale, gradually becomes a more important goal—to know himself. When he returns from the physical ordeal and the spiritual journey, he returns to the safety of mentors who help him interpret his visions. Even months or years later, he recalls his Vision Quest and feeds at the trough of that deep, personal experience.

The Hero's Journey resembles a Vision Quest. Joseph Campbell's *The Hero with a Thousand Faces* could probably be called *The Hero with Infinite Faces*, for the Hero's Journey is the journey of every man. In our own European tradition, King Arthur, Odysseus, Perseus, Dante, Parsifal, Captain Kirk, and countless others face hardship and danger, learn the rhythm and strange demands of the quest, see its visions, discover the Grail or cut off Medusa's head or meet Beatrice or go down to a planet and fulfill the Prime Directive, realizing, as they accomplish the goal, the most important lesson of all—self-trust. Finally they return, welcomed, to their own worlds, to tell the tale and drink, even years later, at its trough.

This book asks you to enter your inner wilderness—your own life as a man in the places you came from and the place you live now. The task of your quest is to heal the wounds you received in your father's kingdom, to become more intimate with those people close to you, and, if you have children, to strengthen your bond with them. The journey will help you know yourself better—it will help you know yourself as a hero, a man of vision. You will find a lot to celebrate as you journey, and a lot to grieve. Both celebration and grief are experiences that build self-trust.

When you leave this quest you will always have its trough to drink from. You the hero, you the quester, will gain lifelong tools, *rooted in yourself*, with which to heal core wounds and gain self-confidence. This book specifically connects this process to our relationships with our fathers because it is in those relationships that we as men gained many of our core wounds and lost much of our self-confidence.

Those relationships left a hole in us that we have been trying to fill with work and other addictions, love relationships, popular-culture heroes, extreme competition, and emotional distance. It is a hole that we must, instead, fill with our own hidden inner life, an inner life most of us as men never have the opportunity to discover.

Consider these familiar words:

> *A man measures himself by what he wins.*
> *The second you relax, Son, they get you.*
> *A man doesn't cry.*
> *Don't dwell on the bad stuff, everything's fine.*
> *Son, you'll never amount to much.*
> *Son, no one woman can ever satisfy you.*
> *Son, a man doesn't really know how to love.*
> *A man can't trust other men.*
> *A man can't trust himself.*
> *Son, don't look inward, it's ugly in there.*

Personal myths like these, often taught by our fathers or modeled by them, profoundly influence, even dictate, our choices and behaviors. They remain largely invisible to us—like icebergs, as Sam Keen has put it. Yet they profoundly affect our relationships and behaviors. Unless we make a quest in search of the unhealthy myths, objects, demons, and gods hidden behind these myths, we blindly follow scripts and blindly live in fears that were programmed into us long ago, and sustained by the culture around us. Unless we recover from our father-son wound and seek *our* spiritual center, we will not be in positive control of our lives.

HOW TO USE THIS BOOK

Use this book in whatever way suits your needs. I have used the process it describes with hundreds of men, some of them finding only one or two parts helpful, others going so far as to write out full episodes of their mythic autobiography. Though *The Prince and the King* helps you focus on your father, many other relationships in your life will also be explored. The wisdom and guidance you discover within yourself will also apply to those relationships.

You can use the book alone, in solitude. I also suggest reading it, engaging in its personal rituals, and making its quest while in the company of other men, either in a men's group or with a therapist or another trusted, older male. I have seen the process work well in both contexts. The advantage of doing it with others is that, as a hero needs mentors to guide and admire him, as an initiate needs ritual elders, all of us need our voices to be heard and our visions admired. Thus, even if you speak to trusted friends or family members only about episodes of this journey, do speak of them.

Don't be surprised if your journey through this book takes longer than you expected. It takes time to discover *your* personal language, *your* personal story, and *your* own path of healing. Deep work is slow work. It is only in lifestyles as fast-paced as ours that we have tried to convince ourselves otherwise.

This book is designed to become a part of your everyday life, as most of us do not have the opportunity to go on the kind of prolonged, uninterrupted quest that Native American culture and mythology dictate. Let yourself go with the slow, gradual rhythm of this process. Your imagination uses powerful tools and performs its transformations at its own strange and mysterious pace.

There is an old story of the Sun and the Wind. In it, they are depicted as two strong old men with long white hair and flowing beards, seated together up in the sky. They see a man with a cloak around his shoulders walking down a road.

The Wind says to the Sun, "I'll bet I can get his cloak off him first."

The Sun takes the bet.

The Wind blows and blows and blows, and the man, chilled, defends himself by wrapping the cloak tighter around himself. It is clear to the Wind after just a few minutes that he will not succeed.

The Sun takes his turn. He throws his rays at the young man. He starts out slowly, then builds the heat. At first the man pulls the cloak back off his shoulders a little, then a little more. Then it's barely dangling from his neck, and finally he pulls it off and puts it over his arm. The Sun is the victor.

The mythology and experience in *The Prince and the King* can act as wind or sun. They can make you draw tighter boundaries around yourself, or they can move slowly through you until your cloak comes off and you welcome the warmth. After the chill and silence that many of us have experienced among other men, and among our fathers, it is that warmth that we need to earn and feel if we are to be healed.

PART ONE

Understanding the Father-Son Relationship

"You talk much to your dad?"
"Some. Not much."
"Me neither. He just kind of did his thing and I did mine."
"But he wasn't such a bad guy, right?"
"My dad? He was okay. Yours?"
"Yeah, mine too, I guess."
"Did their best."
"Yeah."
"I guess I don't know Dad very well, though."
"Me neither."
"He loved me, though. I know that."
"Yeah, me too."
"Something missing there, though."
"Yeah."
"Something real big."
"Yeah. Something real scary to think about."

CONVERSATION BETWEEN TWO MEN
AFTER WATCHING THE FILM *CITY SLICKERS*,
SPOKANE, WASHINGTON, SEPTEMBER 1991

ONE

The King

Rockaby Baby, your cradle is green
Father's a King, and mother's a Queen
Sister's a Lady and wears a gold ring
Brother's a Drummer, and plays for the King.

TRADITIONAL NURSERY RHYME

This book is titled *The Prince and the King* because the archetypal relationship we are born into as males resembles the mythological one between the boy prince and his father, the king. Each of us and our brothers were, during our boyhoods, drummers for the King. It took us a while to realize this.

As we moved within her, and as we grew up in her arms, our mother was a great nurturing Goddess, the Primal Queen. We sucked at her breast, smelled her smell first. Her bond with us was intrinsically different from our father's, especially during the first months of life. We *attach* to our mothers in a truly unique way. Our ancestral cultures and their mythologies have symbolized this primal attachment in figures like the Greek goddess Cybele, with her multiple, gigantic breasts that feed and nurture the world, and the medieval Christian *vierges ouvrantes*, sculpted cabinets of the Virgin Mary that, when opened, reveal Jesus within, a small figure wrapped in her chest.

We are aware of and love our fathers during our early months and years, but our mothers are generally our primary care givers and bathe us, clothe us, and feed us. They carry us around during the day; or, if not, surrogate mothers at day-care centers do. We don't know that we're boys yet, in any psychosexual way. We are just little dependent explorers, getting primal nurturance mainly from women.

3

And so, quite often, fathers will say to me, "I didn't know what to do with my son when he was a tiny infant. It was after he started walking and talking that I figured out I was really a father." The early feeling in the infant boy that the mother is more intimately essential to his life than the father exists also in the father. This is one of the reasons the father's nurturing role in the family remains difficult to define in our culture.

But in the father, too, as the months and years go by, the primal yearning to bless his son as profoundly as his wife has grows and grows. He begins to feel more and more proud of his son. He begins to feel more and more like the king of an expanding kingdom. His youth of sewing wild oats, searching for the right mate, and being the restless explorer gives way, with the coming of the child, to a time to put down roots, buy a house, feel pride of ownership, expand the chest, and see himself as a man connected to the sacred, perennial patterns by which earth and universe live. He becomes, through the fragility of the child in his arms, a man who would be king—a man who must learn to order and bless his kingdom.

He will feel even closer to the son as the son separates from the mother—at two years old, at five years old, at ten years old, at puberty. Each time the son separates from the mother, the son seeks to fall into the open arms of the father, the man in the house, the king for whom he wants to drum.

As we get older, we realize that we are boys. As we get older, we begin to realize how truly powerful our fathers are. By the time we are in grade school, they and their world that lies beyond the house become places of male heroism to us. They and their masculine bodies and voices and handshakings and shaving and mustache trimmings all become important in some primal way we cannot understand. But what we sensed unconsciously from first hearing their male voices in the womb we sense consciously as we live and grow in their kingdom: the unequivocal feeling that our father's nurturing is as sacred and primal as our mother's. Our fathers become an obsession.

By the time we are in early adolescence, we are trembling deep inside with a need to know our fathers, to be blessed by them in a way as primal as the way we were blessed by our mothers. During adolescence Mom is still the beloved mother, but her powers shrivel in our eyes; she is no longer the overwhelming, consuming Goddess of all things. Sometimes we rebel against her violently. We want to know the Great God, the Sacred King. We want more of his time and attention. Why won't he give it to us? His is the most powerful male voice in our lives. We want to fall into his arms and be blessed by him. Without realizing it, we have for years been following him around as a prince follows his king.

What you followed him around for was to learn what a man should be. You followed your father around trying to learn his version of *the male mode of feeling.*

THE MALE MODE OF FEELING

What is the male mode of feeling? There is no definite answer. The territorial feeling a father has for his son, the "I'll raise my son my own way, dammit!" feeling, is rooted in the father's desire to pass his version of the male mode of feeling onto the boy without interference from others. But a father would be hard pressed to put his own male mode of feeling into words. Psychologists have tracked for decades what appear to be biological, but may simply be environmentally caused, differences between the female way of doing things and the male. Their findings are a door into the male mode of feeling, though not a whole picture by any means.

There *is* a difference between men and women. Women, it appears, engage in eye-to-eye contact more than men. Men engage in shoulder-to-shoulder contact more than women. Women will sit down and stare at you and want to know your heart. Men will tend to stand next to each other, working to pull out a stump in the backyard. Men will also prefer what is called *parallel play* to the *feeling talk* of women. Men relate through work, sports, or a game of cards instead of having tea and emotional conversation.

Deborah Tannen's best-selling *You Just Don't Understand* points out a number of these differences. She argues that while men and women speak the same words, they speak, underneath, very different languages, both verbal and nonverbal. Sometimes they react to each other almost as if they had grown up in different cultures.

How much of the difference between the female mode of

feeling and male mode is environmental and how much biological? We don't know. We do know that the differences appear very early. In a study done with toddlers, the girls put their chairs face to face, while the boys put their chairs side by side. Were the boys, barely two years old, already environmentally programmed for shoulder-to-shoulder contact, or was their behavior biological?

Freud claimed such behavior was biological and was based on what he called *psychosexual difference.* Two men standing eye to eye with erect penises before them were brandishing sexual swords and were, in his view, too psychosexually competitive to remain in that position. So they moved immediately to a shoulder-to-shoulder stance. Women have no innately competitive sexual organ pushing other women away.

Whether environmental or biological, there are differences between men and women that boys yearn to learn from their fathers. How does a *man* stand? How does a *man* work, play, relax? How does a man love? How should a man show his anger? How does a man feel grief and joy? How does a man provide and protect? How does he nurture? When does he cry? What is real brotherhood? How does a man help others feel their inner feelings? The answers to these questions constitute the male mode of feeling, which the young son is trying to learn as he follows his father around.

In mythology and archetype, the prince follows the king around, learning what will later be expected of him when he becomes king. He learns by modeling, by receiving direct teaching from his father, the king, and later, by doing the same with mentors. Our culture's association of father with king is perennial. Think of the little sons of Yul Brynner in *The King and I* trying to emulate their father. Think of your own family's personal mythologies: "I'm the father and I'm king around here"; "The man is the king of his castle." Think of the old lullabies, the father depicted as king and mother as queen. Think of your own life and of the power your father had over you. Let yourself conceive of that power mythologically. See yourself as a prince in a magical courtyard, growing up in the house of a king.

When you see yourself this way, you are seeing the archetype of the Prince inside you and the archetype of the King inside your father. This archetypal relationship was going on inside your psyche as your father raised you. To go deep into our relationships with our fathers, and to heal those relationships, let us get a clear sense of how archetypes work, especially the archetypes of Prince and King.

WHAT ARE ARCHETYPES?

Archetypal language gives us words of power like *Prince* and *King* and burns in us with the power of myth. Why is it that father-son myths in deepest Africa and farthest Asia are so incredibly similar to father-son myths in America and Northern Europe? Just as mythology is a common language in all cultures, so too is the archetypal language it uses, the language of archetypes we all share, whether both are evolved by our environment or our biology.

We all heard archetypal language during our early childhood when we were told fairy tales, bedtime stories, and myths. Even our popular culture, from *Teenage Mutant Ninja Turtles* to *He-Man*, tries to use archetypal language. In ancestral cultures, it was the language essential to the initiation of boys into manhood. In ancient men's circles, it was used to ground men in the truth, both the individual truth of a man's inner voice and the moral truths of a culture's guiding mythology. And in our men's circles nowadays we use mythology to do men's work because we are relearning the transformative power of archetypal language.

The Great Forms Within

We call mythology the outward record of our inner world. We call it the song of the soul. The characters reflected in its song are separate elements within us, which we call archetypes.

These archetypes are the great forms within us all. We recognize them as international, intercultural, and universal because we in our culture sing the same sort of song that a man in the mountains of China sings, or a man in a village in Africa, or a man in a mountain city in Nepal.

There are two ways to look at these archetypes: (1) as metaphors for unnameable unconscious forces within all of us;

(2) as neurophysiological components of all human psyches throughout the world.

A strict Jungian believes we are all born with genetically encoded neurophysiological components or archetypes, just as a man is born with genetically encoded physical characteristics like a penis and testicles, and a woman with ovaries and a vagina. Archetypes are, as Robert Moore puts it, the hard wiring in us. They're in our genetic coding. They are within us as neurophysiological legacies that, combined in our lives with activities of our free will and relationships with others, shape who we are.

Archetypes are like an inner blueprint, a psychic skeleton; they are part of our DNA. As such, they form within us an *archetypal system*, just as another part of our DNA forms our physical system. These archetypes, like physical organs, work together to form a psychological system within us that is part and parcel of our own particular physical system. And just as we activate our penis in one sexual circumstance but not in another, just so do we activate an archetype in one circumstance and not in another. We are wired for the archetypes but not bound by them.

Now, you as a reader don't have to believe that archetypes are neurophysiological, or that they are part of our DNA, in order to use them for self-transformation. They are not a dogma. They have what Native Americans call *medicine* (something that heals), even if they are used as spiritual or psychological metaphors for indefinable internal characteristics.

"The King," you might say, "isn't *really* in me. But sure, maybe he is a good label for that utterly self-confident male center that hides inside, still only partially developed." If you are willing at least to say that, you will gain a new understanding of your deep heart's core and its wounds, and you will be able to transform yourself. Metaphor is as powerful a language as "truth."

Women have an internal constellation of psychic "organs." Some of their constellation is similar to the male version, and some of the male version is similar to the female. Supposedly, men and women are 97 percent similar in psychic and physical makeup. The remaining 3 percent is where the mystery lies, and different archetypes explain some of the mystery. Marion Woodman, Barbara Walker, Jennifer Woolger, and Jean Shinoda

Bolen have been involved in mythopoetic and archetypal women's work and have helped women discover their inner constellation of Goddess, Crone, Maiden, and Queen of Love.

In *The Prince and the King* we will concern ourselves mostly with the male archetypes, especially the archetype that most affects the father-son wound in adult men—the King— and his early manifestation, the Prince. Because we were brought up by disengaged fathers, we live much of our adult male lives as Princes, still waiting for full manhood. We have difficulty discovering within ourselves our balanced, immitigable male center, our King. We sense that our fathers were primarily responsible for nurturing that King in us. But we also know that they did not do so to the extent we needed if we were to grow to full, unequivocal manhood.

How can we learn to activate and nurture the King now? How can we finally believe as men that we deserve a loving, wise, and powerful place on this earth? How can we come to a point in life when we will not feel we have a terrible secret: that we are imposters, that there's a terrible hole inside us, that we must fill the hole with damage and distance? When will we feel like Kings?

These are the archetypal questions that run like threads throughout our journey in this book. As you search for the answers, many other important relationships and internal conflicts will come to light.

Activating Your Archetypes

Carl Jung believes that an archetype is like the invisible pattern that determines what shape and structure a crystal will take when it forms. An *activated* archetype is the recognizable pattern of the crystal once it has formed. If my King is activated, evidence of that King's confidence and blessings will show in the crystal pattern of my everyday life. I will act with confidence in my relationships with my family and at work. I will bless myself, taking time for myself yet not losing control of the order and achievement my life needs. I will bless my family and those around me. I will be fair with my kids, fair with my mate. I will feel like a King who sits at the center of a flourishing kingdom.

Archetypes shift in you and change during your life

journey, depending on what obstacles you meet and how you handle them. Jean Shinoda Bolen writes that: "Archetypes might be compared to the 'blueprints' contained in seeds. Growth from seeds depends on soil and climate conditions, the presence or absence of certain nutrients, loving care or neglect on the part of the gardeners, the size and depth of the container, and the hardiness of the variety itself." Your own internal wounds may block activation of your archetypes as you face adversity. In the case of most of us as men, the father-son wound blocks activation of our King archetype. Through the lens of this wound we'll see that activation of the other archetypes— Warrior, Magician, Lover, and Explorer—is also blocked.

We become more creative, more loving, wise, and powerful, the more we access *all* the archetypes in our blueprint. Robert Moore says, "The potential you have is a lot higher than you think. In an archetypal perspective, you have access to creative energies that are grounded in an ancient neurophysiology that you are now accessing only partially."

Rituals help activate our archetypes; rituals are essential for the smooth working of the archetypal system. That's why in Part II of this book you will be provided with archetypal rituals and assisted in developing your own rituals.

Projecting Archetypes during Childhood

When we are infants and boys, unindividuated, with little real sense of our own power, we project the archetypes in the world around us. We learn how to activate our own archetypes by watching how others, especially our parents, activate theirs. We mimic what others do and how they act. We get our first and most long-lasting lessons in how archetypes work from them. We don't yet know our own archetypes, or how to activate them in any consistent way. We are still experimenting with them.

When we are infants, for instance, we have very little capacity to be protective Warriors. We are very small bodies in a huge world. Our parents are basically our protectors. And we have low capacity for magic, though we adore watching it happen around us. Others, like parents, older brothers and sisters, and television characters, are more interesting Magicians than we are ourselves. We can explore only within very circumspect spaces; thus our elders explore the world for us and come back and tell us what's going on. Even in love, we are more receiver than giver, especially in infancy, dependent on parents for love. And we have very little sacred center of our own. We depend on our family structure to make us feel secure in the world. We depend on our mother and father to be Goddess and King; we are still undeveloped Princes.

Only as we grow older and individuate do we learn the extent to which the archetypes are inside us. One of the jobs of male initiation and passage into manhood is to show us that these archetypes are, in an adult man, within and no longer without—that they constitute a man's sacred self.

The fact that archetypes are projected around us when we are young is especially important in understanding how we model and learn inappropriate, shadow, or negative behaviors in childhood. We have no choice: we are modeling our archetypes on the people we trust because we don't have the personal power yet to trust ourselves. When the father, for instance, on whom the boy projects the King, is absent, distant, or abusive, the son models and learns very little about a healthy King. Thus when he individuates in adolescence and early adulthood, the archetype of the healthy King is a very small portion of his life. There is a hole within him, a hole in the center of his being that the King should be filling. From that center, that King, should come the ordering of the other archetypes. But in the lives of most of us, brought up by disengaged fathers—men who are not fully developed Kings—a hole, filled still by an undeveloped Prince, tries to order these other archetypes.

Archetypes of Mature Masculinity

As adult men we have a constellation of masculine archetypes within our psyches: the King (our spiritual center, our self-confidence—the archetype within a man on whom the other archetypes depend for their creative ordering), the Warrior (the energy of self-disciplined action and assertiveness), the Magician (the energy of initiation and transformation), the Lover (the energy that connects men to others and the world), and the Explorer (the energy of curiosity and new search). Each of these archetypes has a sacred manifestation and a shadow manifestation. That is to say, each has the potential to nuture as well as to damage.

In the Appendix I have included a description of the Warrior, the Magician, the Lover, and the Explorer. My descriptions
of these archetypes will resemble other descriptions you have
read, but will also differ in important ways. While a deep understanding of these archetypes is not essential at this point, I encourage you to familiarize yourself with the information in the
Appendix before you move, in chapter 4 and beyond, into the
visionquest. The archetypes act in relationship to each other,
and because the King is the central figure, anything we do with
the King will profoundly affect the other archetypes. So, even
though our primary aim is to activate the King, you will be
working in your journey with all the masculine archetypes in
relationship to the King.

THE KING ARCHETYPE

The King sits in the center of a man's inner world, blessing his
psyche with self-trust, creative order, and a sense of profound
mission.

We have not merely guessed that there is a King archetype
at the center of our psyches. Evidence of his existence is everywhere in our societies, cultures, and mythologies. The King at
the center of our inner kingdom is like the Sacred King in the
center of our cultures and myths, the Sacred King we have
called God, Yahweh, God-the-Father, Brahman, Osiris, the Father Creator, Zeus, Odin, Great Father Snake, All-Knowing
One, Godhead.

Just as a culture feels inexplicably stronger by having a
strong leader—a president, prime minister, or King Arthur—so
a psyche feels inexplicably stronger by having a loving, wise,
and powerful King at its center. Like President Kennedy, Martin
Luther King, Jr., Jesus, Osiris, Brahman, or others who have
acted as Sacred Kings to center their people, the inner King gives
us a sacred connection with important mission and meaning.
Through the King we know cosmos instead of chaos.

Were there no guiding force in the center of the psyche,
that emotional body would not have the self-trust to make important life decisions. It would not feel spiritually grounded on
this earth. It would not know where to place its emotional
boundaries. It would not know cosmos; it would live in emo-

tional chaos and create a false self, a false king, to conceal the chaos. Cultures and mythologies know this tendency universally—the terrible fear of a false king inhabiting the center of the kingdom and leading it into self-destruction.

A male psyche without a loving, wise, and powerful King at its center is easily taken over by the restlessness of the Explorer; the angry, shadow side of the Warrior; the soft, unassertive side of the Lover; and the alienating, hermitic side of the Magician. The male psyche without a loving, wise, and powerful King ends up looking to work, women, addictions, and anything else but the true, genuine self for its blessing.

A loving, wise, and powerful King should not be confused with a patriarchal King. Seated beside Osiris is Isis, the Goddess. King and Queen, Masculine and Feminine, are equal forces in the world, a fact that political systems have neglected for too many years. The Sacred King archetype within each man is respectful of the Goddess. He is too loving, too wise, and too powerful to fear, immaturely, that she is his enemy.

In our culture, the repression of the Goddess has come not because the King has been too powerful in men but because he has been too powerless. The Shadow Warrior in men has moved to crush femininity, which, unguided by a King, it has seen as enemy. We live in a culture that does not help its boys separate from their mothers. Too many men are grown but have not individuated from their mothers. It is especially the Warrior who must individuate from the mother. He cannot remain at her side, being stroked, fondled, and coddled by her. It he does, he'll grow up seeking her surrogate when he marries, and then punish her severely.

Contrary to this unhealthy situation, the loving, wise, and powerful King in a man respects his own feminine side and the femininity around him. And yet he is King, not Queen—just as, for a woman, Goddess, not God, sits at the center of her creativity, ordering, and cosmos.

THE KING WITHIN

Only in the last few decades have we come to understand that our emotional and spiritual growth as human beings does not depend on whether God or Jehovah or Allah or another Sacred

King exists externally. Our belief in them is what matters, for human beings project what they need onto the world and then receive it back. Our religions are and have been ways of projecting the divine that is within us onto the mysterious world that is around us. By simultaneously projecting the divine and seeming to find it *out there,* we are connected to a world from which we human beings can become easily disconnected.

In our day-to-day psychological and spiritual development, what we need in order to grow and prosper are ways to recognize the divine within ourselves. God, in this model, becomes not God out there but a way of experiencing the Great Form within the individual's sacred self, sitting at its center and ruling its cosmos. In this model we, like all other human beings, are a microcosm of the whole cosmos.

As the history of the human race unfolded, pagan Sacred Kings became monotheistic Sacred Kings: Baal (the fertility God of the ancient Hebrews) and Osiris became Yahweh and Allah. Then, in Western culture especially, monotheistic Sacred Kings began losing their power to political kings and presidents. Only in the last few decades have we been in a position to realize that this progression of Sacred Kings from one manifestation to another is not a progression from a better king to a worse one, or a more powerful to a less powerful, or, as many fanatics claim, a good "old" one to an evil "new" one. It is neither progress or regression. Each of the Sacred Kings we human beings have projected onto the world around us has been that era's version of the same King archetype we have sensed inside ourselves. Since we cannot and could not directly touch our archetypes, we projected them outward. Only in the last few decades have men been able to notice the source of those Sacred King projections. That source is the King within us, the King archetype in our own masculine centers.

What, specifically, are this inner King's archetypal qualities? The King's characteristics are the same loving, wise, and powerful qualities of centeredness that Sacred Kings have possessed for millennia. The base of them all is the King's ability to *husband*—in Joseph Palmour's words, "to understand the nature of things before he orders them." Having understood the very essence of things, the King makes cosmos out of chaos. In more specific terms:

1. The King archetype in its fullness possesses the qualities of order, of reasonable and rational patterning, of integration and integrity in the masculine psyche.

2. It stabilizes chaotic emotion and out-of-control behaviors. It gives stability and centeredness. It brings calm and balance.

3. In its fertilizing and centeredness, it mediates vitality, life force, and joy.

4. It feels our essential unassailability and certainty in our masculine identity.

5. It looks upon the world with a firm but kindly eye.

6. It sees others in all their weakness and in all their talent and worth. It honors them and promotes them. It guides them and nurtures them toward their own fullness of being.

7. It is not envious, because it is secure, as the King, in its own worth. (Adapted from *King, Warrior, Magician, Lover,* by Robert Moore and Douglas Gillette.)

Throughout this book, we will travel within ourselves like princes in fairy tales, moving toward this King within. We are seeking to improve and enrich the order we give to our own lives and the lives of others around us. We are seeking ways hidden deep within us to get control of our wounded anger and learn inner calm. We are seeking, in other words, the center of our being, so that we can assert appropriate boundaries around that center.

We are moving toward feeling more vital as men. This will mean taking better care of ourselves: *doing* less and *being* more, living less for mere social survival and the acquisition of goods and more for spiritual, sacred soul time. We are moving toward becoming judgmental and shaming only when absolutely necessary. We are moving toward a time when we can teach younger people with absolute confidence in our own teachings. We are moving toward a deeper sense of personal security and safety in the world. We are moving toward a sense of adequacy that does not need the swamp of envy. We are moving inward to discover masculine powers that bless our inner world with its most sacred, earth-connected, sky-reaching, destiny-filled energy.

These are the things that an activated King can help us accomplish. These are things we wish we had more of. These are things we feel we should have learned better somewhere along our journey. We often come to points in our lives where we cannot make a crucial decision, cannot stay with a mate we know is right for us, cannot feel less than alienated and lonely, cannot feel, no matter how much we acquire and do, adequate as men. What has happened to our King? Sometimes we even go so far as to wonder, "Do I have a King?"—so completely do we live lives of quiet desperation.

In order to discover the King within each of us we must look to our fathers, for the King that sits at the center of every man's inner world is passed into him not by Baal, Osiris, Yahweh, or President Kennedy; it is first and foremost passed into him by his father.

In your boyhood, your psyche projected the Sacred King onto your father. Thus he was your Zeus, your Brahman, your Jehovah at that time in your life when God and Goddess, the eternal and omnipotent nurturers of your life, were your father and mother, utterly powerful. He and your mother ordered your world, provided it with food, shelter, and clothing, possessed almost all the power in it—to such an extent that their power overwhelmed you.

The archetypal development of the King in your boyhood might ideally have looked like this: very early in your boyhood, your spiritual center was occupied by more Goddess than King—as your mother or another female care giver occupied most of your infant world, feeding you at her breast in a way your father could not. Then you grew older. Your spiritual center was occupied by equal parts of Goddess and King as you came to know your father and/or other adult males better, learning from them an art of masculine play and discipline that you generally did not learn from your mother. Then in late childhood and adolescence, your spiritual center was occupied more by King than Goddess—as you broke away from your mother and sought your masculine identity.

During these early years, you were Prince and your father was your King. Slowly, your own King was to develop as you took on a healthy King from your father. Then, in late adolescence and early adulthood, when masculine competition with him became too overwhelming, you shifted your archetypal focus away from him and to other male mentors. In this ideal structure of Prince and King, your father needed to fulfill certain sacred duties that went far beyond merely feeding, clothing, and sheltering you and teaching you some of life's important lessons.

These duties involved teaching you to recognize your own inner voice and bring to the world your sacred, most spiritually empowered self. When a father is untrained for these duties by his own father, or ignorant of the fact that he is a King to his son, or overworked or abusive or absent—he doesn't fulfill these duties. Consequently, his son grows up with an undeveloped feeling of sacredness. This father condemns the son to a life as an eternal prince who will yearn throughout his adult life for his father to give him purpose—a son who will never know his own sacred purpose and power.

DUTIES OF THE SACRED KING

What is a good father? What are his survival duties? What are his sacred duties? We are well aware of a father's survival duties. He (and the mother, too) must provide food, shelter, and clothing for the son. He must either teach a son a craft or seek out the best education possible for the son, given his own financial means, so the son can later make a living. He must teach the son lessons of life, especially responsibility, so the son can later become an active community member and, if he chooses, a father. He must show the son reasonable behavioral limits and how to live by them so the son learns what is socially appropriate.

These are survival skills. They allow a boy to make it in society. They allow a boy to function and to survive. A father's survival duties generally begin with building his part of the nest while the son is still *in utero.* His duties generally near their end when the son leaves home and makes it on his own.

What are a father's sacred duties? They are intertwined with his survival duties and are taught by similar means—

modeling and object lessons. But to fulfill these sacred duties the father must journey with the son very deep into the boy's sacred self, just as a King must journey with the Prince deep into his inner world if that young man is ever to gain the self-confidence and self-trust to later rule the whole kingdom.

The father who fulfills his sacred duties becomes intimate with the son. We are talking now of more than teaching his son how to drive a car, earn a living, use a fishing pole, pick up girls, drink, be a good baseball player. Moments of sacred teaching will occur as these things are taught, but we're talking now of sacred education—something that goes beyond these, into masculine intimacy between father and son. We are talking now about moments and interactions in a boy's life that are necessary for directly and distinctly building a sense of his own reason for being on this earth—his purpose—and his own ability to husband that reason—his power. We are talking about a boy's, and then a man's, personal sense of meaning.

This sense of meaning is the son's foundation for healthy identity. To teach it, his father does not give him a purpose and force him to cleave to it. Rather the father must be intimate with the son in such a way that the son feels, on a daily and yearly basis, that he belongs in the father's kingdom and, therefore—because he has projected the Sacred King onto his father—in the whole cosmos. From this feeling of masculine intimacy and belonging will grow his own emotional empowerment and honesty, his masculine self-love and self-trust.

How, specifically, does the father fulfill these sacred duties? He nurtures the son's imagination and vision. He embraces the son in pain, in joy, in happiness, in grief. He provides a healthy male model by which the son can learn how to love and be loved, how to commit to an emotional equal, how to father a new being. The father takes the son into the world and shows him how to kiss the earth. He guides the son to other men and shows him the strengths of brotherhood. He tests and activates the son's physical and mental strengths with discipline and challenges. He helps the son feel safe. He encourages the boy to dance and sing. Being a King himself, he models kingliness.

The father who fulfills his sacred duties does not need to be ever present in the son's discovery of his sacred self. Often the father need only encourage and admire the son's own discoveries. The father who is fulfilling his sacred duties feeds his son's physical body with sustenance and tempers it with challenges. He builds the son's intellectual body with education and admiration. He embraces the son's emotional body with healthy example and healthy discipline. He stands beside the son's spiritual body with listening and grounding.

These sacred duties give a father a tall order to fill. Yet each father, in his own way, must fulfill them if the son is to feel whole. Each father is the son's Sacred King. If the father—or in the father's absence, some other man—does not fulfill these duties, the son will learn survival skills but not sacred masculine grounding. The son will exist as a man in time, space, and society, but he will lack a deep connection with past, present, and future. That is to say, he will lack a deep sense of his masculine *birthright*—that part of the father and the father's ancestral culture that the son inherits. He will lack a deep sense of *spiritual grounding,* a sense of belonging in the here and now. And he will lack what he must learn as his father gives him *sacred wounds:* the confidence to find spiritual meaning in fate and crisis.

Let's look at each of these separately, and in depth.

Birthright

In a very real sense, *birthright* is the child's right to be born. It is the son's part in the ancestral continuity of a family. Birthright is a psychospiritual container of memories, ancestral legends, family stories, genetic material, and social status that is passed on from generation to generation.

One of the pleasures of having a child is the anticipation of passing this mortal container, with its immortal memories and power, on to your child. One of the pleasures of being a child is receiving this gift.

Birthright holds the son's familial heritage—the country and culture of his origin. It holds his parents' achievements, which they pass on to the son while they are alive, and will pass on with some closure at their deaths. It holds the family's earlier searches for moral values. It holds the story of his family identity, to which he can always return when faced with questions of his own identity. "Who am I?" he will ask in a time of inner darkness. "I am the son of . . ." his answer can begin. It holds what his previous generations have learned about social responsibility, a man's work, a man's relationship with his community. It holds clues as to the son's purpose in the world. It is something he needs to carry into his uncertain future.

In mythology the father's passing on of birthright to the son is one of the most important ritual moments in a son's life. In the mythology of princes and kings, the birthright is passed on to the son over a period of years, with a final ceremony marking the closure of that process, a ceremony in which the Prince is no longer prince, but becomes king. The birthright in this mythology is symbolized by the crown. The father dies in battle or from old age, is killed off by sons or others, or simply retires. The son takes over. The son wears the crown.

Psychologically, we go through a similar journey in relation to our fathers and their birthright. Psychologically this crown, this birthright, is passed on whether we are the firstborn son or fifth.

Often a man will say, "I never really knew myself as a man until my father died." Or, "I never really had control of the business or of my life until my father retired and moved to Arizona." Or, in the case of an inmate charged with patricide, "Now I've killed him, now I'm finally free." For many men, getting to know their own heritage, genealogy, and birthright does not begin in a conscious way until they have a child of their own and start having to decide what to pass on.

In the ideal father-son situation, the father would do and say things—in gestures inherited from parents, in stories remembered from grandparents, in an old language of the old country, in respect for old traditions—that would show the son where the father came from, and thus the son's origins. Like father, like son. The human sense of birthright comes to us through story, through family tales that are often quite embellished. These stories of our father's boyhood reveal in our boyhood imaginations, without our being aware of it, our father's heroism—the development of his King—and much of our own.

"I become immortal by having a child." This is not just an empty cliché. This is an archetypal sense of lineage and birthright. The saying could equally go, "I become immortal by having a father." The son, by learning his father's birthright, connects to his ancestry, all the way back.

Think of the story of Isaac and his twin sons, Jacob and

Esau. Throughout their upbringing, Esau and Jacob yearned to gain their birthright from their father. In rigid biblical times, only one son was allowed the birthright—the firstborn son. The second son would be without the family's most significant legacy and would, after the father's death, be beholden to the first son. Esau was that firstborn son and was his father's favorite, but Jacob had other ideas.

One day Esau came back from hunting, exhausted and near dying. He asked Jacob for help. "Feed me, I pray thee," he pleaded, "for I am faint."

Jacob said, "Sell me this day thy birthright."

Esau thought, "I'm at the point of dying. What profit would this birthright do me if I'm dead?" And so he sold it for food.

Jacob gave Esau bread and lentils and Esau ate and recovered and then got up and went his way.

Years later, when during a deathbed ceremony of blessing Isaac's birthright was to be ritually passed on to Esau, the weak and dying Isaac sent Esau off to get venison. Through trickery, Jacob substituted himself. His blind and dying father blessed him instead of Esau. When Esau found out, it was too late. Esau became a sworn enemy of Jacob, and the kingdom of the Hebrews was from then on divided, a long line of tragedy ensuing, even after the brothers reconciled.

Each son knew that he would gain incredible power from his father's birthright. The whole culture knew it. Each son wanted the birthright. Even Esau, who was forced to relinquish it early, still wanted to have his father's blessing. His identity was at stake in that birthright, his identity symbolized in the Old Testament in his right to rule the kingdom of Israel.

This story goes deep into the male psyche. How can we feel centered if we have not been handed a birthright by our fathers? How can we bless others as whole men if we have not learned and acquired a male birthright of our own? How can we "rule our own kingdom" if we do not know where we come from and how we got here? Isaac lay at his deathbed in the role of Sacred King, ready to bless his son and pass on the final portion of his birthright. His sons hungered for that final portion as we hunger, deep inside, to know our own lineage and ancestry, and to be blessed by that immortal line of men from which we came. In order for us to know that immortal line—to be connected in time with the past—our fathers must do their sacred part in revealing our ancestral and familial past to us.

Once a man I worked with went to see his father in a nursing home. He took with him on this particular day a photograph album. In it were pictures from his own and his family's deep past. He sat down with his father and asked him about all the great-great aunts and uncles and great grandparents and scenes in the old pictures. He and his father, who rarely had much to talk about, spoke for hours, his father remembering pieces of his ancestral past, stories and embellishments of stories, conversations and conflicts. The man who took the album to his father was forty-nine years old. His father was seventy-six. It was the first time the son heard most of the stories. It was the first time he felt the kind of swelling in his inner world that a sense of birthright can give. He understood some of his own barely conscious prejudices and peculiar intelligences. He gained a better sense of where he had acquired the quick temper he had. When he left his father, he was in tears.

In an intimate father-son relationship, the son grows up hearing the old stories, even if many of them are dark, dreary, and painful. The son learns whence he came, even if his father turned away from Grandpa's religion, way of life, or addiction. The son learns what his male influences were like, going back generations, and joins that learning with what he learns of social and political history to form a sense of his own tribe. With a sense of masculine birthright, sons feel connected to the power of the past and of their own tribe of origin as they make important decisions and engage in important activities in their lives. As birthright is passed from father to son, the son's King develops in harmony with past and tribe, even with a past and tribe it may criticize. While we can turn away from our birthrights in our conscious lives, we cannot do so in our unconscious lives. Thus we must know them and love them for what they are.

Spiritual Grounding

To be spiritually grounded is to feel that you belong in the universe. To be spiritually grounded is to feel what R. D. Laing has called *ontological security*. A man who feels secure in the world is a man who trusts and loves his own being. He is able, as a Taoist might say, to live in the Now. He senses an under-lying pattern to all existence and senses his sacred, mysterious place in that pattern. That he feels spiritually grounded does not mean he will never feel fear or sadness. Nor does it mean he will live like a stereotypical monk, without desire or ambition. It means, rather, that he will live with spiritual confidence. He will live life as a meaningful journey, a spiritual quest. He will live the present moment to its fullest.

A man who is not spiritually grounded lives in chronic shame about his past and chronic fear of the future. He feels in-adequate to find meaning and be meaningful. He clings to meanings others foist on him—for example, what his father or mother wants him to be. He asks women to give him meaning. He asks work to give him meaning. He takes on unhealthy ster-eotypes of masculinity. He develops a false male self and puts that front on for the world. His life becomes not a dancing ground but a hiding place.

And one day, if he is lucky, the ungrounded man will fall deep into a midlife crisis, or nearly die of a heart attack, or by some other crisis be thrown into self-examination. If he is lucky, he will emerge from this self-examination with a deeper sense of his spiritual ground, a sense that, though coming late to him, is now all the more essential as he faces death. It is a sense of spiritual ground he should have learned in his boyhood.

The teaching of spiritual ground is the duty of mother, fa-ther, and all other healthy elder influences in a child's life. But the father needs specifically to determine whether a son knows the sound of his own male footsteps on the earth. A father needs to help the son know his own inner visions. A father needs to listen to the son and reflect back, in masculine tones, the son's emerging voice.

Like the Navaho father teaching his son the Medicine Way, a father needs to use ritual and story to help his son to feel that that which is infinite and mysterious in the universe is also a part of the boy; that which is wise in the cosmos is also wise in the boy; that which is warm and nurturing in the earth is also warm and nurturing in the boy.

Mothers and mentors can help with this, but a strong, clear sense of this ground must come from the father because the father holds the sacred male candle and the son yearns to

stand and be admired in its light. Even the spiritual education
that the priest, rabbi, or minister can give is not enough to spiritually ground the boy. The father is the man the son lives with.
The myths of the books must be animated in the sacred father's
world.

Each of us prefers meaningfulness to meaninglessness.
Each of us senses that the world shimmers with mysterious energy. Only a cynic refuses to sense this, and no little boy growing up in his sacred father's house is a cynic yet. However the
mythology of infinite union is spoken in our various native
tongues—whether with God at its sacred center or Brahman or
"the Universe"—it teaches each of us that we are an integral
part of everything around us. "I hate going to church with Mom
all the time," a young son whines. On the day Dad goes, the boy
stands up a little straighter and listens a little more carefully.
Especially after he breaks from his mother, a boy seeks to absorb lessons of spiritual ground from his father; he seeks to
know the King within.

The Chandogya Upanishad, an ancient Hindu text, has a
wonderful story that illustrates this whole idea of spiritual
ground.

When Svetaketu was twelve years old he was sent to a teacher,
with whom he studied until he was twenty-four. After learning
all the Vedas, he returned home full of conceit in the belief that
he was consummately well educated.

His father said to him, "Svetaketu, my child, you who are
so full of your learning, have you asked for that knowledge by
which we hear the unhearable, by which we perceive what cannot be perceived and know what cannot be known?"

"What is that knowledge?" asked Svetaketu.

His father replied, "As by knowing one lump of clay all
that is made of clay is known, the difference being only in
name, but the truth being that all is clay—so, my child, is that
knowledge, knowing which we know all."

Not really understanding this, Svetaketu said, "But surely
these venerable teachers of mine are ignorant of this knowledge; for if they possessed it they would have imparted it to me.
Will you give me that knowledge?"

"Bring me a fruit of the nyagrodha tree," his father said.

Svetaketu fetched a fruit from the nyagrodha tree.

"Break it," his father said.

Svetaketu broke it.

"What do you see there?" his father asked.

"Some seeds, exceedingly small," he replied.

"Break one of these."

Svetaketu broke one.

"What do you see there?"

"Nothing at all."

The father said, "My son, that subtle essence which you do not perceive there—in that very essence stands the being of the true nyagrodha tree. In that which is the subtle essence all that exists has its self. That is the True, that is the Self, and thou, Svetaketu, art That."

Here is the first of two lessons of spiritual ground that the father, acting as Sacred King, must teach the boy. This lesson takes years to teach—that the boy has an authentic self; that he is not just a human *doing* who must trudge around working, making money, sleeping, and doing whatever he does day by day, but that he is a human *being*, part of what is true and eternal. It is a simple lesson, a lesson we wish all our children to know, yet the feeling of self-trust and self-love that comes with the lesson seems terribly hard to come by. It is a lesson the father must teach his son. It tells the son that when he looks inward toward his center and thinks he sees nothing, he is actually seeing the mysterious source and center of himself. Who better to teach this to the son than the man on whom the son, in his boyhood, relies to provide that male center, that King? The story continues:

"Pray, sir," said the son, "tell me more."

"Be it so, my child," the father replied. And he said, "Place this salt in water, and come to me tomorrow morning."

The son did as he was told.

Next morning the father said, "Bring me the salt which you put in the water."

The son looked for it, but could not find it; for the salt, of course, had dissolved.

The father said, "Taste some of the water from the surface of the vessel. How is it?"

"Salty."

"Taste some from the middle. How is it?"

"Salty."

"Taste some from the bottom. How is it?"

"Salty."

The father said, "Throw the water away and then come back to me again."

The son did so; but the salt was not lost, for salt exists forever.

Then the father said, "Here likewise in this body of yours, my child, you do not perceive the True; but there in fact it is. In that which is the subtle essence, all that exists has its self. That is the True, that is the Self, and thou, Svetaketu, art That."

Spiritual grounding, the father teaches, is a matter of body as well as soul. It is not enough to say, "Yeah, I know I've got a soul in there somewhere." The son must feel grounded in his body as well, for his body is an essential part of the cosmos. He tastes the salt, and it remains on his tongue in the same way it remains forever absorbed into the earth where the son threw the water.

And then again the lesson returns to "That is the True, that is the Self, and thou, Svetaketu, art That." Whatever your guiding mythology, whether Christian, Jewish, Muslim, Hindu, Buddhist, Animist, Druidic, there is at its center the idea that each human being is connected to all things, and that point of connection resides in the center of your being. This point of connection in a man is very much the King. The King roots you, the King grounds you.

When you are a boy, your father is that King and he must teach the large portion of that lesson. If he does not, you will never be sure that you belong on this earth and in this life. You will not feel your purpose in your deep heart's core. You will not be able to teach your sons, daughters, and others around you how to feel spiritually alive, how to live in the moment, how to feel confident and whole.

Initiation by Sacred Wounds

There is a wonderful African story of a son and a father who go out hunting one day. The father spears a rat and gives the rat to the boy for safekeeping. The day continues and the boy assumes he and his father will kill better prey than the rat, so the boy tosses the rat away. At the end of the day, after father and son have found nothing but the rat for dinner, the father asks the son, "Where is the rat?" The son confesses he tossed it away. The father hits the boy on the head with his ax handle, knocking him to the ground.

The father starts back to the camp. Holding his head, the boy gets back up. He catches up to his father and says, "I understand." The father nods, letting the boy walk beside him. The son and father reenter the camp together.

A sacred wound, given by the Sacred King to his son, hurts the son but also empowers him. After the son got up and realized his error—that a man does not toss away food when family and community wait for sustenance, even if it's a spindly rat—he came, by the wound of realization, one step closer to manhood. He reentered the camp walking beside his father, accepted again by Dad, feeling a little older and, in some as yet inexplicable way, *stronger*. The process resembles the pruning of foliage. The plant hurts and bleeds when the old branches are cut away, but it grows to be a stronger plant.

Sacred wounds are not abusive wounds. Fathers give sacred wounds to sons from within the context of an intimate father-son relationship, and in order to build the son's self-trust by challenge, adversity, and pain. A wound is not sacred unless it comes from an intimate relationship. A distant father who beats his son continually is not giving his son sacred wounds. He is not punishing the son for the son's sake. He is punishing the son to ventilate his own wounds and spleen. Fathers in our culture have been trained for so long to abuse sons that we have difficulty distinguishing between sacred wounds and abusive ones. Yet a father must make the distinction if he is to fulfill his sacred duty to his son, for sacred wounds are essential to the spiritual development of the son. Without them, the son is not prepared to meet his future with strength, assertiveness, and responsibility.

Why do parents so often say, "Boys seem to need more discipline than girls"? Why do boys seem so consumed, especially in adolescence, with getting into scrapes, doing dangerous things, pushing at boundaries, no matter how painful the consequences? It is as if adolescent boys have a death wish.

But to call it a death wish is perhaps too severe. It would be more accurate to call it a *wounding wish.* Girls have the psychological advantage—though the physical discomfort—of a natural wound that draws their blood and marks their passage into womanhood. In monthly bleeding, they are ritually reminded of their connection to adult circles of women and to the creativity of life and earth.

Boys have no such wound, so they seek it everywhere and anywhere, fighting constantly and bleeding, doing dangerous things and hoping to bleed, going to war and waiting to bleed. A boy seeks anywhere and everywhere to prove he is a man. Physical proof, physical challenge, the final moment of which is the drawing of blood, is a seminal way of proving manhood.

If you remember Mark Twain's story of Huck Finn and Tom Sawyer you will remember the blood pacts those boys made—slicing their palms and shaking hands to mix blood and become blood brothers. You may remember similar rituals you yourself engaged in during your boyhood. At a workshop I do on initiation, a seventeen-year-old stood up and said, "I've had my ears pierced four times, and I was disappointed that it didn't bleed. When it did bleed the fourth time, I knew I had done it right." A boy feels in some deep cellular way that his purpose and his body, his mind and his blood, are disconnected in a way that a girl's are not. He yearns to be equally as connected to his own blood, literally.

Fyodor Dostoyevsky wrote, "Suffering is the origin of consciousness." Sacred wounding is ritualized suffering and the welcoming of consciousness, of knowledge, discipline, and maturity, of spiritual connection to the earth through blood.

In traditional cultures, a boy's break from his mother is celebrated through ordeals that often hurt him. In Pygmy culture, for instance, the mothers beat their sons with sticks in order to send them, at early puberty, to their father's circle of men. In Hopi culture the men take the son from his mother and the break is very painful for the boy. In Sioux culture the boy makes a three- or ten-day fast and Vision Quest, suffering physically and psychologically. Why are these sacred wounds and not abusive ones?

Because in all these woundings, as in the girl's menstrual wound, the wounding empowers. The girl feels more like a woman. If she is not brought up in sexual shame and repression, she feels more mature and empowered. The boy, wounded by the stick, the break, or the cold nights in the woods, feels more mature and empowered. As he fights his fear of the wound and survives the wound itself—like the boy hit with the ax handle—he understands; he becomes stronger in will, in experience, and in discipline.

The Sacred Father's role in initiating his son into manhood involves intimacy, depth of relationship, the passing on of his birthright, the teaching of spiritual ground, and the hard task of sacredly wounding his own son. If the father doesn't do it, not only will the son grow up without a clear sense of responsibility, self-trust, and self-confidence, but he'll probably go far away from the home to be wounded, far into places and circumstances that are unsafe and disempowering.

Every boy seeks wounds, and seeks them from other boys and men, especially during adolescence. The son who is wounded by abuse or from whom necessary wounds are withheld because of his father's distance or permissiveness will be more likely to "get into trouble" outside the home as he seeks to be wounded by men.

Sometimes men will say, "My father hit me three times in my boyhood. I've never forgotten any of those times. Each time he was right and I grew up a little." As I talk to these men, wanting to make sure these weren't incidents of abuse, the men retell the incidents and feel empowered, rather than destroyed, by the father's hit.

"If he hadn't shut me down at that moment," one man told me, "I would have gotten even deeper into alcohol. He pushed me against the wall and slapped me and I was already sixteen—I was pissed as hell. But he got the message through to me. I'm glad he did." These men experienced sacred wounding physically. A man once said to me, "My father never hit me, but he had other ways of getting my attention." In these other ways—withholding privileges, showing disappointment, postponing opportunities—the father initiated the son.

One man gave a wonderful example of a sacred wound that involved no physical punishment. His mother and father said, "You will respect the rules of this house and you will come home by midnight or you will lose car privileges. Fair enough?"

"Yeah, I guess," the son said.

The rule was set up by agreement between father, mother, and son. But the son was sixteen and feeling independent. The rule pissed him off. So he pushed at the boundaries. He didn't come in by midnight. And sure enough, he was punished by the fulfillment of his parents' threat: his father took away his car privileges. But what he remembers well about this incident was the fact that, though he was punished, life went on. He was not shamed. He was not constantly reminded of how bad he had been. He was allowed, like the boy in the African story, to stand up and say, "I understand," and then to walk again at his father's side.

This adolescent knew the boundaries going in, and he did what adolescents do: he challenged them. He suffered for challenging them but was not shamed for challenging them. The inconvenience of his punishment notwithstanding, he grew because of the incident. He trusted himself a little more to rebel and be a man, to push away from Mom and Dad, even as he had to come back into their boundaries. He knew his parents were a sacred structure to which he could return, even in imperfection, for emotional refueling. He was hurt by the punishment, but he felt safe.

"As I look back on it," this man told me, "the whole incident almost seems ceremonialized in my memory. It's like we were going through a dance."

And so they were.

As every parent knows, there are ways of punishing that build up the child's self-confidence and sense of adequacy. And there are ways that break them down. In anthropological and mythological material about sacred wounding we find the same message that contemporary sociology and psychology have been trying to give us: the way you punish and reward your child is the bedrock of his health as an adult.

The key to sacred wounding, as it is to all the inner work we do as men, is trust. If an intimate and sacred relationship is established between a father and son, trust is built, even while the son rebels against the sacred wounds. He will not be able to avoid the power of these wounds, for his father reaches into him through the channel of trust. In the ideal father-son dynamic, family discipline is handled in a sacred way, channeling for the boy the kind of wounding and inspiring energy that builds self-trust, energy he will later need once he leaves the protection of the family structure and has to suffer at the hands of fate and crisis as "his own man."

Just as Moses guided his nation in its purpose, connected his nation to its earth and sky, placed it in the present with a strong sense of its past and future, and put it though challenges and adversities that tested and shaped, so the Sacred Father gives his son a sense of his ancestral legacies and human purpose, a sense of connection with the sacred realm itself, and tests the son until the boy learns to trust his own power. Like Moses, Jesus, Buddha, or Osiris, the Sacred Father connects the son to his birthright, his spiritual ground, and initiates him, through sacred wounding, into manhood.

Our fathers did not generally act as Sacred Kings. They felt that their birthrights were cursed. They felt that the language of the sacred was cursed. They felt cursed themselves in their own process of intimacy with their sons. Our fathers were trained by their fathers and the culture at large to believe that if they provided for their sons and taught them some skills, that was enough. Our fathers brought the curse of their own disengaged fathers and grandfathers to their fathering. They were generally absent, distant, or abusive during our boyhoods. Thus we have grown up with less self-trust, less capacity for intimacy with other men, less sense of sacred purpose, and less sense of male empowerment than we need.

We can lift the curse of masculine distance. We can lift it by admitting that the curse is on us, by exploring the wound that cursed us, and my making a journey that heals that wound. Let us now go further down into ourselves. Let us go down into the father-son wound itself—the shame, the abuse, the physical absence, and the emotional distance we experienced in our fathers' kingdom.

In Our Fathers' Kingdom

*The crisis in mature masculinity is very much upon us.
Lacking adequate models of mature men, and lacking
the societal cohesion and institutional structures for
actualizing ritual process, it's "every man for himself." And
most of us fall by the wayside, with no idea what it was that
was the goal of our gender-drive or what went wrong in our
strivings. We seek the generative, affirming and empowering
father (though most of us don't know it), the father who, for
most of us, never existed in our actual lives. . . .*
ROBERT MOORE AND DOUGLAS GILLETTE

What was it like in your father's kingdom? What was it like
for you, growing up as his son? Was your father intimate with
you? Did he teach you more than just the lessons of life? Did he
spend a good portion of his life passing on his birthright, helping you feel that you were sacred as a male in the world? Did he
give you sacred wounds that only he, relating to you from deep
within his intimate knowledge of your needs, could give—
wounds that empowered you like nothing else in the world? Did
he help you listen to your own voice and see your own visions?
What was it like in your father's house?

If you were like the vast majority of men you now work
with, relate to, are friends with, or live next to, you did not have
an intimate father; you had a disengaged father. Life in his
house has left you with psychological wounds you may not yet
have admitted. Most of the fathers of the last few generations
have been disengaged. They have been disengaged for many reasons, not necessarily because they wanted to be but because
they were trained to be, or because they were tired from hard
work or felt shut out from the emotional life of their families, or
shut themselves out. They were frightened of their sons' emo-

tions as if afraid of their own. They told sons to be strong and tough, or they turned away from emotional outbursts altogether, leaving sons to cleave mainly to mothers. From fathers, sons learned shame. If our fathers did cry, they cried in a movie theater or in front of a particularly moving television show, but not when they sat before us in their own temperaments.

From within that relationship, our disengaged fathers taught us survival skills but not sacred worth. They disciplined us, taught us lessons of life, provided for our clothing and shelter. They loved us in their way. But often they were gone from the home, and were emotionally remote and distant when they were around. They were hurting and wounded themselves, and they hurt and wounded us.

The situation today is not much better than it was during our boyhoods. Today the average father spends between two and seven minutes a day in quality time with his children—about the same as or a little less than our fathers spent with us. And the average divorced father sees his children two days out of the month.

George Vaillant, in a longitudinal study of college graduates, reported that 95 percent of men interviewed cited their fathers as having either a negative influence on their lives or little influence at all. In Shere Hite's survey of over seven thousand men, most said they had not been close to their fathers. Judith Arcana found that 1 percent of the sons she interviewed claimed to have "good relations" with their fathers. In all these studies and interviews men report having had relationships with fathers, but not relationships of intimate trust; the relationships were relationships of distance.

Robert Bly has said, "I've heard one statement over and over from American males: 'There is not enough father.'" There is not enough intimate trust between father and son. There is not enough sacred father.

James Herzog has invented a phrase for what men in our culture feel: *father hunger*. By this he means more than just a hungering for closeness to Dad. He means also a hunger to know maleness at its core—a hunger for the Sacred King within. To *father hunger* other men have added *father fear*, *father grief*, and *father rage*—fear of maleness, grief about what it has become, rage at what it has done in the world. What was it like in your father's kingdom? Each of us owes it to ourselves, our love relationships, our children, and our communities to ask that question and be very careful and honest in answering it.

WHO IS MY FATHER, AND WHERE IS HE?

There is a wonderful Grimms' fairy tale, "Strong Hans," which asks us to look at our own father's kingdom. In the tale, a two-year-old boy and his mother are abducted by outlaws while the boy's father, a woodcutter, is away working. The boy and mother are forced to live in the bottom of the outlaw cave, where the outlaw captain raises the boy as his son, beating him and shaming him constantly. Threatening her with death, the outlaw captain forces the boy's mother to keep from the boy who and where his real father is.

The boy, Hans, and his mother survive in the outlaw cave, and Hans learns many skills of club and sword. But every year he asks the outlaw captain, "Who is my father, and where is he?" Every year the outlaw captain beats him for asking it. Every year Hans, like so many of us during our boyhoods and now in our adulthoods, feels the distance from his sacred father and, as we all seek him in our hunger, asks for him yearningly.

One year, when Hans is in his teens and now a male adult, he asks his outlaw father the question again. He is beaten again. This time he gets his outlaw father and the other outlaws drunk and kills them. He takes a sack of jewels and flees with his mother back up out of the cave and to his original father's house. There he finds his father's house in ruins and his father diminished and depressed. The reunion between father, mother, and son is an emotional one, and with the jewels Hans rebuilds his father's house. But a year later Hans sets out to leave his diminished father behind and find his own way.

Hans, by the end of this part of the story, has experienced life in the hands of the abusive outlaw father and a diminished father. As he leaves his two fathers behind, he still seeks to know the sacred father—the sacred, loving, wise, and powerful male energy to whom he was born and from whom he, as a son, needed to learn who he is. He still seems to ask the world, as so many of us do, "Who is my father, and where is he?"

LIVING WITH THE OUTLAW FATHER:
ABUSE AND SHAME

At a Strong Hans workshop I gave, just as we finished a four-hour section on living down in the cave with the outlaw father, I was verbally attacked by a man in his forties. "I'm not even sure why I'm here," he said. "Sure, my father was an asshole, like that outlaw father, but so what? Everyone screws up everyone else. I'll screw up my kids. You're all just sitting around bellyaching."

I assumed he would not come to further events. But as the months went by I met him a number of times, each time getting to know him better. He was recently divorced. His wife had moved herself and their children across the country. He felt that he was a strong man and couldn't understand his wife's complaints that his rages made him weak. He said he wouldn't give an inch and that was that.

I asked him about his relationship with his father. He described a harsh, abusive disciplinarian. "Never admit to anything" was his father's motto. "Don't show your wife any weakness. If you cry I'll just beat you worse." I asked this man how he felt about his father now. His father was dead now, he said. "And I don't feel like I knew him well at all."

This man had lived a boyhood with an abusive, shaming, alcoholic father. He was asking throughout his boyhood for his father to show his true and sacred self, and his father beat him back each time he asked. A son asking to know the sacred father is asking, "What is manhood, and what kind of man should I become?" Whenever this boy asked his father what true manhood was, what a man's feelings were, he got beaten with belts and vicious shame.

This is the reported experience of at least one of every four boys in our culture. If all significant physical, psychological, and sexual abuse were reported, we would probably find that far more boys experience such abuse than statistics confirm.

When we were little, when our father came home from work tired and irritable, when he took his problems out on our psyches and our hides, our fragile egos took in his aggravated voice and irritation and anger, just as Hans took blows from his outlaw father. This kind of father is not *authoritative*—someone standing as a strong center in our lives, who can give

us advice and learning. He is *authoritarian*—requiring obedience first, the teaching of survival skills second, and emotional nurturance last. It seems to us, as he beats and/or shames
us, that he respects us less than himself. In fact, if we were capable of realizing it as children, we would see that he has little
or no respect for himself and views us as a threat to his
strength.

The outlaw father beats us, makes us feel guilty for our
needs, refuses our requests. The abuse here is shame. It is toxic;
it smashes the son's sense of a sacred, nurturing father. Therefore, it smashes the son's sense of his own sacred maleness. As
John Lee has put it, "If as I grow up I know my dad is an asshole,
then when I realize I'm male I realize I must be an asshole, too."
The birthright passed on from father to son is one so negative
that the son will need, for emotional survival, to turn away
from it. If he doesn't, he will relive his father's pattern and ruin
his own life. The spiritual grounding the son learns from the
outlaw father is abusive, totalitarian, and conquest oriented: a
man takes what he wants, no matter the consequences to others
or the environment. The outlaw father becomes not a Sacred
King to his children and the environment, but a Shadow King.

On the one hand the outlaw father initiates his son
through direct toxic shame: beating us, putting us down,
"you're shit"; "you'll never make it"; "I can't believe a weakling
like you is my son." On the other hand he initiates through indi-
rect toxic shame, treating us with angry silences for hours and
days on end: "I don't want to see your face again." He gives
shadow wounds, not sacred ones.

The outlaw father goes away and brings home riches, but
he is so terrifying to us that we assume, especially in our childhood perceptions, that he is equally terrifying to others. In our
preconscious perceptions he is a criminal, an outlaw, yet we
have no choice but to be his son.

For many of us, the outlaw father may have been an alcoholic; for others, the son of abusive parents; for others, a tired,
disappointed man; for others, a man with a bad temper. His attitude may have been as psychologically abusive toward our
mother as it was physically abusive toward us. He may have seen
our mother not as a separate being but as someone within his
authority who ought to obey him. The message that came

through him to us was this: if you want to be a good son, you should be perfect, you should keep in your place, you should strictly obey *my* rules, you should curtail your experiences of your own free spirit.

Often our own inability in later life to live with integrity and clear, strong values is an outgrowth of our preconscious childhood confusion about this kind of father. He never seemed to get caught for his brutality, but we knew he was criminal deep down. We can't take on his values, though he forced us to obey them, nor can we take on the less defined values of the society that was so stupidly blind to our father's criminality. So what male values are we to take on?

The outlaw father keeps us away from his riches. They are *his*, not ours. The outlaw father has his kind moments. He teaches us skills, like the use of the club and sword. He pushes us toward activities that will lead us to physical strength. But he initiates the Warrior in us in an incomplete, shadow way, moving us toward physical and even mental strength ("Winning is a mental thing, Son. It's all in your attitude"), but with little nurturing of our emotional and spiritual selves. He pushes his dreams and hopes on us, rather than helping us discover our own.

Throughout boyhood and early adolescence, our outlaw father will teach us slowly but surely that we are worthless. He does this most markedly by destroying the *inner male* in us and molding the outer male. He helps us become physically powerful and emotionally closed down. We often respond by turning into adult males whose deepest emotional yearnings are ruled by rage and by perfectionism.

Rage

When our father's kingdom is the kingdom of an outlaw father, we grow up not knowing the difference between rage, hostility, and honest anger. By the time we become adults, our rage gets out of control, or we repress our anger so totally as to lack any Warrior whatsoever. Meanwhile, honest anger—the anger of the initiated, protective, able Warrior, which is necessary to live a healthy, empowered adult life—gets stuffed.

As children we can't feel rage in the outlaw father's presence. His strength and our fear of him preclude it. So we wait till we're not around him to vent our rage. We vent our rage on schoolmates, then on coworkers who are not perfect, on spouses who are not perfect, and especially on children, who are never perfect. We feel completely unified as we are raging, in the same way our outlaw father probably did. After we rage we may apologize, plummeting again into disunity, but in that moment of raging we feel unified as men.

If on the other hand we grow up learning ways to control our rage, we may learn to repress our healthy anger, too. We turn away from rage so completely that we become passive adults, letting others walk all over us. Our self-image is so battered by our father's shame and now, too, our own adult guilt that we just keep on taking abuse from others. In this case, we will never feel unified; we will never even have the advantage of the unifying moment of rage. We will be terminally powerless and ashamed of ourselves, especially of the one predominant male quality we learned from our Shadow Kings, how to rage. Rather than going toward the macho, we avoid confrontation altogether and move toward the wimp.

Pat Pinson has worked in the field of recovery and is now President of the Portland Metro Men's Council. In a recent interview in *Mentor* magazine he describes his relationship with his father and its effect on his life:

> I wasn't allowed to be angry. So I spent a lot of time in fear. I avoided any conflict in relationships. I was the "artful dodger." I'd stay in relationships as long as things were going great. But when I encountered my anger in relationships, I just left. I didn't know how to be angry in a healthy way. For instance, I knew rage and passed my rage onto my children. My kids minded me. I was like my dad, who ruled by terror, not knowing how to nurture.

Pinson's is a poignant statement of the hurt within sons of authoritarian fathers. This kind of son avoids conflict with other adults to protect them from his rage, to protect himself from dealing with his own wounds, and to protect himself from what he knows will be the ultimate conclusion of conflict: he'll lose, just as he lost when he showed anger to his father. He'll be beaten down. He'll end up shamed and crushed.

Pinson continues,

[After life with my father] my self-worth was negligible. I swallowed whole that I was no good. I was paralyzed by fear. I can give you a million reasons why I used drugs, but mostly I found an escape there, until they turned on me. I was slowly killing myself with alcohol until I hit bottom.

If you grew up in an outlaw father's kingdom, it was ruled by a man who himself was ruled by shame. Your father, without ever being able to admit it, felt like a terrible human being—flawed, defective, worthless, always on the verge of failing. Shame was his core identity.

The outlaw father is ruptured from his sacred self. He will know no other way but to teach his son to be similarly ruptured. His son, like himself, will grow up without self-trust. His son, like himself, will live an adult life in which he feels, as John Bradshaw puts it, "as if he is drowning in internal bleeding." His son, like himself, will avoid one thing above all else: exposing to others his deepest, most emotive, most creative and sacred self.

Perfectionism

As much as they repress or overexpress anger, sons of authoritarian outlaw fathers grow up feeling they must be absolutely perfect in everything they do. Our outlaw fathers, often distant, seemed totally engaged when it came to training us in some task or sport that they had their heart set on our learning to perfection. If you lived with an outlaw father, he probably taught you—just as Hans was taught how to use a sword and club to perfection—how to play football to perfection, how to fix the car to perfection, how to do myriad other tasks *to perfection.* Sylvia Plath once said, "Perfection is terrible, it cannot have children." Unfortunately, its worshippers do have children.

Perfectionism is most insidiously taught by outlaw fathers in the way they cut off their sons' emotions. Outlaw fathers teach repression of pain, fear, and grief. A man who is perfect is a man who does not feel anything, except perhaps those feelings required to dominate others. Authentic feeling is a mistake. The outlaw father believes that if you don't feel, you don't make the cardinal *mistake* a man can make: showing feelings and being shamed for them.

Perfectionism is built into our culture's very fabric. Religion teaches it from day one. Not only is "daddy's boy a good boy," but a good Christian had better be perfect in "your Father's eyes." Hell awaits all of us who err and suffer the Father's Final Judgment. That children are taught this is, in my mind, a cultural form of paternal abuse. God the father, we are taught, expects perfection from us and will punish us brutally if we don't meet that expectation.

The outlaw father in "Strong Hans" will brook no deviation from his plan for his son's existence. His son is not allowed to go back up to the surface. His son is not allowed to ask important questions. His son is trapped in the outlaw father's world and must act within its limitations at all times, under constant scrutiny, or he'll be beaten.

When the man who yelled at me in workshop began to see his outlaw father more clearly, he saw how much he had been a victim of his father's perfectionism. His own rages, he realized, rose from his absolute shame at not being perfect. His journey out of that shame is still in process. Like Hans, he and many other sons of alcoholic, abusive outlaw fathers are trying to come to terms with their own feelings of criminality and wrongness in the world—feelings that, until they journey to heal the father-son wound, will come out as rage or be repressed completely, leaving relationships to wither.

LIVING WITH THE DIMINISHED FATHER: ABSENCE AND DISTANCE

While Hans and his mother finally found his father, they found the man in a dilapidated house, living a ruined life. Hans helped his father rebuild the house, but the man he had yearned for all those dark years in the outlaw cave—the man about whom he had asked, "Who is my father, and where is he?"—was diminished. And very soon Hans had to leave him, too.

Beginning at a Strong Hans workshop, and continuing into later sessions, I worked with a man in his thirties who told me something I've heard many times from other men: "I know I'm an adult, but I don't know if I'm a *man*." As I got to know this man and his fiancée, I began to notice the dance they were in together—she trying to help him find his inner strength and becoming impatient with his inability to commit himself, he avoiding "the deep stuff" in himself and his relationship. She wanted a strong *man*, not just a male adult.

He wanted it, too. He knew at some level that he was spending his whole life without the inner male confidence he deserved. He was unable to stand alone, to confront inward or outward enemies with determination and vigor. He held his relationship together by getting his soul fed by his fiancée's feelings. When they had first gotten together, she confessed to me, she liked the fact that he "talked so much, he seemed to be so open about his emotions." But after experiencing troubles in their relationship and then hearing the term *soft soul*, they both understood what was happening. He was a soft soul. He was not actually opening his emotions; he was bedding down in hers. He was bringing more smile to his relationship than soul.

When I asked this man about his relationship with his father, he revealed a typical boyhood. His father was rarely around. When around, his father was emotionally distant.

"When Mom told him to discipline us kids," he related, "Dad would do it. Otherwise, he didn't do much. I think he loved me, and I loved him, but no one really showed it. I remember Dad hugging me once in my boyhood. I felt very close to my mother, very far away from Dad. Dad was at work most of the time and always tired. He slumped at the table or sat dozing on a swinging chair in the backyard. He seemed old to me and quiet and kind of sad. He always said, 'Don't be like me when you grow up.' He just wasn't around, physically or emotionally."

When our fathers are at work all day, we are asking, "Who is my father, and where is he?" We are sons yearning for his attention, no matter how well we understand that he must work and be gone from the home. When he comes home he is tired, irritable. His work has diminished him. The culture has diminished him in its commercials about weak men who can't exist without dandruff shampoos and wives to tie their ties. Often his wife has diminished him. Often divorce has diminished him.

"Who is my father, and where is he?" we ask in our deep heart's core. When we do find him, his internal house is weakened and diminished. We as his sons learn to have low expectations of him. Our desires shift from wanting to learn our sacred self from his love, strength, and wisdom to wanting to rescue him, fix his life, live his dream, rebuild his house, redeem his diminishment. Boys in the house of diminished, distant, emotionally withheld fathers, we learn to be men by default.

The man in his thirties who talked about his diminished father was talking about the kind of father most of us had, a father who provided for us and did as he was taught by his father, but a father who, without realizing it, withheld his Sacred King. His birthright, enmeshed with work he did not love, became a source of shame, worthy only of withholding from his son. He had little spiritual ground himself and had little soul time to learn spiritual ground and pass it on. He was gone so much that he was not around to give us sacred wounds, to build intimate trust with us, or to guide us to rich manhood.

This kind of father affected us as sons with a low-grade but interminable sense of abandonment. The man in his thirties who talked about his diminished father related a terrible grief: "I remember kind of giving up on Dad. I don't know when it was; I was maybe in junior high. I just stopped wanting things from him anymore. I knew he couldn't give them. I've always yearned for him, but I gave up expectations way back then."

This man is now middle-aged, living the wound of his father's distance and diminishment. He lives and loves like a diminished man, with little sense of the King inside him. His manhood, never really taught to him by the most important man in his life, is locked in a father closet he can't make sense of, meshed with a sense of abandonment by this distant father and his own adolescent abandonment of the distant father. He turns to women to teach him emotional life, as he always turned to his mother. There was no intimate father into whose arms he could move when he left his mother. This man is an adult male but does not feel like a loving, wise, and powerful *man*.

"The death of the Sacred King," says Robert Bly, "means that . . . when a father now sits down at the table, he seems weak and insignificant. . . . Events have worked to hedge the father around with his own paltriness." Our fathers, who were great male kings to us at first, became paltry cogs in work machines, emotionally crippled in the face of our mothers' powerful feelings, and emotionally distant in the face of our own. In our culture, the death of the Sacred King, the diminishment of the father, has its most profound sources in the workplace and in the family structure itself.

Fathers Diminished by Work

Until very recently, most men did their work close to home, so that sons could see what their fathers did. A man might own a farm, work at a local post office, deliver milk to the neighbors, run a store, or work at some other business nearby. He might come home for lunch, he might have his son help him in his work, he might teach his son his craft and help his son take over the family business.

Typically, the importance of a man's work was taken for granted. The community he lived in *needed* what he did or he wouldn't be doing it. His workplace helped him to become independent in a healthy way; it provided a way for an individuated man to provide for himself and family while doing something he considered worthwhile.

Is the past all roses and the present all thorns? No. Many of the values passed on during close father-son relationships in the workplaces of the past were patriarchal ones that disenfranchised women. There are many admirable changes that have occurred in the workplace over the last two hundred years. But the diminishment of the father is not one of them.

Most men nowadays, as Andrew Kimball says in the *Utne Reader*, "lead powerless, subservient lives in the factory or office—frightened of losing their jobs, mortgaged to the gills, and still feeling responsible for supporting their families. Their lauded independence—as well as most of their basic rights—disappear the minute they report for work." Our fathers, diminished by work, one of their primary sources of self-image and pride, had more difficulty than we can imagine in coming home and fulfilling sacred duties. They led mechanized, shame-filled lives at work and brought that sensibility and temperament home. For all the good things that industrialization and cultural enlightenment have given us, they have given us fathers who have lost one primary piece of their sense of worth. And sons sense this in their fathers as they sense fear.

Kimball explains the situation powerfully:

As men became the primary cog in industrial production, they lost touch with the earth and the parts of themselves that needed the earth to survive. Men by the millions— who long prided themselves on husbandry of family, community, and land—were forced into a system whose ultimate goal was to turn one man against another in the competitive "jungle" of industrialized society. As the industrial revolution advanced, men lost not only their independence and dignity, but also the sense of personal creativity and responsibility.

How are these fathers to regain their sense of dignity? Fathers who are diminished by the workplace, fathers who work jobs that have little meaning to them, live in a feeling of *spiritual fraudulence*. No matter how hard they work they will continue feeling like frauds. The work will not feed their male spirits. They may even lie about what they do. They will often overcompensate in personal lives for the boredom of their work lives by turning to escape fantasies and addictions. They will seek dignity in the acquisition of goods: a better car, boat, vacation package; a new couch; a microwave; a diamond every year; designer clothes. Whatever the acquisition, it is the acquiring that carries meaning for the man. It is the acquiring that conceals his feelings of spiritual fraudulence.

The values of the fathers are passed on to the sons. Sons see fathers crushed by work they hate. Sons see fathers feeling good by acquiring more and more. Sons go down the same path of spiritual fraudulence in hopes of social acceptance. And, most damaging, men whose spirits are crushed at work can hardly be expected to raise and initiate their sons to healthy manhood.

Has the situation improved for fathers and sons since we were growing up? No. A father's physical absence at work and emotional absence at home are, in fact, getting more pronounced. And now mothers, many by economic necessity, are becoming absent, too. Studies indicate that parents spend 40 percent less time with their children now than they did in 1965. In a recent poll, 72 percent of working men confessed they were "torn by conflict" between their jobs and the desire to be with their families. The vast majority had no choice but to choose the job.

When a father is gone cutting wood twelve hours a day—whether he likes to be or not, whether he has to be or not—he becomes a diminished King. In the emotional life of a son, the father's hands-on nurturance is the transmitter of the King archetype from father to son. Thus no matter how much fame and fortune the father acquires for his wife and son, without the hands-on transmitting of his male spirit, the boy will grow up empty.

Fathers Diminished in the Family System

A few months ago I did a radio interview about mythopoetic men's work. It lasted one hour, with about a half hour reserved for call-in questions. I remember one call vividly. The woman who called in said, "My husband complains to me that the kids and I don't seem to need him. It's like he moans about it. All he feels like is a bread ticket, no matter what I do to reassure him. The problem is, most of the time I don't feel like we need him, either."

It was an honest and frightening comment. It is not as uncommon and as exaggerated a feeling as the talk-show host immediately pegged it to be. I hear this constantly from men at workshops and retreats. The Sacred King's, the father's, essentiality must not be in question; if it is, the kingdom suffers. In our lives, a father's necessity often is in question. In our world a father feels distance, anger, and shame to pathological proportions, unclear of his role as a man and father, forced to be absent, then exhausted and feeling guilty when he's home. He takes on less of a role at home because he must take on an overwhelming role away from home. He comes to be needed less at home and is treated as such. And as he feels more and more exiled, he becomes more the outlaw and/or more diminished. As he moves in those footsteps the mother becomes more and more angry and pushes him further away.

"The critical, dominating father," the family psychologist Augustus Napier tells us in *The Journal of Marital and Family Therapy*, "may try to 'connect' with his kids through the use of traditional male force; the passive father may become an indulgent, nonparental nice guy in order to gain favor with his kids; the addicted man may maneuver to get his kids to feel sorry for him and to take care of him; and of course the violent man is often the one who feels the most isolated and most insignificant, and his violence is a desperate attempt to gain power and influence in the family."

Divorce exiles the father even further from the inner circle of the family. On the average, a divorced father spends less than two days a month with his children. How can he not be diminished by this circumstance? More than half of black male children are brought up without fathers. Psychologists generally agree that boys at all ages are hardest hit by divorce. The father is not around and the son is receiving very little male example, very little King. The son cries out, "Who is my father, and where is he?" The response comes two days a month.

The seeds of the father's exile are planted at the son's birth and during the mother's pregnancy. "Having a child brought us closer together!" men often say. Equally as often: "After we had our first child, something started happening to our marriage." One of the things that happens is the unnoticed and devastating new dance of the father outside the circle. Mothers turn instinctually toward deeply attached care of the new baby. A mother has been moving inward throughout the pregnancy, and with the birth, despite the moments of joy the father shares with her, she still seems far away, obsessed with the child. The father feels as inessential to her as he does to the child. In his book, *Finding Our Fathers*, Sam Osherson has described this feeling very powerfully:

> Many new fathers find themselves without clear guidelines as to what it means to be a father, besides providing financially. A wife has to evolve into a mother, but physiological and social cues help the woman to discover what it means. . . . We underestimate the isolation of the new father. If the husband has depended on the wife to interpret family experiences for him, the wife's attention to the newborn may deprive him of that ally, simply because she no longer has the time or energy to serve that function. The social isolation of new fathers from other men . . . is likely to increase during fatherhood. . . . The husband is left alone with many unexpected feelings amidst a home environment that suddenly seems out of control.

Many of us are tempted to just step out of the way and let our wife do what's important in the home. We are tempted to just accept our isolation, as our fathers did. The child specialist

T. Berry Brazelton once recounted giving in to this urge with his own newborn son and regretting it for years afterward. Many of us, too, become defensive as our wife seems to turn away from us, projecting our own realistic or imagined fears of rejection onto her instinctual bonding with the child. We compete with the son for her affection and feel the loser. Then, as the son grows, we may live in a low-grade anger toward him. Without realizing it, we distance him as a result of that rejection and resentment.

Much of the family's future dance is set up in the parents' resolution of the father's dilemma—his sense of isolation and exile—in this early dance. At the birth of a child, family-of-origin issues in both parents rise up as if from a dark well. And archetypal issues of gender power rise up, too. The new mother and father are often set up to confront the birth of their child in exhaustion and psychological confusion. They will be easily tempted to fall into the comfortable pattern their own parents probably fell into, of a mother who nurtured the child and a father who was diminished and distant.

"What could I do?" a man once told me. "It was like my wife wasn't there for me. And I just didn't know how to make our family work during that first year or so. I just kind of gave up. I started looking elsewhere. I loved my wife and my kid, but I got more and more involved with work. It was like a fever. Then the years went by and it was like my wife and I never reestablished our bond, so I got into other women." That the dance created by his son's birth was resolved in his exile was not the only cause of this man's divorce—but it was a significant cause, and it did later rob the son of a close nurturing father.

As the son grows, the dance gets more and more dangerous. The mother, angry at the father's distances or operating out of gender-power issues of her own, may use the son as a substitute male lover, telling him all her problems with Dad and with other men, turning him, however subtly, against his father, against men, and ultimately against his own masculinity. And the father, sensing his own wounds, failure, and isolation, may try to use the son as his redeemer, leaving the son to grow into manhood without a mission of his own.

If you look back at your own life, you may remember your father's exile from your family. Some of it you'll recall in your mother's attitude toward him. Some of it you'll recall in his own attitude toward his role in the family.

My own father was exiled from our family. My father was emotionally remote and my mother was emotionally over-powering. Should I blame either one for my father's exile? Should I blame both for the fact that he was emotionally de-tached from his sons? I've gone through times of blaming her, blaming him, and blaming both of them. These were useful and therapeutic times. These were times of consciously identifying what was going on, and what formed me.

As I've come to grips with my own past and helped other men work through the exile their fathers felt, I've often heard them say, "I know my father wanted to be more involved. I just don't think he knew how." This is a reason for grief. It is my hope that we as sons are learning how we can be more involved, so that we do not move into the same exile that our fathers went into as if by second nature.

Whether demoralized by spiritless work or absent or dead or ex-iled by divorce or other family dances, our diminished father af-fected our self-trust in a terribly profound way. Our diminished father, who nurtured our inner lives so little, taught us that we were not worth nurturing. By his withholding of attention and love—whatever its external or internal cause—we learned that we were not worthy of archetypal male attention. We learned that we were inadequate Princes of an inadequate King. Is it any wonder we grew up with very little sense of healthy manhood and male empowerment? Is it any wonder we grew up so filled with grief at our distance from our fathers, from other men, from our own emotions, and from those we love?

WOUNDED SONS

We are wounded sons. Like worshippers at the altar, we look back at our outlaw and diminished fathers and yearn to know the sacred father who nurtures the son into manhood. Though we have divided our fathers into two types, outlaw and dimin-ished, we know that there are many types of fathers. And we know that our own fathers did not spend every moment of their lives in one of the two extremes. In mythology, when a Prince searches for the Sacred Father and does not find him, he ends up finding instead an outlaw, ogre father or a diminished, ruined father. It's as if mythology is telling us that when as young boys we look to our fathers for affection and attention and don't get it, we begin to see our fathers in those two primary masks. And we remember them in those two masks. We remember them shaming us and we remember them turning away from our deep feelings.

Our sacred father, hidden behind the two shadow fathers—our sacred father for whom we, like Hans, call out yearly, "Who is my father and where is he?"—rarely showed himself. We spend much of our boyhood going back and forth between the two degraded images of our father, seeking the third, the sacred original father, not realizing how profoundly we have been wounded by the withholding of the Sacred King's presence in our lives.

Stanley Kunitz has a wonderful and painful poem, "Father and Son," about a grown son who still seeks the sacred in his father, never quite finding it. He senses that his father is somehow still "the secret master of his blood." He tries to talk to him, tries to connect with him, tries to bridge the chasm between himself and his father, walking with him through town and country. He does make some connection, but in the final moment, his father turns to him "the white ignorant hollow of his face."

It is that hollow we see in our fathers' faces. That hollow becomes a hole within ourselves. That hole is our wound. Because it hurts us so deeply, we live out whole lives without a spiritual center, without spiritual grounding, without a profound sense of healthy birthright, without empowerment. We who have been brought up to feel strongly independent feel inadequate at our core. We may feel socially independent, but we also feel emotionally isolated. We find a hundred ways to cover the isolation and inadequacy, from overwork to alcohol to depression to escape.

What is the archetypal effect on a man whose masculine foundation, whose sense of purpose and power, is not laid by his father? What is the archetypal effect on a man whose father does not pass on much birthright because he hated his own past or did not consider it important? What is the archetypal effect on a man whose father did not teach his son spiritual ground because he did not know his son needed to have it, or because he was not capable of teaching it? What is the archetypal effect on a man whose father did not do his part to initiate his son into the sacred world of men?

The archetypal effect on such a man is this: his King does not develop; rather, he remains a Prince. For a grown man to have a Prince at his spiritual center is like a ship having a boy at the helm. The ship may get by for a while, but ultimately it will face a storm of crushing proportion, or a journey longer than the boy's patience can endure. A ship piloted by a boy will be forced into destruction or, somehow worse, retreat into a place of quiet and sad longing for the real, the passionate journey. Let us move on to know the Prince. He holds the keys to a number of doors within our psyches.

THREE

The Prince

*Some father-hungry sons embody a secret despair they do
not even mention to women. Without actually investigating
their own personal father and why he is as he is, they fall
into a fearful hopelessness, having fully accepted the
generic, diminished idea of father. "I am the son of
defective male material and I'll probably be the same as he
is." Then, with this secret they give up, collapse, live with a
numb place inside. . . .*

ROBERT BLY

As all of us who have suffered the isolation, exile, and addictions of adult maleness can attest, having a Prince at our helm
often gets us by for a while, but ultimately leads to a time of
realization. Sometimes this realization occurs at midlife. Sometimes earlier. Sometimes later. Having lived for a long time as
eternal adolescents, we feel spiritually hollow, emotionally un-
empowered. Forced to be honest, we feel our wounded selves
hovering just this side of destroying our relationships, our children, others around us, our own lives. Many of us don't remain
on this side; we do destroy the good things we have. Others remain for years on this side of self-destructing, getting by, feeling
emotionally isolated.

We grow up, we call ourselves men, and we are men. But
we don't quite feel like men. We still feel like princes, waiting to
ascend to loving, wise, and powerful manhood. We carry
around a terrible secret: that deep down we are pretenders to
maleness; that we need women to mirror our masculinity and
bring it to fruition; that we must always prove ourselves
through performing, competing, and doing; that we can never

feel centered and whole in the way we perceive women can feel. Even as grown men, our Prince is still following our fathers around, waiting to be taught sacred masculinity.

THE PRINCE ARCHETYPE

History of the Sacred Prince

In mythology, the Sacred Prince is the Sacred King's son. He is Phaeton who wants to gain his father's sun. He is Telemachus who will one day be king of Ithaca in Odysseus's place. He is Richard II who will one day take over for his father. He is Robin of Locksley who will one day take over his father's reputation for fairness and virtue, and one day, as Robin Hood, discover his own kingly power in Sherwood Forest. In mythology, the Prince is male *potential* taught purpose and power by the King and by other healthy males the King brings into the castle as teachers and mentors. Then, when it is his time, the Prince ascends to kingship.

The Prince figure in mythology is the sacred son, sometimes known as the Divine Child, directly connected to the sacred father's realm, as if by a masculine umbilical cord. Jesus is directly connected to his father, God. The newborn Dionysus was a sacred son who was physically connected to his sacred father, Zeus, incubating in Zeus's own thigh.

Like these Princes of mythology, the archetypal Prince embodies the sacred son within, sitting at the very center of our young being. This sacred son is waiting for our father, our boyhood's most powerful King, to teach us how to mature from naive and grandiose Prince to ordering and nurturing King. When the boy becomes a man, the Prince within will give way to the King within. Until then, in the boy's psyche, the father is still King and the boy himself is still Prince. When the boy becomes a man, his own King replaces his father at the center of masculinity.

The Inner Prince in the Adult Male

But what if this Prince doesn't complete his ascension to manhood and kingship? An archetypal schism in men develops. In most of us, biological and social maturity occurs without the psychological transition from Sacred Prince to Sacred King. Most of us, brought up by abusive, distant, or absent fathers and thus lacking a masculine umbilical cord to our sacred masculinity, risk remaining in the Prince archetype throughout our adulthoods.

Because our journey during boyhood and adolescence was too little nurtured and supervised by mature masculine influence, we ascended to social and biological manhood in psychological deficiency. We did not have the opportunity to absorb enough healthy adult male psychology to know what a King should be. We were not able to generate our own King. Thus, when at seventeen or eighteen or nineteen the Prince within us is told by the King, our father, "Go ahead into the world, Son. Now you're a man," we barely feel empowered by the pronouncement. We enter manhood, but we are still immaturely yearning for manhood; we are still Princes. We may not notice this if life is going along fine. But when we come face to face with a business failure, a failure in a marriage, or some other profound form of rejection, we realize just how weak we are in our center, just how inadequate and fearful of adult male life we really feel. The qualities of the Prince archetype in the adult male are these:

1. The Prince pseudo-orders his kingdom. The Prince commands without clear self-confidence. It is often difficult for him to separate his own issues from his guidance of others.

2. The Prince tries to appear as if he has integration and integrity as a man, but more often he feels like an imposter in the world of men.

3. The Prince has difficulty stabilizing chaotic emotion and out-of-control behaviors. He often feels out of control of intimate relationships. When he is passionate he is very passionate; when he is withdrawn, he is very withdrawn.

4. The Prince tries to embody vitality, life force, and joy, sometimes succeeding and sometimes failing, without certainty as to why either has occurred.

5. The Prince gives kindness when firmness is required; he asks the world to lead him to leadership.

6. The Prince gives firmness when kindness is required; he asks the world to give him leadership *carte blanche.*

7. The Prince cannot promote others without feeling he will lose himself. He is not sure of his own talents or what direction they should take. The Prince envies.

When I have given this list of qualities to men I've worked with, the results have been startling. Most of the men end up identifying themselves with more than half of these qualities. This identification should come as no surprise. It is nothing to be ashamed of. It's the logical outcome of being brought up by a disengaged King. It's the logical outcome of the father-son wound. Our fathers did not model intimate and empowering manhood. We, therefore, remain partly boys.

THE PRINCE IN EXILE

When we become adult males, informed by our biology and society that we are complete men but feeling psychologically that we are not, we do more than operate out of some immature patterns, damaging our lives and relationships. We also feel exiled from mature masculinity, exiled from the kingdom of heroic and healthy fathers. We feel that we are pretenders to manhood, and we feel that the kingdom of manhood does not really want us or need us. As boys we were brought up in exile from our fathers' birthright and spiritual ground. Thus we find ourselves exiled from our own birthright, our own spiritual ground, our own sacred masculinity.

Wounded, exiled, what hero's journey do we embark on to gain nurturance of the masculine within us? We don't know a sacred masculine mode of life; much less do we feel capable of living it. We don't live from within ourselves, trusting our own voice. We don't live in a spiritual mode, living from a sense of belonging deep within. What mode of life, then, do we choose?

We choose a survival mode. An exiled Prince, like a wounded orphan, seeks relationships, works, perhaps raises a family, but has very limited spiritual and emotional expectations. Damaging inner myths wound our lives to such an extent that all we can do as men on this Earth is survive as actors in a lifestyle and family script we've had little part in writing. We're good men, we work hard, we provide for our families, we seek personal growth. But we still go to sleep and wake up without a strong spiritual connection to our land and our community, without deep personal empowerment. We, like our fathers, have been taught survival skills with which to earn a living and provide for a family, but not the skill with which to feel intimate with the family we make a living for, the environment we harvest, the other men we compete with.

Many of us are further forced into the survival mode by jobs that don't fit us and marriages we can't make work, by a lack of close male friends and a lack of significant personal rituals and ritual spaces we can turn to in times of need and solitude. The adult Prince goes further and further into exile with each passing year. Other men, it seems to him, are Kings. Why isn't he? He must not belong with these other men. Little does he know that most of those men don't feel like Kings, either. But they appear to be Kings, succeeding in their professions and in their social images. In their company, the adult Prince feels more and more isolated from authentic and empowering masculinity.

How can a person, chronically wounded, his emotional growth stunted, live in a spiritual mode? How can he empower those who depend on him? His wound is gaping; all his strength must go to surviving that wound. Like a wounded animal, the best he can do is remain hypervigilant. The best he can do is survive. When the wound heals, he can return to empowerment. Until then, he must depend on those outside him for his nurturance, and he must fear danger more than anything—the primary danger being close, intimate relationships. He comes to actually desire internal exile. If he can just remain at a distance from others who want to be intimate with him, maybe they won't notice how wounded he is and how powerless he feels.

As adult Princes we turn to one sure place for a modicum of self-image—the society around us. The term *codependency* has been overused in our culture, yet it feels very authentic here. A codependent Self is defined by others, not by internal standards. Women are trained to be codependent with men in ways we have been learning about over the last decades. Our culture created a public atmosphere in which women lost self-hood, lost female spirituality. They quickly learned that to survive they would have to gain selfhood from the man's self.

Men, it has seemed, had some problems, but nothing too startling. The truth is, men have not suffered oppression as deeply as women. But men have suffered *repression* far more deeply. While women have not been allowed their equal place in the society they live in, they have for the most part been allowed to feel their own personal sorrows and joys. Men have not. Until very recently, a man in tears was as shameful as a fallen god. A weeping John Wayne or Ronald Reagan would have shocked the 1950s man to his core. In our culture a wounded hero is not allowed to admit his deepest wounds.

To live in a spiritual mode, to live from within, is to feel a mysterious relatedness with what Paul Tillich has called "the ground of being." This is a relatedness *that we can feel consciously*—a kind of relatedness in which we would thank the deer when we killed it, or kiss the earth when we built on it. To live spiritually is to know and feel mystery around you, especially in your own emotions, yet feel safe with that mystery. To live spiritually is to define your Self by *inner* standards. To live spiritually is to be comfortable with solitude. And most important, to live spiritually is to trust yourself. The spiritual mode does not require codependency.

An adult Prince, a codependent man, living in exile from mature masculinity, does not trust himself. No wonder, then, that he lives in the hypervigilance of overwork. Like Theseus, whose father abandoned him at birth, the wounded Prince tries to prove himself to his father ten to fourteen hours a day. If he stopped working he would have to confront his pain, especially his father-son wound. Hypervigilant, always believing he must do one more project and earn one more dollar or else he won't be a man, he can easily avoid looking within.

Men in many traditional cultures work three hours a day to sustain themselves, their family, and tribe. These men spend more than half their day in *soul time*. Soul time is not the kind of leisure time we think of, where a man has peace and quiet in which to escape his troubles. Soul time, something we allow ourselves maybe a few minutes a week, is time to look within. An adult Prince in our culture is not allowed to be wounded; thus he will turn away from any spiritual activity that will remind him of his wound.

Our male survival mode and our codependency on the addictive society are, in large part, due to lingering codependency with disengaged fathers. We live out whole lives, even after our fathers' deaths, codependent with these men who were themselves wounded and addicted, defining our manhood not from within but by committing our male adult lives to disengaged shadow fathers.

A recent study of four thousand businessmen found that the majority felt they had wasted their adult years chasing financial and social goals only to find their lives empty and meaningless. They had lived so long in the survival mode, in its personal emptiness and social addictiveness, that they had no Self, no spiritual sense of the world. And even in their forties and fifties, entrenched in professions and lifestyles, they didn't know what to do. They were wounded and exiled from spiritual life and knew no other course but to continue the hypervigilance their wounds required of them. Many of them needed to look back at their relationships with their fathers.

THE ADULT PRINCE
AND POPULAR CULTURE

Our adult experiences of living in a survival mode, of seeking to find a Self in fashion and material objects, of seeking to feel whole through peer acceptance, should remind us of our experiences as adolescent males.

In adolescence, our yearning to belong in the society around us and to be initiated into the world was so strong that we tried everything we could, often overdoing it, to belong and to become a man. We measured status by how good we looked. We preened in masks of mature manhood, most of these learned from peers and popular culture. We sought to be noticed above all else. Even if we were very shy adolescents, we hated our own shyness because it didn't fit the qualities of other adolescents. We sought self-image in what was popular around us.

And our popular culture, rather than providing us with models of healthy men living in spiritual modes, provided us models of adult Princes living in survival modes. A popular culture, created mainly by men who were brought up in homes of abusive, distant, or absent fathers, ruled our boyhood imaginations and continues to rule the imaginations of boys today with adolescent heroism—the heroism of boys pretending to be men.

Killing a lot of men (or at least beating them up), sleeping with a lot of women, making a lot of money, remaining ever young (nineteen, twenty, late adolescent), remaining "the best," avoiding embarrassing intimacy—these are the qualities of an adolescent hero, a Prince disguised as King. These are also the qualities of most popular-culture heroes. Most of us, no matter how "developed" we are and how healthy, feel a tug of glory at the end of *Rocky* or *Top Gun*. Most of us have been primed to want endless youth, money, and conquest.

John Wayne, James Bond, the A-Team—in the face of these and countless other adolescents in adult clothing, it's nearly impossible for a boy to believe these men are not really men. It's nearly impossible for a boy to believe that the adolescent mode of love, tending toward prolonged infatuation and sexual conquest, then dissatisfaction and emotional distance, is not the most appropriate. It's nearly impossible for a boy to measure himself by whole men with enough spiritual sense to slow down and wonder what their inner voices are saying. Rather, the boy learns from adolescent heroes to move always with the terrible speed of an adolescent who can't wait to grow up and be *known* as a man.

An adolescent boy lives in terrible fear of a world and body that are changing rapidly and confusingly. He seeks control, especially male control over his own conflicting emotions. When he searches for the answer to that great question of adolescence—"How should I know a man?"—and his father doesn't help him discover it, he turns to a dangerously immature popular culture.

Our popular culture—this entertainment landscape of Princes disguised as Kings—is, of course, a thing of our own production. If we, as men and women, were conscious of what boys need to mature into healthy Kings, we wouldn't create and support a popular culture that teaches men never to leave adolescence. Mothers would help their sons break from them, perhaps in some cultural equivalent to the Pygmy tradition of mothers beating their sons with sticks at a ceremony in early adolescence to force the sons to go away from Mom and toward the fathers. Fathers would be intimate with sons. Mentors would do their part. The social structure would support mature, intimate relationships; it would facilitate soul time. Boys would not have to feel that adolescent heroism and survival modes were the best they could do. Men would not have to wait until a midlife crisis—a "second adolescence," when many men rush back toward adolescent desires—to see how much self-destruction could have been avoided in their adult lives.

A man in his early fifties once said to me, "When I hit my midlife crisis, I hit it hard. I lost everything important to me—my wife, my family. I had to really look at things, at myself. I looked back at my life and felt like I had signed some kind of hidden agreement when I was born into the man's world. It was like someone said: 'If you stay emotionally and spiritually half developed, you'll get all the material success you want.' Which I got. But inside I was empty."

Each of us, by late adolescence, has signed this agreement. The agreement says, "We'll let you work your way up to the top of the world [like Tom Cruise has done by the end of *Risky Business*] as long as you cut off any sacred yearnings along the way." When we do get to the top we discover we are on top of a world ruled by the survival mode—in which Tom Cruise's character will have to make money, dress well, and be clever in order to retain his place. But we signed the agreement, so we must be satisfied. And like a machine that will spend the rest of its life jumping back and forth between lover, money, and personal appearance in a concealed frenzy, we guard the top of the world without realizing that all we are doing is protecting a socially powerful but internally disempowering survival mode.

The mature counterpart of the adolescent hero, the mature hero, gains his maturity when he makes the journey out of the survival mode, stepping out of the need for ego fixes and ego approval. Humphrey Bogart movies like *Casablanca* and *To Have and Have Not* strive to depict Bogart's transformation from adolescent to mature hero. By the end of both these films he has decided to do what he believes in and to do it with courage, rather than to remain socially comfortable in a survival mode. The Kevin Costner character in *Dances with Wolves* could be characterized as a mature hero. He develops within himself a spiritual mode and lives in its authenticity, even though that authenticity means danger and sacrifice. Mark Helprin's recent and brilliant novel, *A Soldier of the Great War*, about the life of one Alessandro Guiliani, recalled by the seventy-year-old Guiliani to an adolescent boy, is a wonderful tale of a mature hero's long, arduous, loving, and spiritually rich life.

The mature hero searches for wholeness in the inner life, which needs less external approval than it does sacred ritual spaces, tasks through which to develop, and other mature people to help nurture it. The mature hero gains his life when he sees his existence as a Vision Quest, not a conquest. The mature hero gains his heroism and the Prince gains his kingship by making a journey through the most frightening wilderness of all—his own. To make this journey is not easy, especially for a male adult who has lived so long in the survival mode, so long in spiritual exile. With a Prince at his center he exists in shadows of masculinity, with no clear vision at all. This is the next part of the archetypal problem the Prince finds himself in. Living in shadows, he becomes like his father—authoritarian or diminished, damaging others and himself as he himself, as a boy, was damaged.

THE PRINCE IN A SHADOW KINGDOM

A Prince in exile *from* his own true kingdom is also in exile *in* another kingdom. That is to say, he will wander in his early adulthood, not settling into any particular healthy behavior pattern, experimenting with his own emotions as he experiments in his relationships. But then, at some point, certainly by the time he has a family of his own, he'll settle into behavior patterns, he'll settle into a self and kingdom.

Because he is an adult Prince disguising himself as King, he will settle into unhealthy, inauthentic patterns, patterns that arise from weakness. His boyhood in the shadow kingdom his father ruled will return to haunt him now, if it has not done so before. He may find himself in the very same addiction or unhealthy behavior pattern his father lived in, or, having rebelled against the most obvious shadow aspects of his father's negative patterning, he may believe he has gone 180 percent away from his father's patterns, only to find that in avoiding them he has nonetheless found new shadow patterns all his own. The adult Prince, in his twenties, thirties, forties, will become a Shadow King.

If you remember the story of Strong Hans, you'll remember that Hans killed his abusive stepfather, returned with his mother to his natural father, but found his father a diminished man and decided to set out on his own adult male journey. He was raised in a shadow kingdom by a Shadow King. When he found his original father, he found not a sacred father but a father sitting in shadows, depressed and diminished. Hans survived these two fathers, learning physical and mental skills from the outlaw and learning some compassion and gentleness from the diminished man. So now, as he enters his own adulthood, what kind of kingdom will he create?

The continuation of the Strong Hans story is very interesting. It illustrates the shadow kingdoms that adult Princes fall into. Hans has grown into an adult. He meets two giants in the forest as he is walking. The first he meets one day when he hears something crunching and cracking. He looks around and sees a fir tree whose branches are wound around its trunk, from bottom to top, like braids of rope. He sees countless other trees wound in the same way. At the top of one of them is a large man with a very skilled mind and hands who is twisting the branches like willow wands.

This man, it turns out, is twisting the trees in this way for no real reason. He was wandering around and thought fir-tree twisting would be fun. Hans convinces him to join him on his adventures and the two set off together. Hans decides to call the man Fir-Twister, and the man likes it. The two of them come to a place in the forest where they hear a huge and heavy knocking sound, like rock crashing against rock. They see another huge man there striking away at pieces of rock with his fists.

When Hans asks him why he's hitting the rocks, this man says, "All I want is to hide from all the creatures and sounds of the forest. I've had enough of them. I just want to build a house out of this rock and hide inside it and hear nothing anymore."

"Indeed," thinks Hans, "this man is big and strong, but

he's lost his spirit." So he invites this man to go along, and he names him Rock-Splitter.

If you have not by now referred to the Appendix to familiarize yourself with some sacred and shadow archetypes of mature masculinity, now would be the time to do so. As you do, you may notice that Fir-Twister and Rock-Splitter embody some very specific shadow aspects.

Fir-Twister, for example, is ruled by the Shadow Explorer and the Shadow Magician. He has no sense of where he is going or where he should settle. He is ruled, simply, by the urge to wander. He creates twisted fir trees for no purpose except to enjoy his magical ability to twist the trees. He is ruled by that magical ability. He is like a man who wanders from relationship to relationship, marrying often, but never settling down to discover what he has married. He is like a man who does a craft well—any craft whatsoever—but does not feel any sacred purpose in what he's doing. He may do insider trading and keep accumulating more money than he knows what to do with, continuing to practice his art just because he can do it. He may create newer types of bombs just because he's able. He doesn't settle down to figure out the ethics of what he's doing.

We are not told much about Fir-Twister's past. We don't know what pathology may have caused him to be stuck in his shadow kingdom. We know only that he is cursed in the kingdom, tying knots in fir trees over and over again. When Hans comes around to give him a mission, he happily joins. Hans serves as a kind of new King for him, making him feel that he belongs. And the two of them move on to meet Rock-Splitter.

Rock-Splitter is a man ruled by the Shadow Lover. Rock-Splitter is desperate to cut off all connections with delight, with touch, with relationship. He seeks his own imprisonment inside a rock that will shield him from all feelings of closeness with anything. Rock-Splitter is someone we may recognize in ourselves or in those around us—the man who distances himself, hides behind his paper or in his garage, turns away from his wife's and childrens' cries for affection, seeks to have no close relationships at all.

We are not told how he got into this shadow place, this warped fermentation of a Shadow Lover. We know only that he is in it and that it is not an empowering place to be.

Fir-Twister and Rock-Splitter, engaged in shadow activity, did not feel whole; they went with Hans immediately. And, as we shall see, the fact that they have no King of their own will contribute to the destruction of their relationship with Hans.

As the story continues, the three men walk on and come to a deserted castle. There Hans kills a wild boar and they roast the boar. They realize they have a lot left over, so they decide one man will stay to guard the meat while the other two go out to adventure and hunt. They all sleep in the castle that night and the next day Fir-Twister stands guard.

A knock comes on the door. Fir-Twister answers it. He finds a tiny, spindly dwarf there. The dwarf asks for meat, but Fir-Twister shames the dwarf and orders him to leave. Much to Fir-Twister's surprise, the dwarf pulls out a club and beats him. When his friends come home he says he fell down the stairs. The next day the same thing happens to Rock-Splitter. He makes the same excuse.

The third day Hans stays home and gives the dwarf meat. But the dwarf asks for meat twice, then a third time. The third time, Hans refuses. "I earned this meat with hard fighting and I've given you more than enough. This meat is now for my friends and me." The dwarf, swift as the wind, starts in on Hans like he had on the other two. Hans turns the tables on the dwarf and is soon chasing him into the back garden, where the dwarf disappears into a hole in the rock.

Peering into the hole, Hans sees that it is dark. He feels a terrible shiver as he remembers a hole in the rock he had known years ago. He goes back to the castle and waits for his friends. This time he'll go down there with some help.

When his friends arrive and see him none the worse for wear, they both confess in embarrassment how the tiny dwarf had beaten them up. Hans laughs at them. "You should definitely be ashamed. First you withhold meat like miserly old men; then you let the little thing whip you. I'd be ashamed, too."

Hans, who served as a King to Fir-Twister and Rock-Splitter, now shames them and hurts them to the core. In the next episode of the story they desert and betray him. Hans, after the encounter with the dwarf, is ruled by the Shadow Warrior, the ridiculing, shaming piece of himself that also ruled his own outlaw father. We know little of Fir-Twister's or Rock-Splitter's pasts, but we know Hans's. We need only think back to the terrifying relationship he had with the outlaw to see how he could end up accomplishing what the Shadow Warrior wants—always propelling himself to separateness and lonely invincibility—but the Sacred Warrior does not: the destruction of brotherhood. That destruction is, indeed, what Hans accomplishes.

The next morning Fir-Twister and Rock-Splitter lower Hans by pail and rope into the hole. When he reaches bottom he remembers every detail of the terrible outlaw cave in which he'd been raised. He wanders in the dark as if he were back in that boyhood place. He sees a faint light down a corridor. When he gets to that light, he enters a room and sees a beautiful young woman bound in chains. Standing next to this maiden is the dwarf, grinning at Hans as if he had Hans in a trap. It's a grin Hans remembers; it's like the grin of the outlaw.

Hans engages the dwarf and kills him with his club. As he does this, the chains fall from the woman. She explains she is a king's daughter who had been stolen away by a savage count. When the count realized she would not give him her love, she was thrown into this cave to be guarded by the ugly dwarf. She explains the kind of sufferings the dwarf has put her through, punishing her worst when she asked to be let free to return to her father.

She and Hans go together to the bucket at the bottom of the hole and Hans helps her in. When his friends have drawn her up, he remembers that they lied about the dwarf and he wonders if he should trust them. He puts a rock in the basket and lets them pull it up. When the bucket is halfway up, it comes crashing back down. If he'd been in it he would have crashed to his death.

Hans looks around, powerless to get back up out of the dark hole. He walks back to the dwarf's cave, finding a ring on the dwarf's finger. Hans has heard of the power of dwarves' rings. He pulls it off the dwarf's finger and with a shudder puts it on his own. As he twists it there, spirits of the air appear. They carry him up out of the hole, where the woman and his former friends are nowhere to be found. He twists the ring again and the spirits of the air take him to the boat that carries his two fomer friends and the maiden. He swings his club at each of his former comrades and throws them in the water. He sails with the princess to her father's castle and there marries her, preparing in this king's house to become king to his daughter's queen, when the time is right, and rule the kingdom happily for the rest of his days.

This, then, is the second and final half of the story of Strong Hans. This story, like so many of the Grimms' tales, ends with the pat marriage and happily ever after. But what the pat ending is doing in relation to Prince-King archetypes is very important. The Prince, exiled from his own boyhood kingdom, can still ascend by making the hard journey to kingship.

Hans went down into dark conflict for a second time and fought his outlaw father again, now transmuted into the authoritarian dwarf. Like so many of us in our adult lives, he went down into grief and darkness to find unresolved family-of-origin wounds, especially the father-son wound. While he was down there confronting the shadows, he rescued a part of his Feminine, the maiden, and he learned something of the Magician—the mysterious powers of the ring. The powers of the ring differ, you will notice, from the powers of jewels in the first half of the story. There he used the jewels to rebuild his father's house. Now he uses the ring for his own empowerment. He is finally, down in the dark, growing up.

Like Hans, when we go down into our wounds and our grief—when we take the adult journey into what we suffered as children—we retrieve parts of ourselves, especially feminine parts our shadow fathers forced us to repress. We learn mysterious powers we never knew we had. We use those powers for our own empowerment, no longer to rescue or redeem our fathers. In other words, we use them to build up the power of our own King, no longer to assuage the King who was our father.

Hans is a Prince just as we are Princes. Only after he has made the long and painful journey into his depths does he rise up and claim a sacred kingship. He is one of the lucky Princes, we might say. Or we might say he is one of the empowered Princes. Like all Princes he finds himself exiled in shadow kingdoms, but like only some Princes, he works his way out of that exile and those shadow places by confronting the Shadow.

Fir-Twister, Rock-Splitter, and Hans embodied adult Princes in shadow kingdoms of Magician, Explorer, Lover, and Warrior. Another shadow kingdom Princes find themselves in, one not revealed in this story but one familiar to many of us, is the male kingdom ruled by the Feminine. We call a man who is in this kingdom a "soft soul." He tries to deny his masculinity in favor of what he believes women want of men. Outwardly it appears he is listening too much to women, trying to get them to teach him what it is to be a man, like a boy yearning for his mother to teach him what she wants. Often a son of a father exiled from his family system finds himself ruled by the Feminine Shadow. Inwardly he is not asking mother or wife to tell him how to be a man. He is asking his own feminine side, and neglecting his own masculine.

SHADOW KINGDOMS ALL AROUND US

Whether a man flourishes by shaming others, wandering without a goal, creating without ethical purpose, feminizing himself to please women, or closing off his emotions altogether, he lives in a shadow kingdom. He is ruled by a shadow archetype who inhabits the King's place, and forces obedience.

Saddam Hussein was ruled by his Shadow Warrior as he took on all of the Western powers. We know that his boyhood relationship with his father was very abusive. As a man he seeks Warrior glories. He sacrificed his country to get those glories. Had he been ruled by a Sacred King—had he lived with a sense of his own sacred masculinity—even putting aside the political and economic tensions inherent in his career, his King could not have invited the destruction of his countryside, the loss of over one hundred thousand Iraqi lives. His Shadow Warrior, on the other hand, occupying his center, could very easily brook this destruction. The Shadow Warrior does not feel responsible for the flourishing of his kingdom. He feels compelled mainly to make war.

The lonely Wild West heroes who wandered off into the sunset—many 1960s Clint Eastwood characters come to mind—are prime examples of adult Princes, spiritually undeveloped, living in kingdoms ruled by the Shadow Explorer. They saved a town, slept with some women, killed a few men, then moved on. That they did not settle in the town was not the only indication of the Shadow Explorer. Rather, the fact that they seemed to want to settle down but could not revealed the schism in their psyches.

Scientists who discover a thousand new mechanical ways to keep people alive who wish to die—these are Princes ruled by Shadow Magicians. They live in the Shadow Magician's wonderful, ethics-less kingdom. It is ethics-less because no King at its moral center blesses certain creations fully and restrains others. It is ethics-less because it encourages endless creativity without a significant moral center.

A man who looks to his wife to tell him how to feel is probably an adult Prince exiled from sacred masculinity in a shadow kingdom ruled by the Feminine. One day, his wife will tire of telling him how to feel. She will become bored with him. For many of us, living in an age of feminine empowerment, the feminine approach to feeling seems empowering to men. And to some extent it is. We dig down into ourselves and find that, yes, there is within us a feminine element, a princess, who has been trapped in the cave. We want to free her. There is a Goddess in us just as there is in women.

Often I hear men say, "I need to become more like a woman." When we rescue and discover the feminine within us we are doing an important thing. We will find ourselves less homophobic. We will understand women's needs better. But we must not let the feminine rule us. As "kind and gentle" as feminine rule seems to make us, it cannot satisfy our masculine self. We will one day have to go back and see it for what it is—an amplified femininity with which we cover up feelings of masculine inadequacy.

Most of us as men have felt, at one time or another, Rock-Splitter's urge to hide from all intimate contact whatsoever. Our Shadow Lover is imprisoned. If we are ruled by that imprisonment, we will seek deeper and deeper imprisonment until we can see no light whatsoever out there. This manifestation of the Prince, living in this shadow kingdom, knows what the other manifestations, living in their shadow kingdoms, do not know: that all shadow kingdoms are ruled by the fear of intimacy. The wanderer wanders, often from one addiction to another, in order to avoid real intimacy. The Shadow Magician busies himself in overwork and ceaseless "creativity" to avoid intimacy with the few people he really needs for his spiritual growth. The Shadow Warrior makes war on faraway enemies to avoid intimacy with his enemies within. The Shadow Lover hides away to avoid any intimacy whatsoever. The Shadow Feminine attaches to female ways of intimacy to avoid intimacy with his own masculinity, a masculinity that may have hurt and neglected him when it was projected onto his disengaged father and other elder men.

In our addictions, our allegiances to cults, our immersion in unbridled technology, our childish love of weaponry; in our destruction of the environment, our inability to stabilize families, our desperation for new stimuli, and our turning away from old wisdom—in all these ways we are acting out the Prince's exile in shadow kingdoms. As men, we turn to anyone but ourselves for centering, without realizing that when a man gives up his own spiritual power to another force, he risks losing himself in the other's shadow. When a man joins a cult—whether a religious or political cult or the cult of youth—when he gives his sacred self over to an addiction, he is compounding the exile of his Prince with immersion in a shadow kingdom.

The break occurs when we become conscious of the fact that the cult has forced us to lose our power. It has forced more than our allegiance to its beliefs: it has forced our surrender. The break we make from mentors often occurs because the mentor's tutelage, once essential in our development, is sending us now into shadows the mentor may need to explore, dark places that we know—now that we've matured and can feel our separate Self—are dangerous or unnecessary for us. The break most of us made from addictions is made because the addiction sends us into life-disruptive shadows. Finally, often through the help of a ritual process like a twelve-step group, we begin a journey of emergence.

The first step toward regaining sacred masculinity is to acknowledge the adult Prince inside you, to feel your own lack of centeredness in masculinity, to notice your sense of exile from other men, and to acknowledge your particular manifestation of the shadow kingdom, whether it is addiction, wandering, distancing, a lack of ethics, feminizing, or overaggression. As you recognize yourself in these archetypes you'll recognize the Prince inside you, and you'll recognize the warped shadow archetypes who, in your adulthood, end up ruling your kingdom.

The next step in moving toward kingship is to recognize the eternal battle your adult unconscious is engaged in with your father. It is a conflict that only a conscious journey of confrontation can resolve.

INNER PRINCE AND INNER KING
IN CONFLICT

We have just seen how an adult Prince exiles himself in a shadow kingdom that probably relates back to his boyhood with his disengaged father. What remains to be shown is that while he serves a shadow kingdom, a kingdom ruled by one of the other archetypes, he knows he has abdicated his own kingship. He knows, like a young Prince who has abdicated his throne, that he himself should be King. Thus, even as it seems a man has surrendered to his addiction or distance or wandering, he is still struggling, desperately and unconsciously, to assert his own Sacred King. And the image he is struggling against is his own disengaged father.

A man caught in this archetypal conflict is like the addict trying desperately to give up the addiction his father lived, but failing. He is the wanderer trying desperately to settle down, but standing his next wife up at the altar. He is the feminized man trying desperately to feel like a man, but giving in again to what he thinks his wife wants of him.

The Prince caught in this conflict cannot give up the addiction or the wandering or the feminization until something drastic happens in his life. Speaking archetypally, he cannot resolve his crisis and ascend to his throne until the Prince and the Shadow King (his disengaged father) finally confront each other. From that confrontation will emerge the son's own Sacred King. The shadow archetype will be banished from the center of the man's psyche, and the Prince will be transformed, by the power of the confrontation, into his own King.

Let me put this another way. Because we have grown up with disengaged fathers, we are wounded initially by their lack of intimate trust. Then, because we don't have ritualized adolescent initiations into manhood—which could ground us in our male spirituality and purpose—we are doubly wounded. We *seem* to make the break from our father—when we leave home or go away to college—but there remains at the center of our being an inner father and an inner son engaged in a lifelong battle. In this conflict, the son is asking for nurturance and the father is pushing him away. The son is asking for a ritualized break and the father is not available. The boy who is Prince and the father who was King are still at war—even when the boy is forty or fifty years old.

To feel loving, wise, and powerful, a grown man who lives in this conflict must bring these two parts of his male psyche into confrontation. The King must replace the Prince. But a boy brought up in distance from the healthy Sacred King within his father will feel what anyone with a low self-image feels: part of him yearns for ascension to full manhood and kingship, and part of him believes only in his own inadequacy as a man. Most of us never grapple with this dilemma.

Yet we must. We must find a safe place and time to challenge and confront our disengaged fathers, who still linger in us with awesome and terrible control over our adult selves. *The Prince and the King* outlines a visionquest in which you can grapple with this issue—in which you can confront and finally surpass your father.

SURPASSING OUR FATHERS

In the mythology of princes and kings, the prince does not ascend to the throne without in some way surpassing his father. In the psychology of Princes and Kings, surpassing the father means a boy does not ascend to manhood without in some significant way gaining a sense of male purpose that surpasses his father's purpose; it is the duty of the Sacred Prince to take the Sacred King's work one step further. All of us feel this instinctually. As parents, we want a better life for our children; as young sons and daughters, we want to do more than Mom and Dad. Youth in its idealism wishes to accomplish what the aged have not yet accomplished.

Our surpassing of our fathers was probably confusing at the time it was occurring, and probably did not occur to any great degree. If you look for a moment at your own life, you'll probably notice that in some work or craft or business, you have undergone the initiation of surpassing: you are better than your father at certain things, and you know it. The important question is, Have you surpassed him psychologically, and is that surpassing complete?

The quality of a growing son's relationship with his father will dictate the character of his initiation of surpassing. If the father was relatively functional, trustworthy, and loving with the son, the son may take over the family business, "follow in his father's footsteps," stay very tribal and close to home in his family associations. He may surpass his father only in bringing computers into his father's furniture store, or by learning even more effective ways to practice law. Internally, he will go through the initiation of surpassing—an initiation that his father will probably support. His father will give him permission to journey, give him space to find himself as a man, and be there to help when his help is appropriate.

"Go to college," the sacred father might say, "go to business school, learn the new systems, be successful in ways I could never be. And be yourself. I support you in your search." The son will break from his father, will journey, then return home to enhance his father's kingdom, build his own kingdom next door as he has his own family, and finally, after his father retires or dies, ascend to his father's throne. In this father-son relationship, the father King will even be able to bless the son Prince if the son journeys and discovers that he does not want to take over the family business—that in fact he wants to build his kingdom a thousand miles away. Each of us must move forward in life asking the question, "Have I surpassed my father psychologically, and is that surpassing complete?"

Perhaps your father was an alcoholic and you discovered that you were, too. If you've now been sober for a good while, then you have surpassed your father in that psychological way. Perhaps your father was a child abuser. If you've been through therapy or personal-growth work and broken the chain of abuse with your own young children, you've surpassed your father in that way. What the therapeutic community calls *recovery* is surpassing when that recovery involves breaking a psychological pattern, a family curse, your father has passed on to you.

If you have gone through experiences of surpassing like these, you may have had the kinds of archetypal experiences I am about to describe. You may not have realized their mythological and archetypal character, but you have been through them. You may even have completed your surpassing of your father—an initiatory process that can last decades. You may also have further surpassing to do. One of the things the next chapters of this book are designed to do is to help you discover the ways in which you have already surpassed your father, and to encourage further initiation away from your father that you need to accomplish.

In the sacred context (in ideal father-son relationships), the King—the father—is healthy and simply needs an heir. The functional King wants to pass on his male lineage and craft to his son. But even then, the son will often not feel like the complete heir until his father, the king, dies. Male psychology works in a similar, more symbolic way. We do not murder our fathers to become men; rather, *killing* means breaking from them. We must break from our father to feel like a king. This break is the first, rudimentary step of surpassing him. If we were brought up by disengaged fathers, we cannot break from our fathers without killing off much of what they stood for and much of what they taught us. This fact makes our break with them terribly difficult.

Killing Our Fathers

The Oedipal myth, on which Freud based some of his most important theoretical reflections, and in which Oedipus kills his father and sleeps with his mother, is perhaps our best-known mythological case of patricide, a kind of patricide that dramatically symbolizes the son's break from his absent father. Strong Hans kills his abusive outlaw father. And Zeus had to kill his father, Cronos, for Cronos had the tendency to snack on his own sons. In the "killing the father" myths, the father is not redeemable. No amount of blessing will redeem him. He must be killed so the son's self can emerge.

Oedipus killed Laius without knowing Laius was his father. Hans killed his adoptive father without knowing who his biological father was. Zeus killed his father knowing full well who his father was. In each case, the son gained strength and purpose from the killing. In Oedipus's case that purpose ended in tragedy. Freud has done more than enough to analyze this tragedy; we won't remark further on it here. In Hans's case, the killing of the outlaw father gave him freedom to seek his real father. In Zeus's case, the killing of Cronos gave him power to rule all the world's kingdoms.

When we have to become Oedipus, Hans, or Zeus, we become very afraid. We don't want to kill a father we barely knew. That would be like killing off what little father we had. As John Lee says, we feel like there's a thin cord that connects us to this father, a very thin cord. If we cut it we might just float away.

And thus many of us don't kill our fathers. Some of us are killed *by* our fathers. When it came time to do the killing, we slunk away, or we still slink away. Our self-image is still aching from his brutality yet is also still aching for him, the man who killed our insides, to resurrect us. If you are this kind of man you know in your head that he cannot redeem you. You know *you* must take control. But in your heart you are still waiting for him.

It's frightening to kill your father, whether you and he have had a close relationship and in breaking from him you feel afraid of being on your own, or whether killing him is part of your recovery process but makes you afraid of the unknown in an equally powerful way. But it must be done. When you do it, what you thought of as a thin cord linking you to him will become a golden rope that will connect you to the sacred archetypal father, the Sacred King who is very healthy and waits to be discovered inside you.

Oedipus killed his father but did not discover the archetypal father within. As a story of male development, a primary root of his tragedy lies in that deficiency. We must realize that when we kill our fathers we are not like Oedipus. We don't kill the *whole* father, only a portion of him. We kill the shadow father so the sacred father can emerge. Strong Hans killed the shadow father in order to discover his sacred father. Zeus killed his shadow father and found his own divinity. He went on to rule omnipotently and immortally. When as modern sons we kill our fathers, we're killing his shadow side while trying to help the sacred side emerge. Until we have engaged the Sacred King in our vision of our father, we cannot discover it in ourselves.

Replacing the Shadow Father with the Sacred Father

Those of you who have said, "I am not going to be an alcoholic like my father," and have changed have killed the shadow father. But often in the recovery process, finding the sacred father who will replace the shadow father is equally difficult. Believing in a higher power is a first step in accepting the sacred element back into your self. Yet a higher power is not your own King; it's not your whole archetypal story.

Perhaps you go home for a visit and step back into the dysfunction your father still curses with his drinking. Perhaps you stand there, feeling your own dysfunctional adult-child role taking over, and you cry within yourself, "I've changed, so why don't I feel better now, when I need to most, here with Dad?" Or perhaps you are able to separate yourself from Dad but are unable to bring your new strength into present relationships.

You may be feeling the cry for the sacred. You may be back in your father's kingdom yearning for it. Yet his kingdom cannot give it. You no longer drink. You've surpassed him, yet you haven't completed the surpassing. You still have to go deeper into your own darkness and discover the sacred father that's buried within *you*. You are still acting in a Prince mode, waiting for the Sacred King to bless you from without. You now have no choice but to look within.

Most of us are faced with this kind of situation during our personal growth process. Whether it is substance or sexual addiction, numbness, distance, closed-off feelings, overwork, or wandering, we work to surpass it and stand before our father, or his memory, still asking him to acknowledge the redemption. He, for his part, is usually still caught up in his old pattern. In the inward journey of killing and surpassing, we do something more: we find a way to allow the sacred father within us to bless the little Prince still inside us and thereby bring him to his kingship.

It is exactly this that occurs in the second part of "Strong Hans." In the first part, Hans fights his shadow father many times, losing initially because he is not yet physically and mentally strong enough to win. The outlaw father hits him and shames him, forcing him to come back year after year. In our own lives our fathers might say, "Come back, Son, when you can take me on. Until then, don't shake your fist at me." On the last try Hans does finally kill his abusive father. But then in adulthood he must go back down into the cave and do it again, within his own inner darkness. It is from this adult journey downward that he emerges to discover a mature kingdom.

The vast majority of us are like Hans. The Oedipus myth, with which our culture is so familiar, is deeply complex in its treatment of mothers and sons, and deceptively simple in its treatment of father-son issues. In it, the son, separated from his father at birth, kills his father the first time he meets him. Most of us have not lived this. Most of us have lived like Hans, fighting our fathers all along, fighting for their affection and attention, and fighting against their shadow side, trying all through our childhood, adolescence, and especially adulthood to be our own man.

Our fight with our fathers, even after we've wrestled ourselves free of one of their addictions or negative patterns, will still remain archetypally constant unless we do something consciously—as, for example, you are offered the opportunity to do in the next chapters of this book. Unless we *do* something, we'll go to men's workshops and raise our families and carry on relationships but still never quite feel like our own Kings. We must not only walk away from our fathers' negative patterns; we must also walk into our own positive center. This we accomplish in the full initiation of surpassing them. This we accomplish in whatever is our equivalent to the second part of the Strong Hans story. This we accomplish when we confront our fathers, grieve for them and, finally, accomplish the hardest task of all: forgive them.

FORGIVING THE SHADOW KING

The outlaw father and the distant, diminished father have counterparts throughout world mythology, counterparts with which Princes must make peace if they are to succeed in their quest for kingship. This final step of the Prince's journey, forgiving the father, is psychologically negated in our religious culture to such an extent that it becomes nearly impossible for us to forgive our own dads.

While we preach forgiveness from every pulpit, we don't preach forgiveness of the Father. In fact, we preach just the opposite. As much as they teach us self-respect and respect for others, our culture's ancient religions and guiding mythologies also teach us that fathers should rule sons from a distance and require from them absolute perfection. This is not something to forgive fathers for. Just the opposite: it is we who should be forgiven for not having met their expectations. According to our religious culture, we have no power to forgive him, the Father. He must forgive us. It should not surprise us, therefore, that forgiving our mothers, our friends, our lovers, and our children is often easier than forgiving our fathers.

In *Wonders of the Invisible World*, published in Boston in 1693, the Puritan preacher Jonathan Edwards scares the hell out of every son and daughter he can. He gives us the same message people have gotten for three thousand years: the King is angry with us. We Princes have screwed up. "The Bow of God's Wrath is bent, and the Arrow made ready on the String; and Justice bends the Arrow at your Heart, and strains the Bow; and it is nothing but the mere Pleasure of God, and that of an angry God, without any promise or Obligation at all, that keeps the Arrow one Moment from being made drunk with your Blood. . . ."

The curse of paternal abuse and distance that we experienced in our own homes has been entrenched in the male (and female) psyche by the beautiful and morally rich Old and New Testaments. Whether we were avid churchgoers as kids or merely heard our friends quote Old Testament and New Testament material about God, we were bred to expect rage and shaming and distance from the Father.

God the Father requires that Abraham kill his son to prove his faith. The Abraham-Isaac story is a story of father and son that has been so romanticized in our culture that we've forgotten the real truth it teaches: that a son is the father's to slaughter without explanation. Abraham is in a state of self-doubt concerning his faith in God. Whom will he sacrifice to assuage that doubt? His son. When our fathers beat us with fists or with distance, often taking out their own aggressions for their own self-doubts, their eyes were not on us. Their eyes and hearts were not pointed toward the nurturance of our Prince and the future ascension of our King. Their eyes, like Abraham's, were looking upward toward a Father who would discharge their own self-doubt by accepting the son instead.

When you fight internal and external battles of healing with your father, you are fighting a battle with God himself. God's eye has always been lodged deep in your father's eye, especially if you are a churchgoer and accept the God of holy books as a father figure. In the Abraham-Isaac story, there is never any mention of the fact that Isaac needs to go through a process of forgiving his father. Isaac never processes his near-death at all. The Father is sacrosanct. The Father is God (the Sacred/Shadow King). The Father does not need to be forgiven; he is the forgiver.

In the New Testament the Abraham-Isaac story becomes a God the Father–Jesus story. The New Testament is certainly a gentler book than the Old. A great deal of militancy is replaced with mercy. However, the old father-son pattern is still intact. Again a son must be sacrificed if the Father is to see the worth of his children. Christianity, as much as Judaism, buys into the destructive Oedipal patterning of fathers and sons, perpetuating it like a disease throughout our culture. The son's worth is never to be real in the father's eyes except by the absolute sacrifice of the son.

Nowadays we sons do not, like Jesus, offer up our lives as a sacrifice. But we do sacrifice something that makes up our lives: our feelings. We have been taught for so long that sons gain worth in their fathers' eyes by their own destruction that we have destroyed that part of ourselves our fathers seemed the most uncomfortable with—our deep emotions.

We wonder why women say, "You don't feel anything. Where are you?" Our isolation from our feelings was part of the father-son pact we made with Dad. He's isolated from his feelings, yet must be redeemed. So we become isolated from our own to justify him. Like Isaac, we allow ourselves to be sacrificed. Like Jesus, we are sacrificed.

I've often heard men say, "I don't know how to approach, much less change, my father. He was distant and enraged and capricious and never satisfied. When he was hurting me it was sometimes like he didn't really see *me*."

This kind of father was Abraham at the moment of raising

the knife. Our cultural mythology does not teach us that a son
has the right to grieve the fact that his father doesn't really see
him (the son's inner self, the son's deepest emotions), nor does
it teach us that sons have a need to forgive their fathers for that
distance. It teaches us, instead, to accept the situation and live
with it.

The pressure of our culture's archetypal imperatives,
passed down through religious institutions, cannot be under-
estimated. It is partly because of these imperatives that Isaacs
like ourselves accept as a matter of course our fathers' destructive, emotionally repressive behavior, and later perpetrate it on
our own sons. We were brought up with it, and unless we take
experiential and conscious steps to separate ourselves from that
curse, we cannot forgive our own fathers.

There is little we can do to change our fathers. Many of
them remain lonely, distant men, and for some of us they're already dead. There's not much point in saying to them, "The
whole culture teaches me that I must accept you and that I have
no right to grieve or to forgive you, but I need to do that." There
is little time even to approach these men.

But grieving, surpassing, and forgiving our fathers is not
done for them. It is done to establish in us an archetypal inner
Father who, once established, will initiate us into further manhood throughout the rest of our lives. Forgiving our fathers is a
final step in a process that we go through in order to find male
sacredness within ourselves. Without forgiving the father, our
inner father cannot be established.

THE PRINCE'S JOURNEY

Men are in spiritual danger. Compelled to become men without
initiation beyond the boy Prince, we're forced to look into
warped and opaque mirrors, until we cannot see anything except inadequacy and shadows. We're in danger of losing contact
with our sacred selves, our deep feelings of connectedness, our
souls.

For years we have treated the repression of male feeling as
a mainly emotional question and sought the answer in our
female lovers and their way of doing things. We've learned a lot

from women, but recently we are turning to other men for answers, for emotional and for spiritual answers. We are turning to other men, and looking back at our relationships with our fathers, so that at least we know the right male questions to ask. We are seeing ourselves as exiled princes who yearn to come home.

"What I do now will affect the next seven generations," say the Sioux. The destructive father-son patterns we live have gone on for more than seven generations. If men of our generation do not reclaim the male soul, we will simply pass on our curse and our wound to our sons, as our fathers did to us. We will force our sons' inner Princes into exile. Our sons will never know what a whole man is, what a mature male hero is.

The next chapters of *The Prince and the King* ask you to go on a visionquest. In it you will move toward your own mature male heroism, a heroism that will seem opposed in many ways to the heroism you've been trained to seek, for it is a heroism based on spiritual self-definition rather than public expectation.

The ground of this spirituality, the ground of a mature hero, is self-trust, trust in your maleness, a trust that cannot be gained until you go back and fully understand, and confront and forgive, and finally make peace with your father. Once that trust is nurtured, the mature hero within you can rise up and be counted. Once that trust is nurtured, your Prince can become King.

PART TWO

Healing the Father-Son Wound: A Guided Journey of Initiation

Everything we do affects the next seven generations.

SIOUX INDIAN PROVERB

FOUR

Beginning
Your Heroic Quest

*Somewhere in our early education we become addicted to
the notion that pain means sickness. We fail to learn that
pain informs the mind that we are doing something wrong,
not necessarily that something is wrong. . . . We get the
message of pain all wrong. Instead of addressing ourselves to
the cause, we become pushovers for pills, driving the pain
underground and inviting it to return with increased
authority.*

NORMAN COUSINS

*I asked myself, "What is the myth you are living?" and found
that I did not know. So I took it upon myself to get to know
my myth, and I regarded this as the task of tasks.*

CARL JUNG

In the remaining chapters of this book, I will act as an invisible
mentor-guide who will help you discover pathways to your
sacred self. I will guide you on an odyssey through your own internal landscape, your memory, your present relationships, and
your future potential. The quest you embark upon will be a
search for information, understanding, inspiration, and recovery. You will be asked to perform a series of tasks, some very
difficult, that will constitute an intense journey of initiation
into mature masculinity.

Some of the tasks involve asking yourself questions. Others involve asking questions of other people, some of them people you knew decades ago. Some of these encounters may be

confrontational. All are likely to involve very deep communications. You'll be encouraged to make phone calls and even visit people in other cities, especially mentors and old men who have been significant in your life. You'll be directed to make very specific lists and genealogical maps, to gather photographs and to write letters. You'll be helped to confront demons that still haunt your inner life. You'll find your father waiting for you, and you'll be supported in confronting him, whether he is living or dead. Through guided meditation, you'll be taken on inward journeys by means of which you can probe your psyche and unconscious memory.

Like all heroes and visionquesters, you will be in search of your authentic self. As you find pieces of that self, you'll be encouraged to take the intensity of your experience to partners, spouses, friends, and groups of other men.

The goal of this personal odyssey is ultimately the journey itself: to rediscover and to live what is sacred within yourself. And like so many heroic quests, it has a specific, tangible goal, a grail: the healing of your father-son wound. If you can accomplish that, or at least take significant experiential steps toward recovering from that wound, you'll have made it through an initiatory experience like no other. You will have gone back down into the cave, like Strong Hans did, afraid but strong. You'll have challenged the shadows of your father and risen back to the surface again.

The personal odyssey you are invited to undertake in this book is similar to initiatory Hero's Journeys and Vision Quests. It involves a good deal of ceremony and ritual. Its tasks are like those faced by the heroes Jason, Hercules, Arthur, Parsifal, Telemachus, Gilgamesh, and Indra. It involves connecting to your pain and grief by going through painful ordeals. And it involves the return to sacred stories. We'll continue to find challenges, "Medicine," and our own archetypal patterns in stories about Princes and Kings from around the world. These stories will help us through the initiation process in some very specific and subtle ways.

The most useful Prince-King story I know is that of Telemachus and his father, Odysseus. Their story will become our map as we journey together, explorers into your mythic and emotional depths. If you had more than one father, more than one Odysseus, in your childhood—perhaps a biological and an adoptive father or stepfather—you may find that you have more than one Odysseus toward whom you need to journey.

The story of Telemachus and Odysseus was recorded by the great Greek storyteller Homer. It is one of the most translated and influential epic stories in human history. If you look at that story as a basic map of a man's inner landscape, you find that in significant moments of the son's search for his father, he is searching for his own sacred self as well. Telemachus meets mentors, understands his own strengths and needs, visits the old men who guide and inform his life, meets his inner Warrior, encounters the Goddess, makes mistakes, makes painful decisions, encounters the Lover, meets his father, leaves his mentors, and discovers his own King.

As you accomplish tasks equivalent to those faced by Telemachus, you move through the archetypal stages of the search for the King. You will find that you have already completed some of these tasks, though their completion may be unremembered—and you will find that other pieces of the journey are beginning now. With Homer's Telemachus story as a base, we will make the experiential journey that mythology has told for millennia, the journey in which a man transforms himself from Prince to empowered King.

James Hillman says, "Psychology as religion [we might substitute "Psychology as spirituality"] implies imagining all psychological events as effects of Gods in the soul." These "Gods" (and goddesses) are not out there, on Mount Olympus, in Homer's ancient Greece; they are our own archetypes. As Telemachus listens to the gods in his mythic landscape, you will listen to the gods (and goddesses) in your own soul. As the gods and goddesses helped Telemachus dig into the dark corners of himself during his search, your sacred archetypes will help you dig into the dark corners of your own empowerment.

You can make this journey without reading (or rereading) Homer's *Odyssey,* but a reading of that great myth would help a great deal. Many translations exist. Most are adequate for our purposes here. When I make references to the tale, I will be referring to W. H. D. Rouse's translation.

THE STORY OF ODYSSEUS AND
TELEMACHUS

Odysseus, you may remember, was the hero of the Trojan War. In this war the Trojans attempted to withstand a siege on their walled city by the Greeks, who'd come from across the Mediterranean. Odysseus was the cunning Greek general who suggested that his soldiers build a huge wooden horse to be given as a gift to the Trojans. This legendary Trojan horse was, of course, the strategic gift that led to a Greek victory in the ten-year war.

The war between the Greeks and the Trojans probably did not begin for the reason Homer gives—that the Greek beauty, Helen, was stolen from her husband, Menelaus, by the Trojan prince, Paris, and taken to Troy. It probably began, as the British archeologist Michael Woods has argued, because of a trade dispute with the Hittites. But in mythology it began for love, as so many of our emotional and spiritual journeys do. So for our purposes we'll let it be as Homer tells it. The great Greek generals and armies stood alongside the wronged Greek husband, Menelaus, outside the embattled walls of Troy, ready to rescue Helen and "show their stuff."

In Homer's tale, by the time Odysseus came up with his idea, great warriors had already been lost and other warriors, once unsung, had found their places of greatness. Achilles had been shot dead in the only vulnerable spot on his body, his heel, where long ago his mother had gripped him as she dipped him into the waters of invulnerability. Hector, too, was dead. Odysseus, among other greats, remained. As he commanded the huge wooden horse to be built, he also ordered a contingent of warriors to hide in its hollow belly. Then he told all the Greek armies to recede and he called to the Trojans to accept his so-called gift of truce.

The Trojans, late that night, wheeled the wooden horse into their walls. At midnight, while the Trojans were asleep, Odysseus's men climbed out of the horse's belly, opened the gates for the Greek armies, and the Trojan war ended with a brutal sacking of the city of Troy.

It is of this battle and many other legendary feats that Telemachus heard back in Ithaca, where he was growing up with his mother, Penelope. The son heard of his father's greatness but felt sadly distant from it. His own male identity was unclear to him throughout his father's twenty-year absence. And, as in "Strong Hans" and in so many myths of sacred fathers disengaged, remote, or gone, outlaw fathers stepped into the father's void: twenty years old but still a boy-prince, Telemachus stood meekly by as ugly, brutal suitors pillaged his father's treasures and kingdom and wooed Penelope, doing everything short of raping her.

Telemachus had no strong feeling of his own personal power. He could do nothing to counter these outlaw fathers. He yearned for his own King, his own sacred masculinity, to rise up and be counted. But for this to happen he first had to find his father. So he decided, finally—with some good advice from the gods—to search for him.

Telemachus's sacred father, Odysseus, had seemed heroic to him in legends. But when Telemachus was twenty the Trojan War had been over for ten years, and still his father was missing. Our boyhoods, too, have been over for years, and we feel, like Telemachus, that with every year we get further and further away from understanding and knowing what was and is sacred in the first man we knew.

Let us begin our journey and our visionquest in the same place Telemachus began: ready for the pain of seeking the father, ready for the danger of seeking the King.

Homer begins his tale of male self-discovery, self-empowerment, and self-trust with the line, "This is the story of a man . . ." We begin our tale with the same line. We are men, yet something is missing within us. Become Telemachus for the ritual space and the ritual time of your heroic quest. Become him and know yourself as mythic, as sacred.

Know yourself as an ancient prince in sandals. Feel the rocks of the earth pressing against your heels and soles. Know that the landscape of your soul is a masculine landscape of ancient things. It invites you to walk on it, to search for yourself everywhere in it, like a man beckoning a boy to great power and wisdom.

Discover the epic story of one son and one father that sings within *you in particular.* It will be a piece of the universal story of fathers and sons. It will be your own story of a son who, in search of his own mature masculinity, must make a search for his lost father. If you had two fathers in your upbringing—if, for instance, a stepfather became your father for a large portion of your childhood—you may need to do the rituals in this book for both these men. Use the process to fit your life.

As much as you can, seek support throughout your quest. Share your experiences with other men and women in safe places, in safe ways. Undertake this quest with a therapist or trusted friend, or in a men's group. If you can be part of a Prince-King group specifically formed for men to make this quest together, consider joining or forming such a group. To make this quest privately will be initiatory: it will help move you from one stage in your life to the next. To make this quest in the company of other men will be initiatory not only for you, but also for them.

I have learned as I've facilitated this work that any adult male can practice and experience this process of self-initiation. It is necessary only that you open yourself to it, and bring to it diligence and energy. The guided meditations, the stories, the revised mythology, the memories, the grief, the journaling, the letter writing and oral storytelling will rise up out of you. Even if you dislike self-disclosure, you will find yourself *wanting* your own mythic story to come, because it will be *your* mythology, personal to you, available uniquely to you, and as powerful to you as you're willing to let it be.

SEVEN BASIC TENETS
OF A MAN'S HEROIC QUEST

As you move through this process, you may at times want to re-fer back to the tenets given here. For this process to be effective, it needs to be woven through your life; it needs to be returned to at some personal ritual time you set aside for yourself, away from family and commitments.

James Hillman has connected personal growth with what he calls *slowness*. Slow discovery honors your inner voice in a way that quick change does not. Until we slow down we cannot get to the depths of our spiritual selves. Your personal odyssey work needs this slowness, this ritual rhythm. And because it needs that, the precepts are likely to be forgotten. When you need to, repeat these seven tenets to yourself as a way of bringing yourself back to the objectives of your inner search.

1. A *man* is a loving, wise, and powerful male adult. I strive to live in the fullness a man deserves. I strive to live with spiritual connectedness to my deepest self, my friends and family, and my surrounding world. I strive to live in more than a survival mode. I strive to know my sacred self.

2. The human unconscious is a mythological story. It unfolds in my outer life with chaotic, day-to-day complexity, while unfolding in my inner story with the epic simplicity of mythology. Certain universal myths (what Native Americans call *medicine stories*, or *stories that heal*) reflect my inner story.

3. My outward behavior and inward yearnings are guided by countless personal myths I rarely articulate. Many of these ensure my survival and the survival of my loved ones. Many of these enhance my spirituality. Many of these inhibit survival and inhibit spirituality.

4. My personal myths are not written in stone, just as wounds are not permanently damaging. I can change my personal myths. I can heal my wounds.

5. Not all damaging personal myths and wounds respond to personal odyssey work. Some need twelve-step groups, men's groups, transformative therapy, even hospitalization. I need to seek help when I need it. I will make the right choice about how to pursue my growth.

6. There is no such thing as a perfect man. We are all wounded. We gain strength by honoring our wounds. I am wounded. I gain strength by honoring the wounds I received in my father's house.

7. For centuries, our male culture has turned away from the magic of the inner story and toward the radiant distractions of external stimulation. To change myself, I must look inward toward the dark center of my being, where my sacred self lives.

TOOLS FOR YOUR QUEST

Now let's look in some detail at some of the techniques and tools you will use on your quest.

Personal Rituals

All significant human growth needs ritual. A ritual is a personal or communal act, using symbolic objects and sacred places, that marks an important event or process. All societies and all human beings create and discover rituals of importance to them. You already have many in your own life. You may not feel you have enough *sacred* rituals. This book will help you develop personal rituals in which you can feel safe as you undertake the odyssey of this book and through which you can celebrate your inner world.

RITUAL SPACE AND RITUAL RHYTHM. Ritual space is the safe place that used to be called a sacred place or church. In this safe place we slow down to a ritual rhythm and are thus able to hear the truth, however we define that word.

We each need to develop personal rituals of enough depth to create our own personal churches and sacredness. This is not to say we shouldn't seek community in churches and synagogues. This is simply to say that going to church on Sunday is not enough to facilitate deep growth, to heal father-son wounds.

We create and discover ritual spaces more than we realize. A ten-minute session every morning on the toilet with the bathroom door closed can give you the only peace and quiet you get all day. An act even that mundane can create a kind of ritual space for you.

In seeking personal growth, the ritual space needs to be sanctified not only in the feeling of peace and safety it gives you, but also in the content of your actions in it. The shock of insight in therapy is grounded in ritual space and ritual rhythm. The weekly lunch you have with your wife to discuss important family matters can be a ritual space and, if uninterrupted by phone calls and outside stresses, can settle for that hour into a ritual rhythm. It can feel very safe.

In the process of working with this book, you will want to discover a quiet place where you can do the meditative, memory, and writing work of the quest, a little bit at a time, uninterrupted by family or work concerns. If you undertake the odyssey of this book with your men's group, then that is a ritual space. If you do so on your own, make sure to find a place of peace. If you can go out into the woods, someplace away from anyone else, your ritual space and ritual rhythm will be all the more connected with the original landscape, the natural world, from which your body and mind originate.

Finding a safe time is part of finding a safe place. Many rituals, like the journal writing that is part of the quest of this book, go deepest into the self when they are done at a similar time every day. Professional writers will tell you how important it is "to get up every morning and write," or to "write every night after dinner." You need to find the time of day when your mind and heart are most open, most imaginative, and least distractible.

SACRED ACTS AND OBJECTS. For your writing process to have significant power, and for you to be able to move as easily as possible from your busy working life to the slower rhythm of your inner story, you need to discover symbolic objects and acts around which to focus your transition from busyness to slowness. When the truth stick is passed from one man to another as a Native American men's council begins, this is done not only to allow each man to say where he is on this particular evening, but also to slow things down, to make the transition from the nonsacred space of the busy life to the sacred space of the ritual world.

Maybe you'll choose to always write with a certain kind of pen. Maybe you will write on a certain kind of paper. Maybe you will read a poem before you start writing. Maybe you will listen to some music, light a candle, say a few words, drum, chant. Whatever you do, find symbolic acts and objects by which to make the transition to the ritual space and rhythm. Later, as you journey, you will find and create further sacred objects.

Guided Meditation

Many of the rituals this book provides involve guided meditation. These guided journeys need some preparation. Whenever you get ready to do one of the guided meditations or other tasks in this book, it's important that you go through some kind of personal ritual by which your ordinary mental chatter is silenced. Your body, too, must be ready to turn away for a while from its usual hypersensitivity to external stimulation, so that it can sense, for the time of the meditation ritual, its inner rhythms.

Your very breathing needs to be slowed down, disciplined, and opened up in ways it has not been before. As Nathaniel Branden says, "Opening the breathing is generally the first step to opening the feelings. It creates a condition of stillness, a condition in which we stop running, so that our emotions have a chance to catch up with us." Take deep breaths, and pace your breathing evenly as you move through the meditations.

If you already have your own style of meditation, bring that style to this book. If you have never meditated before, always remember to work toward three things: relaxing the body, evening out the breath, and clearing the mind.

To make the guided meditations flow more easily, you might want to read them into a tape recorder, then play them back as you do the process. You might also ask someone else to read them to you. If a men's group member or other man can read them to you, his low voice can resonate with the journey toward the father. Read the meditations slowly and deliberately. Avoid hurrying. Avoid losing the ritual rhythm. Stay as relaxed as you can. If you wish you may order tapes that include the guided meditations in this book set to background music. See page 272 for more information.

Your Journal

Many of the tasks in your quest will involve writing in a journal. Many of the questions and answers, confrontations and memories, letters and meditations will need to be written and recorded. A thick journal is the best way to hold all of these writings together in one volume, a volume that will become sacred to you.

We could just perform tasks and not keep a written record. But writing is a powerful experiential tool of healing and growth. Truly, its power to raise consciousness and to heal emotional wounds cannot be overestimated. If you can do a task and then describe the experience in writing, it's as if you are doing the task twice, gaining empowerment by claiming it in words. Gabriele Rico explains the healing power of writing very well:

> The language of the emotions is elusive, fragile, multi-faceted, because our emotional being is logically undefin-able. The very act of putting pencil to paper is an act of giving shape to amorphous feelings. Whatever our crisis, whatever our sorrow, whatever our feeling, to name it is to frame it. Expression empowers us to transform our feel-ings; it permits us to connect our stories with the stories of others, to bridge the gulf of our essential isolation from one another.

For your journal to become a powerful tool of self-discovery and self-transformation, you must use it as a knife: pare with it, trim with it, treat it with sacredness as it reveals to you the powers you have. You are on a visionquest, and the words you use in your journal are your knife, one of your most sacred and important tools. Journal and journey come from the same root. The knife is the warrior's ritual tool and the journal is the traveler's ritual tool.

There are effective and ineffective ways to use your jour-nal, just as there are effective and ineffective ways to use your knife. A journal that stresses analysis of events rather than the feelings the events caused; a journal that records other people's notions and explanations rather than your own; a journal that worries about grammar and details of formal English—such a journal will be of little help in making a journey into deep imagination and deep feeling. Write freely, and focus on "I feel" and "I experienced" statements.

PREPARING THE NOTEBOOK. Find a blank notebook, relatively thick, in which you will record answers to questions, letters, memories, interviews, stories about your feelings, and re-sponses to meditations.

Draw straight lines vertically on every page, beginning at about five inches from the left or right margin, depending on whether you are left or right-handed. Leaving this open space will allow you to come back and record in it a feeling or memory whose description was left unfinished at the last sitting.

FREE WRITING. Always free-write during first sittings. Don't be concerned with surface mechanics or missing a thought. If, a day later, you want to bring out another aspect of a feeling or memory, then do so in the open space. Free writing is essential for keeping an open channel to the heart. Formal and self-critical writing is good for college papers and business memos, but not for early sittings of personal odyssey work.

A PRELIMINARY TASK. Finding your own rhythm of writing and discipline of feeling in written language will take some time. Set aside a week or two for preparation. During this time, pick a subject and write about it for twenty minutes to a half hour four days a week. These subjects should be profound and central to your life. What follows is one suggested pattern. Respond to the following questions and statements.

DAY 1. WHO AM I?

  1. How do I look physically to myself?

  2. I describe my personality as . . .

  3. My strengths as a man are . . .

  4. My limitations as a man are . . .

DAY 2. WHAT AM I LIKE IN RELATIONSHIPS?

  1. How do I look physically to my partner, spouse, or best friend?

  2. How would this person describe my personality?

  3. My strengths in my relationships are . . .

  4. My limitations in my relationships are . . .

DAY 3. HOW DO I FIT IN MY COMMUNITY AND SOCIETY?

  1. Where am I headed as a man in this society?

  2. Where do I want to be headed, especially where my work is concerned?

  3. My strengths in social situations are . . .

  4. My limitations in social situations are . . .

DAY 4. WHAT IS MY RELATIONSHIP TO THE NATURAL WORLD AROUND ME?

  1. How do I explain the mysteries of the world?

  2. Do I sense a presence or presences in nature greater than myself?

3. When have I sensed this?

4. If I have not, is that okay with me?

In all your journal writing, stick with memories and feelings. Try to avoid a mind/body split, a head/heart split, as much as possible.

You'll notice that in the preliminary subjects suggested above, there is no explicitly mythological material. As you are practicing the writing experience, it's best to save the mythological journey and reliance on its language until you are comfortable with journaling. Get a feel for the journaling process for a while before actually starting chapter 5.

JOURNALING ON TAPE. Can a journal be done by voice, on tape? Yes it can. You may feel that in giving some of your responses to the episodes and experiences of this quest, you will benefit from oral journaling. If you choose this route, make sure to catalog your tapes carefully. One of the benefits of journaling your quest is that you can go back a week, a month, even ten years later and look at what you experienced. This is less possible with tapes, since they get more easily lost, erased, or misplaced. Finding a particular day's entry on a tape weeks later can mean rewinding and fast-forwarding and frustration. Writing can also be more effective than taping, since in writing your feelings you have to slow down a little and engage them.

Nevertheless, taping can be advantageous, especially for those times when the feelings and memories are coming too fast for your pen to keep up.

If you do choose to journal on tape, think about doing some on tape and some on paper. Perhaps you can make a ritual out of this choice, choosing to journal orally after each guided meditation but in written form during other experiences.

For ease of direction, I will generally instruct you to write things in your journal. If you have chosen to use tapes, interpret *write* as *speak*.

GETTING THERAPY
AND FINDING MEN'S GROUPS

As you go through the process of this book you may find yourself experiencing some difficulty and pain. Old feelings concerning your father and other members of your family will arise. The wounded child inside you will relive some damaging experiences. The sacred self is not discovered without substantial and painful growth.

If throughout any of this process you believe interaction with a therapist would be helpful, don't hesitate to make the phone call. You honor your sacred self by doing so. Therapists serve the role of mentor and ritual elder. Therapy can be a very powerful initiation ritual.

Similarly, men's groups are initiatory, especially groups led by qualifed leaders. If deep issues should arise, especially issues concerning intimacy with other men, a men's group might be an even more useful place to find ritual space than a therapist's office.

YOUR FIRST TASK:
MAPPING YOUR FAMILY HISTORY

You stand at the threshold of your quest. In part I of this book and in this chapter so far, you've been sitting at the entrance to the dark wilderness, hearing medicine stories and receiving inner and outer guidance about what your quest needs to accomplish, what its tools are, how you can best experience it.

When a man enters upon his quest, Native Americans sometimes say he has a trail of light and darkness behind him. This trail is his personal and family history, which every man brings to his quest.

At this time, as you are preparing your journal and your ritual times and space, spend some time identifying important lights and shadows on your own behind-trail. Give a brief, emotionally detached history of your life up until the present day. In this brief history, places and people are more important than emotional entanglements.

1. Write where you were born and where you lived as a boy.

2. Write who your parents were and what their family histories were.

3. Write who your siblings were and are and what directions they have gone.

4. Write who your first girlfriend was, your best male friend, what you did in high school.

5. Write of your partners and spouse or spouses.

6. Write what your first job was, and your next.

7. Write how you got into your present career, what you sacrificed to get there.

8. Write about your own children, if you have children.

In this part of the ritual I'll give an instruction I will rarely give again: curtail your free writing whenever you feel emotional entanglements entering it. If you feel yourself starting to say, "I think it was when I was four years old that I felt my father didn't completely care about me," stop the sentence. Return to an emotionally detached life history. Give the facts—names, dates, places, and not much more. Many of your entries will not be full sentences, just listings and notes.

I ask you to curtail emotional entanglements in this instance because as you move beyond the threshold, you need to have an emotionally detached reference to life events that will serve as a frame for the emotionally entangled picture of your inner life you'll be painting and repainting throughout the rest of the journey. Later, you'll want to refer back to where you were at a given time, to your parents' and their parents' histories, and you will need your reference to be clean of entanglements.

Grief needs boundaries. Despair knows no boundaries. The journey I am guiding you on is a journey of grief, not despair. For your grief to be nurtured, a strong frame needs to hold you. The people, places, and things in your life history constitute a very strong frame. It has held you till now and will hold you till death. The "facts" about your life represent your destiny up to this point. That destiny is strong because it's vibrant and alive. It is strong despite the negative beliefs your self-image, wounded by your father-son relationship, may reflect. You are a man, and your destiny is a frame for everything else in your life. Write your history without entanglements, and view its milestones with pride.

Do more than writing or taping here. Get a ream of large drawing paper and draw a map with times, dates, and places on it, including your parents' and grandparent's histories. In other words, do a genealogy and much more. To complete this map you will probably have to call your relatives, even your parents, and ask many questions about your family's origins. You'll need to ask where your ancestors emigrated from. You will want to ask what the emotional relationships were between spouses in your lineage—"What were Great-Grandma and Great-Grandpa like?"; "What kind of a man was Grandpa so-and-so?"—but without getting emotionally entangled.

Attach photos next to the people you're representing as points and names on the drawing paper. Write short descriptions that capture these people and places. You may find yourself using up a whole wall with this kind of "family album." Assert yourself in the space of your own home. Find a wall that can be yours and use it. Your whole family will benefit from seeing your history on its walls.

Begin this task now and continue it over the days and weeks ahead. You don't have to finish the entire history before continuing on to chapter 5. What you need to do now is to get down on drawing paper and plastered on the wall the following: the dates and places of your growing up and significant life experiences; and a beginning history of your parents' and other ancestors' significant life experiences. It you have kids, bring them in to help you. Have one of your kids call Grandpa and ask what Great-Grandpa did and where his family came from. This whole life-history project can become a wonderful game.

When you have a map of your life and your family's life to frame your journey, move on to chapter 5, in which you cross the threshold.

Standing in the Wind
and Saying Who You Are

The "call to adventure" signifies that destiny has summoned
the hero and transferred his spiritual center of gravity from
within the pale of his society to a zone unknown.
                                        JOSEPH CAMPBELL

Everyone who begins an important journey hears the call to adventure. When Strong Hans set out to walk the forest as a man, he heard the call. When a young Sioux boy prepares for his Vision Quest, he hears the call. When, early in Homer's *Odyssey*, Telemachus yearns to find his father and his own kingship, he is hearing the call. Your own call to this particular adventure may have begun in some previous work you've done concerning your father. Now, in reading this book, you become like Hans, the Sioux boy, and Telemachus.

What will a man do with the call? That is the important question. Will a man set off on his journey out of mere curiosity, or will he answer the call to adventure with honest vulnerability? If he does the former, he will gain some skills of the Explorer and the Magician. To gain his King he must do the latter; he must get in touch with his deepest needs.

Early in Homer's story of the sacred son, Telemachus stands up to say who he is, and why he must journey toward his father. In describing the state of his house, he describes the state of his soul. "There is no man at its head," he cries, "no one like my father, to drive my curses out." Because he has not made the journey that will help him discover his own King, he yearns for his father to be his King.

Like Telemachus, we too have felt the wound of our lost fathers. Our relationships have suffered, our solitude has been spoiled, our masculinity damaged. Sometimes we hide in addictions; other times we survive in a constant, low-grade shame. We feel, like Telemachus, that if people really knew who we were they'd recognize our missing center; they would discover that there is no man at the head of our house. They would know us as Princes lost in the larger world; they would not know us as whole men, as Kings.

Telemachus, in admitting the hole he feels in his center, is like we are when we make ourselves vulnerable in a men's group, or with a therapist, or with a trusted friend. We are speaking our private need to the world; we are owning it. In some Native American traditions, this is called "standing in the wind and saying who you are." No man can fully answer the call to adventure without speaking his vulnerability. Mythology has expressed this for millennia. Only recently have men been trained so repressively that they're encouraged to make life's adventure without speaking from their souls.

As Telemachus's internal kingdom is at risk, so is yours. Each of you knows your own risk differently. Each man suffers the risk differently. Each man must therefore speak his own risk with his own voice. In the tasks that follow, you're guided to seek out your own particular curse and speak it to the wind as truthfully as you can. It is in this truth that your journey begins. The man you reveal now is the man who will be transformed by this journey.

TASK 1:
RECALLING YOUR FATHER'S KINGDOM

As you fulfill this task, you are asked to stand, as Telemachus stood, and define yourself in your father's shadow. You are asked to see your father archetypally, from the inside out, rather than as you've usually known him: a man who stood far outside of you so you could barely guess his remote insides. You'll then be guided to see yourself as his son, strong and skilled in some ways, wounded and vulnerable in others.

In this, as in later tasks, I'll invite you to enter into your wounds and entanglements using archetypal rituals. In this way, you won't enter the wounds and entanglements unprotected. You'll be holding a sword and shield. You will have the tools of grief, risking much less the despair and defensiveness that usually terminate journeys through our wounds.

To recall your father's kingdom, you will need a comfortable sitting position, a pen or pencil, and your journal. (In all these steps, of course, you may choose to substitute a tape recorder for pen and journal.) When you are comfortable, enter whatever personal ritual of relaxation you have developed. Beat your drum, meditate, do your mantra, concentrate on an image, picture, or point on the wall; however you can invoke your ritual space, do so. Go out into the woods if you can, away from any distractions.

When you have done your breathing and centering, concentrate on the father who brought you up. In this task, as with all others in this journey, if you had a significant stepfather, or a substitute father, like an uncle or grandfather, or an adoptive father, fulfill this task in relation to that person as well as to your biological father.

As you recall your father and the qualities of the King he may or may not have expressed, you will be guided to recall both how your father ordered his home/world and how he seemed to be ordered within himself. In performing this task, as in others later in this journey, recall what images come to you first, your first intuitions. Recall exact incidents, conversations, memories of yourself and family. Recall objects in rooms, the picnic table out back. Recall the way your father spoke, what he said, how his eyebrows drooped, what shoes he wore.

If few or no significant memories rise to your consciousness, or to enhance your memory process, try dividing up your childhood into four-year intervals. Spend time on where you lived from birth to age four. Recall your neighborhood and house. See yourself and your father in it. Then move to you from four years old to eight years old, and so on. Even if your father was distant and angry all the time in your conscious memory, you may discover surprising recollections of his attempts at nurturing and love.

Like Telemachus, you begin this journey in search of your father by defining yourself in his distant shadow. You are your father's son. Spend time now, in this ritual, understanding as exactly as possible some of the myths that make you that son.

You will now be asked many questions. You don't have to respond to each one. Write the questions in your journal. Respond to the ones that strike you as most important. Write for as long as you need. (You may recognize the descriptions of the King's characteristics from chapter 1. I am indebted to Robert Moore and Douglas Gillette for significant pieces of these.)

Did Your Father Know How to Use Power in a Healthy Way?

The King orders his world and guides others toward fullness in it.

1. In what healthy ways did your father lovingly order your home, your life, and the lives of your siblings, mother, and other family members? In what unhealthy ways did he do so?

2. In what healthy ways did he order the lives of other men and women who respected his leadership? In what unhealthy ways did he do so?

3. In what healthy ways did your father guide you to fullness? In what ways, especially, did he help you find fullness in loving others? In what unhealthy ways did he repress your fullness?

4. In what healthy ways did your father order his own life? In what unhealthy ways did he do so?

5. What healthy rituals gave him inner order? What unhealthy rituals did so?

6. Write down things he said during your upbringing that indicated his internal order. Write things he said that indicated his sense of internal chaos.

See him, and write him down in memory and image.

Was Your Father an Honest Man?

The King exudes integration and integrity as a man.

1. In what ways did your father exude integrity as a man in his dealings with others in your family and in the community? In what ways did he not?

2. In what ways did he defend and nurture your evolving masculine identity against outside attack? In what ways did he not?

3. In what ways did your father seem confident as a man? In what ways did he not?

4. In what ways did your father admit his mistakes to you? In what ways did he deny them?

See him. Write him down.

Was Your Father a Man of Self-Control and Stability?

The King stabilizes chaotic emotions and out-of-control behaviors. He brings maintenance and balance.

1. In what ways did your father bring stability to the lives around him? In what ways did he not?

2. In what ways did he calm others who were in crisis? In what ways did he not?

3. In what ways did your father calm his own terrifying emotions? In what ways did he not?

4. Was your father in control of himself? When did he tend to be the most out of control? When did he tend to be the most in control?

See your father. Write him down.

Was Your Father a Man Who Loved Life?

In his fertilizing and centeredness, the King embodies vitality, life force, and joy.

1. In what ways did your father bless and fertilize the gifts of others around him? In what ways did he not?

2. In what ways did your father bless and fertilize your gifts? In what ways did he not?

3. How did he make the world a place where you and others are safe to feel joy? How did he not?

4. Was your father full of life? Was he a joyful, vital man? When did he seem the most full of life? When did he not?

5. In what ways did he take care of himself so that he could remain focused on his passions? In what ways did he not?

6. What made him feel safe? What made him feel unsafe?

See him. Write him down.

Was Your Father Balanced in His Disciplining?

The King looks upon the world with a firm but kindly eye.

1. In what ways was your father kind and loving to you, your mother, your siblings, others in your family, and his acquaintances?

2. In what ways was he firm and loving with you, your family, and his acquaintances?

3. In what ways did your father balance kindness and firmness? In what ways did he not?

4. Did your father carry himself with healthy authority? Do you recall times when you wanted to emulate his way of judging?

See him. Write him down.

Did Your Father Honor and Promote?

The King sees others in all their weakness and in all their talent and worth.

1. In what ways did your father accept weaknesses in your mother, your siblings, and others around him? In what ways did he shame their weaknesses?

2. In what ways did your father accept, without shaming you, weaknesses in you? In what ways did he not?

3. Did your father shame his own defeats? Did your father honor his own victories?

4. In what ways did your father promote himself appropriately in the world of men? In what ways did he not?

See him. Write him down.

Was Your Father Secure in Himself?

The King is not envious or covetous.

1. In what ways did your father envy others? In what ways did he not?

2. In what ways did your father envy you? In what ways did he not?

3. What personal rituals did your father have for controlling his envy?

4. In what places and circumstances did your father feel the most secure in himself?

See him. Write him down.

After you have completed this part of the ritual, take some time before moving on to the next. Let your father as King move around inside you. Share some of your memories with friends, groups, or spouse. Live with the memories. If you are making this quest with a trusted friend or therapist or in a men's group, share this piece of your journey with that person or group. Let your memories of your father be heard and your visions of him be seen.

TASK 2:
SEEING YOURSELF IN YOUR
FATHER'S SHADOW

Within you, as you were growing up in your father's house, a Prince watched your father's King archetype very carefully. That Prince, a boy in training, was (and still is) unfinished, prone to pseudo-order and behaviors like those described below.

1. Shaming of other princes (Hey, asshole, where'd you get that face? At the pizza parlor?)

2. Envy (Jimmy's better than I am at football, so I'm nothing.)

3. Grandiose masculinity (I'm the greatest. I can do anything in the world!)

4. Undeveloped integrity (Well, you know, stealing a little of this won't *really* hurt anyone . . .)

That Prince was prone to a terrible fear of dishonoring himself and his castle but had no clear sense of what honor truly is ("I'm trying to do it right, honest I am . . ."), felt confusion about his role with women ("Girls—can't live with 'em, can't live without 'em"), and displayed a tendency toward extremes of harshness and apology. The Prince, in other words, is very much like an adolescent boy in transition to manhood.

You have written and spoken of your father's character and his relationships in terms of the archetype of the King. Now you can see yourself as his reflection in the archetype of the Prince. Speak about your current adult life—who you are, now, at this moment—being very honest about two things especially: how you feel ordered within yourself and how you order your family and world.

Have You Used Your Power in a Healthy Way?

A Prince lacks a center of self-confidence; he pseudo-orders. He cannot separate his own issues from his guidance of others.

1. In what healthy ways do you order your own life? In what healthy ways, especially, do you order your loving relationships?

2. In what unhealthy ways do you order your life and your love?

3. What feelings, statements, and behaviors indicate your internal order?

4. What feelings, statements, and behaviors indicate your lack of internal order?

5. In what healthy ways do you order your home, your life, and the lives of your family members?

6. In what ways do you wish you could?

7. In what ways do you order the lives of other men and women who respect your leadership?

8. Do you guide others to fullness? In what ways do you not?

   See yourself. Speak in memory and image.

Have You Been an Honest Man?

The Prince tries to appear as if he has integration and integrity as a man.

1. In what ways do you feel confident in your values? In what ways do you not?

2. Do you feel like an imposter in the world who can never ultimately be respected for who he is?

3. In what ways do you exude integrity as a man in your dealings with others in your family and in the community?

4. In what ways do you not? Recall incidents.

See yourself. Speak in memory and image.

Have You Been a Man of Self-Control and Stability?

The Prince has terrible difficulty stabilizing chaotic emotions and out-of-control behaviors. He often feels out of control in emotional relationships.

1. In what ways are you in healthy control? What rituals help you calm your own terrifying emotions?

2. What buttons get pushed to make you the most out of control?

3. Does your control seem artificial and therefore frighteningly on the edge of disappearing?

4. In what ways do you bring stability to the lives around you?

5. In what ways do you calm others who are in crisis?

6. When do you make things worse?

See yourself. Speak in memory and image.

Have You Been a Man Who Loves Life?

The Prince tries to embody vitality, life force, and joy, sometimes succeeding and sometimes failing without certainty as to why.

1. Would you describe yourself as a man who is full of life? Are you a joyful, vital man? When do you feel most full of life?

2. In what ways do you take care of yourself so that you can remain centered?

3. What makes you feel safe? What does not?

4. In what ways do you bless and fertilize others' gifts?

5. How do you make the world a place where you and others are safe to feel joy?

6. How and when do you not?

See yourself. Speak in memory and image.

Have You Been Balanced in Your Management of Others?

The Prince gives kindness when firmness is required; he asks the world to lead him to leadership.

1. Are you a kind and loving man?
2. Are you too kind? Do you know the place of firmness?
3. Do you believe in your heart that consensus is always better than leadership?
4. Are you satisfied with this belief?
5. In what ways are you kind to your family and others? How and when do you mix kindness and firmness?
6. Would you describe yourself as permissive, assertive, or authoritarian in your parenting style?
7. Do you give sacred wounds as blessings upon your children and others in your family?
8. Do you curse others with your firmness?

See yourself. Speak in memory and image.

Have You Been Generous in Your Honoring and Promoting of Others?

The Prince sees others in all their weakness and must resist sinking with them. The Prince cannot promote others without feeling he will lose himself.

1. Do you know your own talents? Do you honor yourself?
2. Do you survive defeats by honoring yourself?
3. What rituals do you have for enduring life's sufferings? Are they healthy rituals?
4. How do you promote yourself in the world of men?
5. Do you accept weakness in others?
6. Do you work to promote others in the world?
7. Do you feel detached from others' gifts or do you feel you must be as good as others at certain things?
8. Do you feel ashamed in the face of others' weaknesses?

See yourself. Speak in memory and image.

Are You Secure in Yourself?

> *The Prince envies. The Prince turns away from enjoying others' talents.*

1. Are you an envious man? Do you envy others for the things they have?
2. What personal rituals do you have for controlling your envy?
3. How do you feel society treats and values you?
4. Do you envy men more, or women more?
5. Do you envy your children?
6. How does this envy hurt your relationships?

See yourself. Speak in memory and image.

TASK 3:
PLACING YOURSELF BESIDE YOUR FATHER

To see who you are, you were first taken back to your childhood home to look through the windows of that home at your father. Second, you were taken to your own home, to look through the glass at your own life.

Now see yourself beside your father. Discover which of your behaviors as a Prince come from legacies of your father. Though he was your projection of King during your childhood, he was also probably much of a Prince himself, passing on legacies of his own repression, adolescent shame, and lack of consciousness.

Your task now is to write letters to your father, letters you will probably never send. Write them after rereading your answers to the questions above. Write them after letting everything you've just written sit for a day or two.

Letter 1: A Positive and a Negative Memory

In this letter, describe your father to himself, touching on the memories, moments, conversations that really stood out for you during the seeing and writing above. Though we have used the word *seeing*, we mean it to include all the sounds, smells, tastes, and touch feelings you associated with your memories.

Center your letter on two incidents, one positive, one negative. Describe to your father how he was a Sacred King to you and how he was a Shadow King and how this made you feel, picking out only *one* incident or memory for each aspect. Tell him your feelings during and after the positive and then the negative memory.

> For example, *Dear Father*, you might begin (use whatever epithet you used for him), *when I was ten years old you came to visit my school. I remember it was the only time you came. I was having trouble and you and Mom came. The teacher wanted you both to come in. I remember you kept your hands folded because of the grease under your fingernails. You were embarrassed because you worked in the factory. You were nervous, but when the teacher accused me of stealing Jenny Pentwright's two dollars you looked me in the eye and asked if I did it. When I said no you believed me and I felt like you really trusted me. I felt like I was okay. I remember I felt . . .*

You might begin the negative memory this way:

> *Dear Father, I remember you took me to your factory when I was eleven and I remember you kept fidgeting with your tie. You seemed mad at me and I didn't know why the hell you took me in the first place. Every time I asked for something, you shut me down. I remember there was a man who came to you and got mad at you and told you to do something and you stood and took it. Then when he was gone you told me to get my butt home, I just got you in trouble anyway being here, you had to get to work. I felt . . .*

Letter 2: Legacies

Now begin a new letter to your father. Imagine that he has read the previous one and absorbed your memories of him. Then write a letter to him about your current life, who you are now. In the first part of the letter, describe yourself to him. Describe what you do well as a man, what you do not do well. Connect your behavior and feelings as a man to incidents, memories, unconscious scripts and patterns, and personal myths you learned from your father.

> *Dear Father, when I took my boy Dave down to go fishing
> and he dropped the fish in the water I lashed out at him
> and God he looked at me the same way I looked at you
> that time on the Missouri River when we went fishing
> and you lashed out at me. . . .*

Free-write this letter so that it flows between your own
pain and your father's life, back and forth, feeling for legacies in
the mud and grime.

Letter 3: Owning Trust and Fear

Begin now a third letter that focuses on the two feelings that lie
at the heart of your father-son wound. When you are acting in
shadow, you're acting out of *fear*. When you are acting sacredly,
you're acting out of *self-trust*.

As you write to your father, touch the trust in you that
was given to you by life with him. Touch those pieces of yourself you trust, pieces he helped you develop. Recall incidents
and memories of going hunting with him, playing ball with
him, talking to him about girls, family life, or manhood. Write
how the self-trust he helped you learn still manifests itself in
your life. As you write, address him directly.

When you find yourself touching the fear in your wounds
with him, spend time with this fear. Recall incidents of fear and
work with them. Notice fear in yourself as you relate to your
spouse, your children, your partner or friends, and recall the
fears your father had, the limited sacredness he was able to live
in and give to you. As you write, speak to him directly, showing
him how he helped set up patterns of fear in you.

> *Dear Dad, you taught me the lessons of life pretty well. I
> learned how to fix the car and how to earn a living. But as
> I look back at you I see how afraid of Mom's feelings you
> were, and of mine and Sarah's and John's. You tried to
> shut them down all the time. You wanted things to go in
> an orderly way and you shouldn't be bothered by crying
> and weeping. Emotion was some kind of long-suffering
> duty to you, no more. . . .*

Let your emotions move on the page (or in the tape recorder) as you write to your father, for not only are you writing

to your father who was and may still be alive, but also—most important to your quest now—you are communicating with the father locked inside you, who is still ruling your inner world.

As you end the letter, ask your father to help you let go of the shadow legacies you've received in your wounds from him. Ask him to meet you later in this journey. Ask him to come out of his outlaw anger and absence. Tell him he has no choice. You will be finding him, no matter where he hides.

You need him. Tell him this in your own words, for you are ready to journey. He still is the man he was in your boyhood— the man who must see you most lovingly and supportively, and the man you most need to confront as you seek yourself.

CLAIMING A SACRED OBJECT
FOR YOUR QUEST

You are on the threshold of your journey. You've heard the call to adventure and answered it by standing in the wind and saying honestly who you are. It's as if the gods and spirits have asked, "Who are you who claims time in the sacred realm?" and you have answered, "This is who I am. I deserve time in the sacred realm."

Before you proceed to the next chapter, claim a sacred object, something—from your own home or from the woods you walk in—that gives you feelings of empowerment and safety. Maybe it is a walking stick, maybe your drum, maybe a stone or crystal, a piece of art, a picture or photograph. Because you are choosing this object now, at the end of this episode of your quest, the object gains some of its sacredness as a memento of what you've been through so far. It commemorates and captures what you've done. Maybe it's an old coin, a baseball card, one of your father's tools that he passed on to you, a stone, a ticket stub with profound memories for you.

Don't pick an object that draws you into unresolved issues, anger and pain, or bad memories. Make sure the object activates feelings of safety in you. The purpose of claiming a sacred object is to claim sacred and positive energy.

Claim the space where you're performing the quest of this

book; perhaps it's in your study, your basement, or your tool shed. Place your sacred object on a table, mantel or other surface there. This surface will serve as your altar. At the end of each episode of your quest you'll be directed to claim sacred objects and place them on the altar you've created. As your quest grows, so will the significance of its sacred objects.

Sacred objects in a sacred space help center a man in his journey on this earth. In our culture, a man's sacred objects tend to be shoved down in his pocket. And, except for his house keys and pictures of his children, most of his sacred objects involve making a living—business cards, money, credit cards, gas cards. Even his driver's license, while it marks his identity, is connected with material acquisition.

Claiming other kinds of sacred objects balances a man's psyche. It returns a sense of sacred space to a man's life and home. Walking down the streets of Istanbul, you'll see Turkish men, even agnostics or atheists, running their fingers through black worry beads. For religious Muslims, these beads are sacred in direct relation to their connection with religious tradition. For many other Turkish men, however, they are sacred simply because they center a man in some constant, intimate physical activity. At night, Turkish men lay the beads next to their watch and glasses on the night table.

Claim your own sacred object, whether it originated in a religious tradition of your ancestors or comes from a place where you feel inherently safe. Let sacredness and safety come into your home.

CREATING A SACRED OBJECT: WRITING A SCROLL

Some sacred objects exist around you, like the pinecone or ticket stub, a stone or worry beads. Others you have a hand in creating yourself. At the end of each episode in your quest, you'll be invited to follow the claiming of a sacred object with the creation of one. You will be invited to create a scroll that is a testimonial of what you've been through.

For the episode of your quest now ending, it would be appropriate to stand in the wind and say who you are. The first step in doing this is to actually write a statement that encompasses or crystallizes what you've been through in this episode. Since this episode has centered around how you exist in your father's shadow, your statement needs to speak to that. And since many positive legacies and attributes have also emerged, you need to speak to them as well.

Take some time now to write a statement of what you celebrate and what you grieve in your father and his legacies, and what you celebrate and grieve in your own present life. Once you've written the statement, consider making it or pieces of it known to other trusted people. Perhaps read that statement to a men's group, a trusted friend, or a therapist, or in another safe setting. Read it to your spouse. Read it aloud, even, in front of the mirror. Hear it out loud. After you've literally stood in the wind and said who you are, place that written statement on your altar. Here is one such sacred statement by Rick, which he read aloud to a church congregation as part of a Father's Day service. He read pieces of a poem, and then said:

> This poem speaks of a garden. The garden is like what is inside of me, my life, or the who and what I am, my soul, my center.
>
> My garden has been nurtured by a variety of factors including parents and grandparents, school, peers, and other significant adults.
>
> The garden is also influenced by the choices I made growing up in my late teens, early adulthood, and even now.
>
> The poem notes that only the flowers are dead, not the garden.
>
> I feel that for a long time I've known my flowers are all dead. There have been many times that I've looked into the mirror and ignored the other self that speaks in a very honest and direct way. You know, that little voice inside of you that doesn't let you off the hook. Some of the questions that are reflected back are:
>
> Who are you? What are you trying to become?
>
> Why do you do the things you don't want to do, and the very things you want to do you can't or you refuse to do?
>
> What is a mature man like?
>
> What do you stand for and what are your principles?
>
> Through the years, I've locked these issues up, hid-

den them from others, so that I could be in control and look good.

Machado wrote: "Look for your other half who walks always next to you and tends to be who you aren't."

I've reached the point where I've begun pulling the feelings, the personal doubt, the pretensions, out from the bag. In other words, I'm trying to be who I am and who I want to become. Think of it like Scrooge in the Charles Dickens story A Christmas Carol. My life is flashing before me . . .

One of the struggles is my relationship with my father.

My father didn't speak to me of being or becoming a man. There was never discussion about feelings, about relationships between other men or with women.

I didn't learn from him how to be a husband, a best friend to my wife, or a better father. Very simply, I don't know the person I call my father.

My father died when I was about twenty-two, from liver cancer. Even in his illness and death we didn't share close moments. As I look at me today, I sense that I'm just like him in many ways.

I'm sad that he's not alive today so that I could share my struggles with him and ask these many burning questions. There is no promise that he would understand, respond, or accept me as I am today. That's maybe the most troublesome; I simply don't know.

I know I have to break the pattern and not be like my father in every way. It's difficult and scary, and it will take time. I know it has to be done for a lot of reasons and for a lot of people.

Rick was in tears as he read this, and so were many men and women in the audience. Rick's statement became sacred in the church, in the minds and hearts of his listeners, and in his own life.

Write your own sacred statement. Promulgate it if you wish. Set it on your altar, celebrating and grieving what you must celebrate and grieve as you stand ready to make your journey. When you have created your sacred scroll, move to the next chapter, where you'll walk further into the journey itself. There you'll meet the Magician in your inward life, the Magician who is like the mentor every hero and initiate meets as he moves forward on his quest.

SIX

Who Walks with Me?

The first encounter of the hero-journey is with a protective figure. With the personifications of his destiny to guide and aid him, the hero goes forward in his adventure.
JOSEPH CAMPBELL

In Homer's *Odyssey,* Telemachus' house is being ruled by outlaw kings in the absence of a sacred father. "Something is wrong with me," Telemachus cries out, standing in the wind. Telemachus sheds tears of grief and asks for the help of the gods of Olympus. Telemachus gets help in the form of a mentor sent by the gods.

The goddess Athena appears to Telemachus disguised as an elderly man, later to be called Mentor. Athena is a unique figure in Greek mythology, for she is as much connected with male energy (she was born not from a mother but from the head of Zeus—the Sacred King) as female (any man who looked on her naked virtue was blinded). He/she (this divine combination of goddess and wise man) instructs Telemachus that to discover himself he must set out on a ship in search of his father.

As Telemachus begins his heroic quest, he yearns for divine and elder assistance. Like Telemachus, we also need mentors to help us in our heroic quest. As Telemachus stands calling out to the gods, we stand calling inward to whatever powers we possess.

Like Telemachus, we are ready to journey. The book we are reading is a ship to sail on. Prepared, we stand and ask now, "Who will walk with me?"

We seek within ourselves, and we seek in the lives around us, the inner and outer presence of magicians and crones who can help define us; mirror us; discover our gold, our talents, our wealth; and guide us to self-trust as we move through hard times of self-discovery.

In mythology and in our own male lives, there are two kinds of male mentors. One is the mentor who teaches us *skills* and physical/mental discipline, which help us compete and survive in the world. Thus teachers and coaches teach us business or athletic skills that give us a strong warrior base to go into the world and compete in the work we choose. We are not as emotionally and spiritually intimate with these mentors as we are with the second kind.

From the second kind we learn more than skills and physical and mental discipline. Though we try to learn from our fathers the male mode of feeling, as sons of absent, abusive, or distant fathers we cleave instead to a high-school coach or college teacher or grandfather or uncle or, having no healthy elder around, to an older brother or other older boy, seeking to learn how we should know a man. In Homer's *Odyssey,* Telemachus had learned from mentors various warrior skills. But he never knew his father, so he had not learned the male mode of feeling. While mentors teach him what lessons they can in his father's absence, he seeks to learn the male mode of feeling as he sets off to find his father.

While in most cases mentors are benevolent guides, in some cases they are nasty in their provocation. In "Strong Hans" the mentor is a provocative dwarf. In Goethe's *Faust* the mentor—Mephistopheles—often teaches by deceit. In Dante's *Divine Comedy,* which describes a medieval heroic quest, the mentor Virgil, who will guide Dante through spiritual growth, is both benevolent and provocative. Dante finds himself in a mythopoetic world. He is dazed and he sings:

> *As I fell to my soul's ruin, a presence*
> *gathered before me on the discolored air,*
> *the figure of one who seemed hoarse from long silence.*
> *At sight of him in that friendless waste I cried:*
> *"Have pity on me, whatever thing you are,*
> *whether shade or living man."*

Virgil, the long-dead Roman poet, Dante's "shade or living man," tells him what all mentors must tell their heroes:

You follow me and I will be your guide
and lead you forth through an eternal place.

Later in his journey, Dante meets Beatrice, who becomes both a figure of youthful female love and a pristine elder female mentor. In Homer's *Odyssey*, Telemachus, too, has both a female and a male mentor, as well as many others. In many mythical journeys there is more than one mentor for the young searcher.

In your own life you meet many mentors. As you were developing, you projected the Magician or Wise Man onto many elders around you. Just as a Prince projects his King onto his father and Goddess onto his mother, so does he project the Magician primarily onto important elders in his community and culture. After he is grown, he no longer needs to project the Magician onto others; he has learned from those others what a Magician is and now carries the Magician within him.

In the heroic quest of this book, you will be aided in recalling the various mentors you have had in your life. You will then be asked to focus on one of them, a man. Finally, you will be assisted in discovering within yourself your mentorial energy, your Magician or Wise Man. This will be a composite of the energies of the mentors and teachers you've had, energies that wait to be activated within you. The Wise Man within can rise to help as you call out at any time in your life, "What wise man walks with me?"

A grown man has less need for living mentors than has a boy or adolescent. A grown man needs supportive brothers more than lesson-giving mentors. While he still calls out to mentors, and while they are an essential part of his life, he calls out less to other older men for guidance than he calls inward to his own strengths and wisdom. Your inner Magician is the power within that you've often called upon in your adult life, a power whose language you may not have known. Thus this power remained dormant. Once you have discovered your own inner Magician, he reveals himself as a seat of strength in your soul throughout your life.

In the context of this book, your inner Magician walks with you as you confront your father—a task that is perhaps as difficult as any in your life, a task for which you need to be in intimate contact with the Wise Man within.

TASK 1:
WHO HAS WALKED WITH YOU?

Spiritual Mentors

Recall the men and women from politics, literature, art, and culture who have been spiritual mentors for you, or role models. Perhaps Gandhi was a spiritual mentor. Often a writer, through his or her work, becomes a spiritual mentor, teaching us for the first time how wonderful it is to have a spiritual vision, helping us to move from one of the stages of our development to another. D. H. Lawrence has been this kind of writer for some men, Hermann Hesse for others.

Sit for a while and recall those mentors whom you never met but whose work helped you see your own purpose. Concentrate here on the actual men and women. If a particular character in Hermann Hesse's work was an influence on your development, but Hermann Hesse himself and his body of work were not, then reserve that character for later, when we discuss mythic and literary heroes.

As you write the entry, focus on your age at the time the man or woman became important to you, the medium through which you gained knowledge of this spiritual mentor, and how that mentor's teachings manifest themselves in your life. You might want to include an important incident that epitomizes your relationship with this particular spiritual mentor. Here are two examples of entries men have written:

> *Joan of Arc. I remember being amazed as a young boy— maybe six or seven—with Joan of Arc. My mother, who was a pretty devout churchgoer, told me about her, painting a glowing picture. I looked her up in the encyclopedia. Then, just by happenstance, I saw a book about saints at a friend's house and read about her there. Her courage is what got to me. I was brought up in a pretty chauvinistic house, and so the fact that she was a woman and fought so physically also amazed me. My mother was not assertive like Joan of Arc. There are still feelings in me I can't quite connect around this. I respected Joan of Arc in some way I couldn't respect my mother, even though I love my mother very much. I look for some of Joan of Arc in women I think.*

Chaim Potok. When I was sixteen I discovered The Chosen, *Chaim Potok's first novel. I later read all his books. When I was in college I heard Potok speak. He was wearing a* kepa [skullcap]. *It was then I realized I wasn't just into his books but also into him. I was brought up Jewish and broke away from that tradition pretty badly. I spit in the face of my parents' belief system. Potok broke away from his Orthodox tradition but managed to do it in a classy way, retaining what he valued without still being sucked into its medieval dogmas.*

After I heard him speak about the hell he went through, I went back to my folks and talked to them. I tried to help them understand why I had done what I'd done. And I apologized to them. It was a very powerful moment. Because of a model like Potok, I feel more comfortable passing on some Judaism to my kids. I feel like the traditions can be passed on without all the dogma taking over.

Mythic and Literary Mentors

After you've recalled spiritual mentors, recall mythic figures and literary heroes who have been your models and guides. Zeus, Captain Kirk, Pip in Dickens's *Great Expectations*, Athena, Apollo, Iron John, Rupert in D. H. Lawrence's *Women in Love*, King Arthur, Steppenwolf, the boy in *The Yearling*, Spiderman, Superman, Shane—any of these or other fictional characters may have had profound effects on your life. All function as heroes after whom we model and in whose presence we feel empowered.

If you have done archetypal work before, you may have identified mythic figures like Zeus or Iron John as archetypes in your own psyche. For most people, heroes from Greek mythology, the Grimms' fairy tales, literature, drama, and cartoon books all blend together in a landscape of imaginary heroes. These figures were mentors to us as kids (and can still be, in more sophisticated mediums), teaching us lessons as they themselves learned them or taught them to the boys and girls in the cartoons, novels, fairy tales and legends they appeared in during our childhoods.

Among these mythic and literary mentors were some unhealthy heroes. They've caused sickness in us because they are fantasy heroes whom we've confused with mythic heroes. A fantasy hero often grows out of meretricious formulas for entertainment, whereas a hero of myth or a mythic hero in a literary medium grows out of a cultural and personal quest for meaning. In our popular culture, a figure like John Wayne was a very limited male model. He taught many of us an unhealthy mode of relating to women, the environment, and other men. We confused his fantasy maleness with mythic masculinity. As you recall your mythic and literary heroes, be honest about which ones were mere fantasy, yet were powerfully influential in your life. As you write short entries for each hero, focus on your age at the time the hero became important to you, the medium by which you gained knowledge of this hero, what qualities you modeled from that hero, and how that hero's life now manifests itself in your life. You might want to include an important incident that epitomizes your relationship with the particular hero, especially an incident where you felt that hero guiding you to a specific kind of action.

An entry might read like this one:

> *When I was in my teens I loved Westerns, especially Clint Eastwood movies. Was it that his characters, so silent, reminded me of Dad? Maybe so. But I also liked the fact that he was so skilled, so good at getting what he wanted. Like every boy, I had played cowboys and Indians, probably from watching John Wayne movies. But when I saw Clint Eastwood, I knew what kind of man I wanted to be. Now I look back and I see how limited he was, but at the time I felt like I kind of knew Clint Eastwood, I kind of knew what he would be proud of in me.*
>
> *It might sound strange, but another important hero of mine was the man from Mars in Robert Heinlein's* Stranger in a Strange Land. *I read that book as a teenager, really getting into how alone he was, and yet how strong he had to be. The press and everyone made him into a hero and a villain both, and he just had to take his isolation and make the most of it. I guess I've always been a little like that.*

Living Mentors and Teachers

Take some time now to recall in your notebook men and women who have been your living mentors and teachers. Recall those men and women who, alive and active in your immediate world during a certain time in your life, influenced your life significantly. Recall even those mentors with whom you have made nasty, painful breaks. Recall grandparents, aunts, uncles, neighbors, teachers, coaches.

Write a small piece in your journal about each of these men and women. Note the person's relationship to you and note the period of your life when you related with that person. Note what life skills you learned from that person. Then note which of the mentor's teachings still manifest themselves in your adult life.

Put a star beside the name of each person with whom you had a relationship of intimate trust. For each starred name, recall not only what *skills* you learned but also what *modes of feeling* you learned and modeled. Especially with starred names, recall an incident that epitomizes your experience of learning with this mentor. If one male mentor among all those you recall feels the most important to you, don't enter him here; wait until the next section.

As you recall your male mentors especially, you may discover that none of them taught you the male mode of feeling—nor, really, did your father. You yourself have thus become a man disengaged from his male identity who has had to teach himself, in fragments from spiritual mentors and mythic and literary heroes, what a man should be. The inner mentor you meet later in this episode will be the embodiment of the self-teaching you've done, and he will take you further. An unstarred entry might look like this:

> *Mr. Anderson. He was my best friend's dad. I knew him when I was in elementary school. We were never very close but he always took his son and me fishing. I learned a lot about the outdoors from him. Part of my love of camping comes from those times with him.*

A starred entry might be a little longer and look like this:

> *Uncle Sanders. He was my father's brother. He was the father of three boys, my cousins. Every summer from about my eighth birthday to my thirteenth, I went to stay with him and my aunt and my cousins. My dad was in the*

*Navy. He was gone a lot. Uncle Sanders took me and my
cousins to his factory and played ball with us. Sometimes
he told me, "You're like a son to me, my summer son."*

*Once I remember he took me and my cousin Stan to
his factory—he worked in a factory that built conveyor
belts. I remember his boss, a tall, lanky man with pol-
ished shoes, was mad that we two boys were there
"mucking up the works." But Uncle Sanders told the boss
to mind his own business. He and the boss yelled at each
other in the boss's office. When Uncle Sanders came out
he was red in the face, his fists clenched. He took us back
to his place on the machine and as he began to relax he
said, "I coulda lost my temper but I didn't. I coulda hit
the guy but I didn't. If I don't ever do anything else in my
life, I'll still remember keeping my cool with that asshole." My father and his two brothers all had tempers,
but Uncle Sanders always tried to keep his. I think of
him when I want to lose mine.*

Your Most Significant Male Mentor

After you have recalled your spiritual mentors, mythic and literary mentors, and living mentors, recall the one man besides
your father who has had the most profound effect on your life.

Perhaps you can say of this man, "I learned at least as
much from him about how a good man lives, acts, feels, loves,
and behaves as I did from my father." Or, without any com-
parison to your father, you might be able to say, "I learned an
incredible amount from him about how to be a good man, how
to live, even how to love."

As you recall this man, focus on your age at the time he
became important to you. Recall the man's relationship to you
in some depth. Remember what life skills you learned from that
person, as well as what you learned of the male mode of feeling.
What did he teach you about how to love yourself and others?
What, especially, did he teach you about how to love a mate?
How have his teaching and modeling manifested themselves in
your life? Here is a recollection of one man's most significant
male mentor:

*Dr. Mark Johnson. One of my English professors in col-
lege. Was I attracted to him because I felt like a weak*

young man and he was so strong, so substantial! He was physically muscular. More than that, he carried his inner being with confidence. Once when I told him I thought a faction of students was gossiping about him and trying to hurt him, he responded, "If they have something to say, they can say it to me. Otherwise, I won't pay attention. The only people who intimidate me are people who speak a deeper truth than I speak."

Mark was not only strong, he was strong in ways that felt true to me. He had integrity as well as strength. He didn't seem grandiose and false. He hurt me often, better at verbal jabs and sarcasm than I was. In fact, this sarcastic quality of his I worked hard to avoid. I was eighteen and he was thirty-five, and the only way, in my opinion, an eighteen-year-old can withstand the kind of verbal jabbing he did without damage to his self-image is if he falsely pumps himself up to become equal to the mentor. So I don't believe in the kind of severe sarcasm he put me through.

But, I must admit, now that I'm a teacher and his age and a mentor, I do see that some verbal sparring with the young students is empowering. It builds their warrior a little.

Another thing he did that hurt me at the time but that I see now was his way of teaching me the male mode of feeling was to challenge my feelings. I often practiced a kind of concealment by candor. I seemed to be very honest about my feelings. I talked and talked and talked— yet most of it was bullshit. He would say, "That's not what you really think, is it? That's not what you really feel." And I would become defensive. But he was giving me permission to have real feelings as a man. I never realized this until years later. I was in a phase of wanting to have feelings I thought women wanted me to have. He challenged that, trying to get me to figure out what my feelings were.

I remember, he let me come over to his house for dinner. I baby-sat his youngest child. He gave me responsibility. I watched him interact with his wife and family. He modeled good and true interaction. Although again, he was not without his faults, and many of the things he did I think I now do better.

> *Mark lent me some money to go to Europe. It wasn't much—I earned most of my own—but just the fact that he lent me the money to go make a journey that intimidated me was another way of his helping me to learn the male mode of feeling. I remember he said, "I think you need to go to Europe. I think you need to see where your people come from. I think you need to get out of this university and get into the world and see what you're made of." He didn't just push me into the world of fear. His money was a support, a promise of support.*

After you have recalled a most significant male mentor, wait a day or two before going on to the next task in your quest. Use this time to read over or listen again to all of what you've recalled about all your mentors. Form in your mind a composite picture of all the positive attributes of the mentors you've had, weighing your composite more heavily toward the positive male influences in your life.

The inner Mentor you'll soon be guided to discover will be male. Your masculine quest will be more productive and more empowering if you feel strong, supportive male energy around you. When, for instance, we do our inner work in men's groups we are seeking this kind of male strength and support. We feel that we trust the men in our group enough so that making a sacred promise to another man (the kind fathers and sons make to each other) would actually feel safe. And once we get near this feeling of safety and trust with other men, we can confront our father with real strength.

There is within you a very male mentor. If you activate him, you can have this feeling of trust inwardly. There is within you a male mentor who fits all your personal mythologies of what a man ought to be, to whom you can promise cooperation, and whose promises of masculine blessing and support you can absolutely believe. It is that man within you that we now seek. This inner mentor has formed in you, especially during the first two decades of your life, as a composite of all the positive male influences you experienced. He is an embodiment of your Sacred Magician archetype. He waits in your active imagination to be discovered. The guided meditation that follows will help you discover him.

TASK 2:
MEETING YOUR INNER MAGICIAN

If in doing this guided meditation you encounter a female presence, or an animal or spirit presence that feels female to you, wait a day or two and do the meditation again, perhaps preparing for it by doing more memory work and writing about the male mentors you've had. Value the female presence, but remember that at this point in your quest it is masculine energy you seek.

Remember that the inner Mentor, the Magician you discover, will come from whatever spiritual tradition feels closest to your soul. We are using the Telemachus story and its Greek landscape in our model of the heroic quest—but your Magician may be a Buddhist monk or an old Sioux warrior or a biblical figure or a composite of your living mentors. Let him be who he is.

Enter now the spirit of meditation. Find a comfortable position. Quiet your breathing. Enter your personal ritual of relaxation. Take three deep breaths, quieting your inner chatter. Concentrate in your third breath only on your own breathing. When you are relaxed and ready, see in your mind's eye an ancient landscape filled with forests.

Picture yourself in ancient dress in a room in a castle that sits in the middle of the forest. See yourself standing before a group of older men and women. You are speaking to them, but many of them are talking to each other, not paying attention to you. You stand in vulnerability and need; you want instruction and protection. You know that you must stand here like this and speak who you are and ask for help and support if you are to make a hard journey. Why are they paying so little attention to you? Perhaps you are not speaking loud enough.

Hear your own voice murmur, "What man walks with me?" No one in the crowd hears you.

"What man walks with me!" Say it a little louder. Now see some heads turn.

Cry out, "What man walks with me!"

See a change in this room of old people. A man's last comment hangs in the air as he turns to you. A woman in middle age turns from her partner and looks at you. Some old men and women raise their eyebrows, leaning forward a little, looking to you. Some dogs are wrangling with each other for a bone in a back corner, but their growling quiets a little. Old men look you in the eye. Enjoy that attention for a moment.

Then close your eyes and feel yourself traveling through air. Open your eyes and find yourself standing in a forest. This forest is an even deeper place in your inner life, a place that most people in the castle fear. This forest is your inner wilderness. In it you are dwarfed by huge trees and vines. Cries of animals are all around you. Your call, "What man walks with me?" still rings in your ears.

Walk a few steps toward shadows and light that emanate from behind a mass of trees and vines. Cut through the vines. The work is hard, and it is difficult for you to breathe. Feel your perspiration and deep breaths. Your face and arms are scratched. Your arms and wrists are tired. Feel the exhaustion that this inward effort causes.

Push through the last mass of vines and see a tiny open meadow, surrounded by small trees. In the center of the tiny space is a huge carved stone, jutting upward. Statements about you are carved on it. They are statements that describe how you feel as a man at this point in your life. Some of the statements are statements you want never to change. Some are statements that make you sad, for they reveal your inhibitions, your open wounds.

See some of these statements now. Read them to yourself.

Walk up to the monument. Touch the carved statements. Run your fingers on them. As your fingers touch the tiny rivers in the stone, see images of boyhood, images that the statements remind you of. Some images make you happy. Some make you sad. Don't judge the sadness. Celebrate your stamina for having survived your boyhood. Run your fingers along another statement, and then another, until you have run your fingers on them all.

Your sweat is passing; the air is cooling the moisture on your skin. Walk now to the other side of the monument. See there a photograph of your father when he was exactly the age you are now. You look a little like him and he looks a little like you. It is only a photograph you see. It does not talk to you.

You feel at your back a warmth, a vague heat. Turn your back to your father's photograph now; walk toward the heat. Before your eyes is no fire, and yet your body feels a heat. Before your eyes is the huge forest around you and the light growing dimmer now as you leave the meadow. Before your eyes is a darkening place in the forest. Walk slowly toward it. What will you find?

Before you are two huge trees. Their branches form a beautiful archway. Walk toward the archway. Walk under it. Walk forward along the path into a small meadow, a meadow just like the one your monument was in. There is someone waiting in the meadow for you. Do you see someone there? Look at him in the center of the meadow. He is a piece of yourself. Go closer to this man. He comes to meet you from the deepest region of yourself. Note how he is dressed; who he looks like, if anyone; what epoch he seems to hail from; how old he is.

Come up in front of him and let your eyes meet. You are meeting the eyes of a deep and strong masculine part of yourself that you can trust absolutely. Let your vision enter your Magician's eyes and move into his body. See his eyes doing the same with your body. For a moment be in total connection. Hear your Magician's voice. "I will walk with you," he says. "You are the man I have been waiting for."

Celebrate this moment. Feel how absolutely your Magician believes in your worthiness. Feel his affection for you. You are worthy of that affection.

Hear him ask you, "What do you most fear as you begin your journey toward your father?"

Answer him with honesty. If your Magician has a response to your answer, hear that response. Continue your conversation with him in whatever way you need to continue it. Let your Magician say to you what you need a caring elder to tell you at this moment in your life.

When the time is right, hear him say, "Go back. I will see you soon and we will find your father."

Thank him. Take a moment to express to him how being with him has made you feel. When it is time to part, let your-

self feel a moment of awkwardness, of nervousness. Who will turn away first? Your Magician stands waiting for you to turn. Is it frightening for you to turn away? What if this Magician disappears and never appears again? Your feelings for him and his feelings for you are so clean, so bottomless in their warmth, so strong in their girding. Must you move away from them?

Your Magician stands waiting for you to turn. He seems to say, "Risk turning away. You will be rewarded. I will not disappear."

Close your eyes. Feel yourself moving on air. Feel yourself returning to the room of old men and old women. One dog has managed to snarl the bone away from the other. The men and women are still looking at you. Your cry, "What man walks with me?" has died out. But now, standing up and coming toward you in this castle room is the same Magician you met in the meadow. True to his word, he has not disappeared.

Watch him weave through the crowd, moving between people who are chatting again, paying little attention to you. Let yourself feel how special your Magician's attention is in this room of noise. Let him come up to you. Let him embrace you. Go with him through the side door and out toward the shore, where a ship is waiting. It is dusk. You will not be able to sail until tomorrow. Tonight, you can be certain, you will sit together in candlelight in the forward cabin, together.

From that seashore and at that shipside slowly leave your mythopoetic landscape and return now to ordinary reality. Do it in whatever manner works best for you. Take three deep breaths. Open your eyes. As you open them, cover them for a moment with your palms.

When you have returned, write what you need to write in your journal. Describe your experience as you stood in the community of elders. Describe their faces and the room. These men and women are the society that we always feel judging us. No matter how hard we strive for inner peace, there are judges. Who judges your manhood the most?

Describe the forest, the meadow. Describe the monument and its carvings. Describe your father's photo and face. What feelings arose for you? What memories?

Describe your inner Mentor, your Magician. Describe your feelings as you met him. Recall what he said to you and you to him. Write what you need to write. If at this time or other times in these rituals your pen can't move fast enough, speak your experience into a tape recorder.

If this first guided meditation experience did not reveal your Magician to you, do it again. Do it until you find the male mentor who feels right to guide you forward. You are on a visionquest. There is no competition and no judgment. You don't have to get it the first time. Do this meditation ritual as many times as you need to, without self-criticism.

CLAIMING AND CREATING
YOUR SACRED OBJECTS

At this point, claim another sacred object and place it on the table you have set up in accordance with the instructions in the last chapter. Since you'll be invited to do this at the end of each episode of your quest, you needn't wait until the ends of chapters to claim these objects. Perhaps you already know what you're going to claim and have known since doing some work on literary heroes or spiritual mentors.

There are myriad ways to claim sacred objects. However you do it, claim a talisman that lets you feel, even for a second, the energy of positive mentors in your life—a photo of your football coach, a program from a violin teacher's recital, a professor's term-paper critique, a book by Hermann Hesse.

Hold the sacred object in your hand. Feel the energy of it. Put it on your altar and enjoy its presence there.

Once you have found this object and placed it on your altar, begin to create a letter, a *sacred scroll*, written directly to your father, though you may never send it. Let this letter begin with "Dear Dad" (or whatever epithet you use for your father), and make in it a written (or spoken, if you are using a tape recorder) testament of the experience you've been through in this episode. Like the claiming of a sacred object, the creating of this kind of scroll is something you'll be invited to do at the end of each episode of your quest.

When referring to yourself in this scroll, focus first on the positive experiences you've had in this chapter: recall important mentors, what they taught you, how their lessons are still manifested, how they filled holes left by your father's disengagement. Recall your inner landscape of meditation and the Magician you met there. Claim the mentorial powers you've gained, powers that allow you to mentor to others and to yourself.

Move to the negative when need be. Recall how mentors have misguided you, how they couldn't quite fill in for Dad, how fantasy heroes have confused your masculinity, how you feel afraid of mentoring. Celebrate and grieve as you must. Help your father see how important it was for you to recall your mentors and seek the mentorial energy within you.

Encircle this letter with stars or some other design to set it off from the other writing in your journal, thus making it a sacred scroll. Use this same symbolism or something like it around the letters you'll write at the end of each of the episodes in your quest.

In these sacred letters you will have both a summary of what you've been through and a sacred object—like an amulet, walking stick, prayer bead, fossil discovered in a cavern, arrowhead, or scroll—that embodies the energy of a sacred place and time. In letting your father listen to and visualize your experience, you're doing what a man does on a visionquest: he brings his visions to the father and elders so that those visions can be *seen* and *heard*.

Many of us never got a chance to have our fathers see and hear our most intimate feelings and visions. Now is that chance. Again, remember that even if you don't send the letter to your father, he'll still see and hear you from within. Even if your father is dead, his ghost that still lives inside you will see and hear.

When you have finished this letter, place it on your altar with your other sacred objects, beside or beneath the maps and legends of your family history. If you can, read your letter to your men's group or to another trusted friend, or in a church or other sacred setting.

When you feel satisfied that you've finished this episode of your journey, go on to the next chapter. In the next episode of your quest, you'll move further into the male lineage from which you and your father have descended, your mentor walking at your side.

SEVEN

A Visit with the Old Men

*It is becoming clear to us that manhood doesn't happen by
itself; it doesn't happen just because we eat Wheaties. The
active intervention of the older men means that older men
welcome the younger man into the ancient, mythologized,
instinctive male world.*

ROBERT BLY

When you were a boy, did you have a grandfather or uncle you
respected, an old man you loved to hear talk? When you went to
visit your grandfather did you enjoy his stories about your father when your father was a boy? Was there an old man down
the street who sat on his porch and talked about the old days?
Did you hear about old cars and railroads? Did he make jokes
about women?

While we were growing up there were old men all around
us. Even those of us who, because of family feuds or long physical distances, were cut off from older relatives—even we noticed old men around us. Our feelings toward them were am-
bivalent: on the one hand their long, wandering conversations
bored us; on the other hand, they said one or two things we
would never forget.

These old men played a large part in our lives, even without their knowing it, or our knowing it at the time. Even if our
fathers had not been disengaged, the old men would have been
important. But because our fathers were disengaged, these old
men played far larger parts. Perhaps we modeled our manhood
after them—these grandfathers, uncles, neighbors—as we
avoided our fathers' addictions and rages. Perhaps we modeled
manhood after them as we found our fathers still at work or
tired from work or concentrating more on the beauty of the
lawn than us.

In the archetypal male journey, the sacred son visits the old men. In Native American tradition, Grandfather is a presence everywhere in the young man's progress. In Hopi tradition, the boy who is ready to be initiated into manhood not only visits the old men, but goes to live with them. In ancient Greek tradition, the old men sit in kingly state and the journeying hero visits their kingdoms to see himself reflected in their old eyes. The old men give the young prince tasks—acquire the Golden Fleece, fight in such-and-such a tournament. They give him food and drink and hear of his voyages and tell him, in great detail, of their own.

While some old men function as significant mentors in a boy's growing up, the kind of old men we're discussing here have another, separate place, too. Rather than walking with the young man, the old men tend to sit and wait for him. Unlike traditional mentors, they don't lead him. They are Kings more than Magicians. As such, they are *visited* by young men.

"We sit here after a long life of success and failure," the old men are saying. "Now, here is what we want to tell you."

As he visits the old men, the sacred son is initiated one more step into mature manhood, often without conscious action or deed. Visiting the old men is an ordeal. It requires humility in ways that, for instance, sitting with old women does not. The son can more easily blow off what old women say to him. The son can more easily make fun of them. What they say is like what Mom says to him, and as he breaks away from Mom he allows himself a lot of smirking. But the old men are of the father's world, and it is the father's world for which he hungers.

Visiting the old men requires that the son find the guts to rub shoulders with accomplished kings, kings such as he himself aspires to be one day. It requires that he hear the kings out and then, once given the floor, that he speak his own piece. In the presence of the old men, "who he is" as a young man is judged, found worthy, often criticized. In the presence of the old men, the sacred son hears his own voice in the great male chorus.

In Telemachus's journey, a major step in his connection with his disengaged father is taken when he visits the kingdom of King Nestor in Pylos and that of King Menelaus in Lacedaemon. Telemachus's experience with each of these old men mirrors the stages of any man's initiatory encounter with old men, especially in relation to his discovery of his father and his own King. It is an encounter broken roughly into three stages.

Listening to the Old Men's Tales

First, the young man must listen to the old men. He must learn to hear what wisdom and glory really sound like. He must let them talk about their lives in great detail. Thus he learns about the past, pieces of his own birthright, what male greatness is.

He must especially listen to the old men talk about his own father. He must hear what the old men know of his father. Listening to that, he learns a most significant piece of his birthright—his father's young life, his father's strengths and weaknesses as seen by old men who knew (and know) him well.

Telemachus sits with each of the two old kings in turn and hears stories of their lives and deeds and stories of Odysseus's great deeds and innate goodness. Hearing his father's manhood lauded by the male chorus, Telemachus is not only more impressed with his father than he was before, but also more connected to his own sacred masculinity, his birthright. His own sense of self is bolstered as he hears great kings laud his father.

Receiving the Invitation to Speak

At intervals during their respective conversations, the old kings invite Telemachus to speak. In the wake of their lengthy portrayal of Odysseus's greatness, and in the intimidating presence of great kings, Telemachus is understandably shy. But he manages to transcend his shyness—thus moving through the second stage of the initiating encounter with the old men. He tells each of the old kings of his troubles and why he journeys. The old men accept and support him. They enjoy his voice and who he is. They say to him, "Oh, you do resemble your father!" On hearing this, Telemachus, like any man in search of his masculinity, feels his sense of self bolstered one step further. He feels spiritually grounded in his birthright.

Had the great kings gone on and on about how terrible his father was, their remarking on the resemblance between Telemachus and his father would have had the opposite effect. And in every tribe or family there are old men who would, perhaps accurately, go on this way. But what is sacred in a man's father will be known to some old men. Each of us, to gain what Telemachus gains, must find the appropriate old men—the men who can help us see what was good in our fathers' birthright and ours.

Why is hearing the old men say, "Oh, you do resemble your father!" an initiatory moment for a man? While it is powerful to hear Mom say, as we're growing up, "You look just like Dad," or "You're turning out like your father," it is especially powerful to hear respected old men say it.

By recognizing the father in the son, the old men, the old kings, give communal, social, and masculine recognition of the prince's claim to his birthright in a way that a mother, for instance, cannot. "Oh, you do resemble your father!" they say, nodding and smiling. "You have a lot of your father in you," Grandpa will say. "When your dad was your age, he did such-and-such, just like you do." "You've got your father's broad shoulders," your uncle will say, as you help build a fence on his acreage. "You're getting muscles just like he had." "I saw your dad the other day," Mr. Ferguson down the street will say. "I'll bet he's real proud of you." The old men connect you to your father.

If we visit the old men enough, even those of us who had alcoholic or abusive fathers will hear positive aspects of his character and being. You as prince are inheritor of both aspects of your father's legacies. They both form a large portion of the masculine birthright your father passes on to you. As you visit the old men in your own life, both aspects are claimed. The negative you hope to surpass, the positive to own with more power.

Being Known as a Man

The third initiating moment with the old men occurs when these old kings look at you as a man, not a boy. In mythology this moment is often symbolized by the old men giving the sacred son a gift or sacred task. In seeing the young man as a man in his own right, the old men accept him into the brotherhood, the circle of men.

"That young man has a birthright like all men have," they are saying. "That young man is spiritually grounded. He will be a healthy member of our circle."

One of the reasons many of us join men's groups is to feel this equality of manhood, this brotherhood, this groundedness, even in our middle age. We are seeking a brotherhood we can feel now, as we earn it in the hard work of discovering our masculinity. We are seeking it now even if as boys we did not feel connected to our fathers and the old men in the way we needed to.

In *The Odyssey*, when the old kings send Telemachus on his way, he feels he knows his father better, and he feels he knows himself better. The moment of the story that captures his new station as a man in an old man's eyes happens when, as he leaves King Menelaus's kingdom, he refuses Menelaus's gift of horses. The shy boy who came to visit Menelaus would not have been capable of such a refusal. The new Telemachus is. He makes a very mature decision. He says to King Menelaus:

> If you should offer me a gift, let it be something for me to treasure. But horses I will not take to Ithaca. I will leave them for you to enjoy; for you are lord of a broad plain. Here in your kingdom there is plenty of clover, galingale, wheat, spelt, and broad-eared white barley. But in Ithaca we have neither wide roads nor meadows. It is a goat country, much pleasanter than a horse country. None of the islands in the sea is good for driving or good for meadows and Ithaca least of all.

This is a decision of ordering the kingdom that a King makes. My kingdom thanks you for your offer, he is saying, but it needs something else. For a young man to order his kingdom in the presence of a man who embodies a King means that the sacred son has gained strength enough to stand up and be counted. Meneleus does not respond with a reprimand; he responds with the respect another King deserves. He gives Telemachus a more useful gift.

Had each of us had the good fortune to go through the three initiatory stages with the old men in our own families and communities during our late adolescence and early adulthood, we would have been admired while we were growing up as extensions of our fathers, then promoted and listened to as men-in-the-making, then accepted as men in our own right.

"Oh, your father's quite a man," our old men would have begun.

Then, "Oh, you do resemble your father!"

Then, "Oh, you are a fine man."

Some of our mentors in school and at work help us realize the final stage—that we are becoming fine men. But because in our culture we don't spend enough time with the old men to be connected through them to our fathers or to our whole ancestral lineage, what mentors do for us is often very little and comes too late.

Whatever amount and quality of contact you have had with the old men in your life, you can make a visit to them now. It is that visit, and the empowerment that can result from it, that constitute your task in this episode of your journey.

TASK 1:
CONTACTING THE OLD MEN

In our own lives, the old men are not kings like Nestor and Menelaus, but most often grandfathers, uncles, and other men in the family and neighborhood who knew our fathers. It is time now to reconnect your life with theirs.

To do this, you'll need to make a lot of phone calls. You may even need to fly to another city. Have your journal by the phone as you make calls. Take your journal with you as you visit the old men. Some of the connections can be made by letters, but it may take a long time to get responses.

Call old men in your family, or any old men who knew your father, and ask questions about your father and his male lineage. You might call on your mother and father and other family members to help you get in touch with those men whose names escape you but whose faces, from far back in your boyhood, you do remember. While you could call every older man you can think of, I would suggest calling only those whom you respected and still respect as men.

As you talk to these old men and the conversations take on a rhythm of their own, loose and undirected, make sure to ask questions that particularly further your quest. Ask about your father's *deeds* and *character*. Only you will know the questions to ask.

> "Grandpa, do you remember that time you hugged Dad at that family picnic? What was going on there? Why were you so pleased with him?"
> "Popper, what was Dad like when he confronted so-and-so?"
> "Mr. Ferguson, remember that time you and Dad did such-and-such? What made you two such good friends?"

Only you will know how to form the questions so that the old men will not feel too vulnerable to talk. Only you, like Telemachus, will know how to fit just the right amount of humility into your request for aid. Many of the old men will not want you to visit them. Don't be surprised or worried. Many of the men of previous generations would consider the journey you are on in this book to be unbecoming of a man—too "emotional," unnecessary. Some of the men may speak candidly with you, though. They may even be honest about your father's dark side. Let them be honest—but always circle the discussion back around to the positive. There will be a number of opportunities during your quest for you to return to the negative legacies of your father. In this visit we are concerned with positive deeds and character.

As carefully as you ask the old men about your father, also ask them if they remember things he said about how he felt about *you*. Don't be surprised if some of the comments hurt and some of them fill you with unexpected joy.

Go even further with the old men. Ask each of them how they saw you as a boy and adolescent. Ask them especially to recall incidents when they saw you as your father's son. Ask them to recall incidents when they saw you and your father together, doing a task or visiting them side by side. Ask them to speak to you about how you seemed to be your father's son.

Some of their memories may be negative ones, especially if your father was the kind of man who elicits negative memories. But keep pressing the old men to recall positive memories, and to see you as a son who resembled his father in those positive memories.

Finally, ask them when it was that they began to see you as your own man. Ask them to recall as vividly as possible the moment or moments when they, as old men in your family or neighborhood, had to give you credit for manhood.

> *Grandpa, when did you first see me as a man?*
> *Uncle Rufus, when did you know I was a man?*

Old people remember the world and everything in it, if we ask them the right questions and give them the time to answer. And their memories are powerful markers and transformers in our lives. Let the old Kings in your world recall your manhood and give these recollections to you as their gifts.

Call the men up in their nursing homes and cottages and family homes. Go to their gravesites and wonder over the conversations you might have with them. Listen to their old masculine voices, raspy on the phone wire. Stare into the wrinkles on their faces. Shake their hands and embrace them. If some of the old men live in the same city you live in, take an evening or weekend to connect with them; set the phone aside. Bring one of the old men to your men's group, or bring your group to him. Do anything you can do to connect your past to the life of the old men in its lineage and along its boundaries.

When you have gathered the information you feel you can gather, when you have connected with the old men as much as you can for now, move on to Task 2.

TASK 2:
MAKING THE ANCESTRAL
JOURNEY WITHIN

In the following ritual, you will be asked to find your father's male lineage within your own psyche. You will be asked to go back four generations. As you move through the following ritual, pay special attention to what your inner world reveals about how you see your father in the context of the other old men, and how you see yourself as their grandson or great-grandson.

A guided meditation similar to the one I offer here can be found in David Feinstein and Stanley Krippner's *Personal Mythology*, where they make a very important point: in guided meditations like this one it does not matter if the people you meet within you are still alive, or even if you knew them personally. What matters is what responses about them rise in your activated imagination.

If you have done the previous task of contacting the old men of your family, you'll know some of the characters you are about to meet better than you would have before. Even if we as men are removed from our fathers and old men, we can turn inward and find pieces of the old men inside us. Our ancestors sit staunchly within our psyches. Where you don't remember certain old men's bodies and the facts of their lives, hear echoes of family mythology surrounding them. These echoes sing, sometimes faintly, often powerfully, of your heritage.

Pick a place in the room where you have a few empty yards behind you, and a few empty feet on each side of you. Stand comfortably and close your eyes. Take three deep breaths. With the first breath, tense your body, then relax it. With the second breath, begin to quiet your inner mental chatter. Use personal meditative rituals you've developed, or concentrate on an image from nature that is very relaxing to you. With the third breath, concentrate only on the sucking of your own breath.

Take a step backward and now imagine that you are stepping into the body and being of your father. Physically assume his posture; physically dramatize it. Take a few moments to sense what it felt like to be in this body and this personality. (Pause)

Take another step backward into the body and being of your father's father. Physically assume your grandfather's posture. Take some time to get it as right as you can, whether you remember it or imagine it. Take a few moments to sense what it felt like to be in this body and this personality. (Pause)

Take another step backward into the body and being of your great-grandfather. Physically assume his posture. Re-

member it or imagine it. *See the place he lived, in whatever country on this earth; see his world. Take a few moments to sense what it felt like to be in this body and this personality. (Pause)*

Finally, take a fourth step backward into the body and being of your great-great-grandfather. Physically assume his posture. See the place he lived, in whatever country; see his world. For a few seconds, let it be your world. If you know nothing about this ancestor, allow whatever comes to rise from your imagination. Take a few moments to sense what it felt like to be in this body and this personality. (Pause)

How would your great-great-grandfather, whose body you inhabit now, answer these questions were he now your present age?

1. What worries you most in life, Great-Great-Grandfather?

2. What makes you the most happy?

3. How do you feel about your position in your society?

4. If you know a God, Great-Great-Grandfather, how does this God treat you? (Pause)

Answer these questions for a few moments. Then step forward into the body and being of your great-grandfather. Assume his posture again. Feel his being. Ask the questions of this man, as you stand within him. Visualize him as if he were your current age.

1. What worries you most in life, Great-Grandfather?

2. What makes you the most happy?

3. How do you feel about your position in your society?

4. If you know a God, Great-Grandfather, how does this God treat you? (Pause)

Step forward into the body and being of your grandfather. Assume his posture again. Feel his being. Ask the questions of this man, as you stand within him. Use whatever name of endearment you used or still use for him. Visualize him when he was your current age.

1. What worries you most in life, Grandfather?

2. What makes you the most happy?

3. How do you feel about your position in your society?

4. If you know a God, Grandfather, how does this God treat you? (Pause)

Now step forward into the body and being of your father. Assume his posture. Feel his being. Ask the questions of him, as you stand within him. Use whatever name of endearment you used for him in your childhood. Visualize him when he was your current age.

1. What worries you most in life, Father?

2. What makes you the most happy?

3. How do you feel about your position in your society?

4. If you know a God, Father, how does this God treat you? (Pause)

Now step into your own body. Find your own typical posture. Take a few moments to return to yourself, in body and soul. Ask yourself the questions. Use your own name as you ask and answer each one.

1. What worries you most in life?

2. What makes you the most happy?

3. How do you feel about your position in your society?

4. If you know a God, how does this God treat you? (Pause)

When you have explored these questions to your satisfaction, come to a resting point. Take three deep breaths, moving slowly back toward the outside world.

When you are ready, write or speak what you have experienced and understood in your journal or tape recorder. Don't force yourself to write every single detail, many of which are still moving around uncontrollably in your head. Write what feels important for each man in your lineage.

After you've written what you need to write, answer these questions:

1. How does my ancestral lineage manifest itself in my present life?

2. How does my ancestral lineage empower me?

3. How does my ancestral lineage inhibit me?

4. What has my ancestral lineage taught me about the qualities of a man?

You have taken a journey back to your male progenitors, old men who still live in you, old men whose voices still echo in your personal inner landscape. You might want to repeat this ritual sometime later. You might want to do it for your mother, her paternal and maternal heritage, and also for your father's maternal heritage. If you are adopted, you might want to do it for your two sets of lineages. Like reading a great book or seeing a great film or hearing a great myth for the second, third, or fourth time, each time you do this exercise, you will learn new things. Just as the book or film relinquishes new secrets each time, so does the greatness in your inner story.

Rely on your journal as much as you need to here. Read and reread it, underlining passages that hit you the hardest.

CLAIMING AND CREATING
YOUR SACRED OBJECTS

It is time again to claim a physical object that you will place on your altar. This object might be a picture of a significant grandfather or old man in your life. In your hallway or living room you might find family pictures; take one of them and put it on your altar for a while. Or if you went specifically to visit one of the old men in your family, some object from that trip might go on your altar—a photo, a ticket stub, a program from an evening at the Rotary club that honored your grandfather for a lifetime of service.

Once you have found an object that holds powerful old masculine energy, move into the last piece of this episode. Write a letter to your father. As with all these letters, it is not a letter you will necessarily send. In it, recall your visit with the old men. Recall especially a visit with one of the old men in your family, a visit that helped you feel a little more initiated, spiritually grounded, connected to your birthright than you did before. As you write this letter you are creating a scroll that embodies your growing closeness with your masculine lineage.

In the letter refer to hearing the old men talk about your father and your birthright, then hearing them admire you as your father's son, then hearing them admire you as a man in your own right. If you went to visit an old man rather than doing everything by phone—perhaps this visit provided your sacred object—write to your father about this man.

Randy flew his family recently to a city 2,500 miles across the country to visit his grandfather. He did this "so that my children would have a memory of their great-grandfather and so that I might learn more about him, and about me." His experience was a powerful one for all involved. During the visit, he learned about his own parents' lives and his grandparents' lives. Much of this is reflected in his scroll. He said the part that was especially powerful for him was learning about his great-grandfather, hearing about that old man and sensing how that old man's story filtered through the stories of all the men and women in his family. He discovered a pain in his male lineage while visiting with this old man. Here is a piece of his story:

> I asked Bampa to tell us about his father, the founder of the family dental-equipment business. When Bampa was a teenager, his mother and father divorced. That was a difficult event in the 1920s in part because adultery was one of the few grounds for divorce and the grounds had to be "arranged."
>
> At the time of the divorce Bampa's father was an officer in the family business. He was fired from the company and joined a competing business. He vowed bitterly to regain what he had lost. But Bampa's mother was a shrewd businesswoman, and she was now in charge of the affairs of the family business. She asked Bampa to help her, and he did. Within a few years she had bought the competing business that Bampa's father had joined and she again fired him. Bampa's father stayed in the field of business for many years and the only time Bampa would see him was at business trade shows.
>
> Many years later at a fall trade show, Bampa's father came up to him and asked Bampa to publicly acknowledge and accept him. Bampa refused. The next fall, at the same trade show, Bampa's father again asked him to publicly acknowledge and accept him. This time Bampa recalls hearing a voice he can explain only as the voice of God telling him that this will be his last chance to accept the invitation from his father. So, against his mother's wishes, he talked to the group and publicly acknowledged and accepted his father.
>
> Three months later Bampa received a telephone call from a family friend who said that his father was in a hospital in New York City and that he should come right away. Bampa picked up his sister outside New York and

together they went to the hospital to see their father. The next day Bampa's father died.

Bampa's voice cracked and wavered and tears filled his eyes as he finished this story of his father.

We sat in silence for a few moments.

I tried to think of how I had thought of the life of Bampa's father. It was not the kind of life I had imagined. It sounded like a lonely life filled with scorn and failure. It seemed like a story I should have heard of long before, when I was younger. It seemed like just the beginning of stories I needed to hear about the men in my family.

When you have finished your own letter to your father, take some time to sit with what has happened in this episode. When you are ready, move on to the next piece of your quest: an encounter with the feminine.

Freeing Your
Imprisoned Lover

A man's femininity is a part of his core.
HERB GOLDBERG

*Is this the face that launched a thousand ships
And burnt the topless towers of Ilium?*
CHRISTOPHER MARLOWE

In every hero's quest there are meetings with female figures. Because the journey depicted in the myth or fairy tale is gender specific to the male hero, we know these are meetings with the feminine inside the male as much as meetings with women outside of him.

A hero will meet the Goddess, as a Native American initiate meets spirits of Mother Earth in the soil and in animals. He is also meeting the mother within him. A hero will meet the Princess, as Strong Hans meets the maiden in chains in the cave. He is also rescuing the feminine within himself. A hero will meet the Queen of Love—as Telemachus meets Helen, a queen of great beauty and warmth.

From Goddess, Crone, Maiden (or Princess), and Queen of Love the hero learns certain things the Feminine can teach him. That often these encounters with women teach him about nurturing emotion does not negate in any way what he learns about nurturing emotion from male figures. What it does do is honor the teaching role of the feminine in a man's journey. And a man seeking his King cannot discover a full, rich King without knowing the feminine within the man.

Like those of us who can remember meeting an older

woman who altered the course of our loving, Telemachus meets his Queen of Love *after* he has begun to learn, through other trials, ordeals, and relationships, a large chunk of who he is as a man. In these trials, ordeals, and relationships—like the visits with the old men—he seeks male identity among men, male mentors, and male figures. Not until he has established some masculine identity does he meet his Helen.

This learning order is important in a man's journey to his King. Since it is a masculine center he is seeking, its foundation must be laid before he knows the feminine. If a masculine foundation were not laid, the Prince would be devoured by the wonderful feminine that reminds him so much of his early childhood at his mother's breast.

Mythology is generally very wise about the masculine/feminine tensions involved here. Myths of many cultures acknowledge that a man cannot be King without knowing his own feminine, but also that he must first know some of the width and depth of his masculine. Even when a female figure is the first mentor met by a young hero, that female will often disguise herself as a male. It's as if the myth acknowledges that the Prince, broken from his mother and seeking his father, cannot begin with his mother again. Thus, as when Telemachus first met Athena and she disguised herself as the male Mentor, even the Goddess pushes the hero toward male influence. Even she knows that if he starts out the whole journey smitten by a woman, how is he to focus on his father and discover his own inner male?

In your own growing up—especially in your adolescence and early adulthood—what was your experience? Did you have romantic and sexual encounters with girls and women before really having a sense of your own masculinity? Did you use those encounters to *define* your masculinity? Many of us do this. Our fathers are distant; our birthright, spiritual grounding, and self-discipline are unclear to us and/or consumed in hormones, in needs for social acceptance, and in rebelliousness against authority. We don't just experiment with girls or become friends with them; we define ourselves by our relationships with them.

We are men if we've "had" a lot of girls. We are men if we have the right girl on our arm. We are not men if we can't get a girlfriend. Of course we develop our masculinity through sports, academics, first jobs, and the other developmental activities of adolescence and early adulthood, but often, not getting enough intimate attention from our fathers and older males, and unable to go back to the intimate attentions of our mothers, we move to the intimate attentions of other females for emotional sustenance.

We are too young to realize that we live in a developmental and archetypal schism. The schism shows up when, often, we seek conquests. Then, when we've "gotten the girl," we become quickly distant from our conquest, feeling an almost instinctual fear of being devoured by the feminine. Without a well-developed masculine center, it stands to reason we will behave this way.

In this episode of your quest, you will be guided to meet feminine elements within yourself. No matter your actual adolescence and early adulthood; in this quest you have reoriented your archetypal development to begin with deep masculine development. You have traced important pieces of your relationship with your father, with close male mentors, and with grandfathers and old men who influenced you. You have specifically explored what your father and mentors taught you about how to love. You have come to the point in your quest when you meet your Helen with some strong grounding in your own masculinity.

MEETING YOUR HELEN

We encounter, seduce, are seduced by, love, leave, pine for, and bleed for many girls and women in our first couple of decades of life. Our Helen is special among them. She is the woman we love for a time who, unlike the other girls and women we've fallen for, does not make adolescent demands upon us.

Like mythological figures, you may have had an affair in your adolescence and young adulthood with an older girl or woman who honored your budding masculinity, taught you important things about what a woman wants from love, and, if your relationship was sexual, about what a significant and comfortable thing sex can be. In some cases these relationships may have been part of your adolescent rites of passage, as roman-

ticized in the film *The Summer of '42*. Or they may have occurred in college, or later. Your Helen was more than a peer. She
was older, beautiful in an experienced way, deeply satisfying.
And your relationship with her probably didn't last more than a
year, or a few months.

She was a female mentor. For a brief confidence-building
time, she gave you a chance to transcend some of your youthful
anxieties, alienations, and self-deceptions. If you were, for instance, the son of a disengaged father, wounded by his abuse or
distance, she let you transcend the legacies of your father-son
wounds for a while. She saw you and your Lover for who and
what you and he were—beautiful. She admired your youth and
vitality, not worrying too much over the insufficiencies you
worried over and, with most people, concealed. She taught you
some things about love that would help your Prince change his
way of loving, bind him to deeper intimacy with women, and
further develop his King.

When at some point this female mentor started having expectations you weren't ready to fulfill ("Let's have a kid." "I'm
getting older; let's be committed") or when you met someone
more your own age with whom you fell in love (or whom you
just wanted to be with), you broke from this female mentor.
Often the break was painful, but still you retained a lot of what
you had learned about loving from this female mentor.

Our outward journey tends to mirror our inward journey.
When you were with this Helen, you learned things only an experienced woman could teach you. Your inner feminine was not
developed enough to teach you these things, so you found a
woman who could give voice to what your inner feminine was
only murmuring. In the archetypal journey of this book, the
Helen you meet will be a voice for the mature feminine within
you, which needs to be known consciously, as part of your own
voice.

THE DARK SIDE OF MEETING HELEN

I have thus far painted the meeting with Helen as a bright and
beautiful experience. It has a dark side, too. Many of us—
perhaps most of us—are too undeveloped during our youthful
adventure to recognize the dark side. Yet it is a dark side that

affects the rest of our love relationships. This dark side directly involves our father-son wound.

When our fathers are disengaged during our boyhood and adolescence, our masculine foundation is not well constructed. Consequently, we learn very little about loving partners that is healthy and fulfilling. We enter our adolescence and young adulthood unconsciously convinced that there is little the masculine can teach us about love. We seek out only the feminine for lessons of love. We meet Goddess, Maiden, and Queen of Love. Wanting to love and be loved, we give our Lover over to them.

"Come," we are saying, "I am lousy at loving. You show me how." After a few years of this, what we are really coming to say is: "Listen, since I'm so bad at loving and since you, being a woman, are so good at it, why don't you do the loving for both of us?"

This terrible relinquishment of personal power is rooted in our father-son wound, our lack of deep connection with healthy male energy, and our archetypal confusion about female mentor and female lover. The women we mate with must be lovers, not mentors. While mates teach each other things, they are first and foremost loving partners. Men in our culture, however, lacking sacred masculine foundation, confuse lovers with mentors, asking women to be their female mentors as much as their sexual, reproductive, and supportive lovers.

This is the dark side of the relationship with Helen. Each of us needs to be honest about just how much we have been confusing female mentoring with female loving. In myth and archetype, the meeting with the Queen of Love is a *meeting*, not a lifelong pupilship of men to women.

Thus the tasks of this piece of your journey will have two intentions. First, we'll ask Helen to help us concentrate on our modes of loving. As your male mentor has and will continue to teach you lessons from his masculine point of view, let your feminine elements help you in this chapter to learn lessons from your deep feminine well of wisdom.

Second, I'll encourage you to look at ways you may be confusing female lovers with female mentors. Some of these ways will directly relate back to your father-son wound. While certainly our relationships with our fathers are not the only, and for some of us not even the primary, locus of our adult confusions about love, they are a crucial one. If we are to become Kings, our meeting with Helen, in both its sacred and its shadow moments, is a rich learning ground.

HOW DO YOU LOVE?

Before reading on, take a moment to go to the Appendix and review the information about the Lover archetype.

The Lover is the part of you that takes absolute delight in the world, is capable of unconditional love, and is most vulnerable. It was the first archetype to activate within you and it was the first to be shamed and imprisoned. It has no defenses, so it relies on the Warrior to defend it. It loves everything, so it relies on the King to bless some of its relationships more than others—especially, in adulthood, its primary relationships. The Lover is easily swayed this way or that, easily tempted, and so when a King is not developed within a man, the Lover will often love the wrong woman; it is the King that guides the man toward the woman who is most healthy for him, the one who will best bless him. The King is capable of judgments that the Lover, passionate and unreserved, is not.

You can see, therefore, how knowledge of how our Lover is functioning within us directly relates to our journey toward our fathers. The father-son relationship activates the King more than any other, and if we have dysfunction in that relationship, our way of loving is affected in profound and, as we shall see in this chapter, identifiable ways. Douglas Gillette speaks to the relationship of King-center and intimacy in this way:

> In the end, only one strategy for achieving Self-empowerment, and, hence, for achieving intimate relationship, will work. That strategy has several facets. But it has one goal—a calm but vitally alive, firm but creative, centeredness. When a man finds that centered place in his own psyche, he is the owner of his own legitimate power. . . . When he has achieved this inner condition, the condition of realistic self-esteem, then he can be welcoming of *truly* intimate relationship.

The King is that piece of ourselves that centers us in realistic self-esteem and from that center guides our Lover toward partners who will enhance and support that self-esteem.

What does realistic self-esteem mean? It means a man knows his own limitations and is comfortable with them. It means he brings as much emotional and spiritual power to a relationship as his partner does. Instead of being the man who says to his spouse or partner, "I love you because you make me feel like I'm worth something," he is the man who says, "I feel like I'm worth something, and I love you." Many of us, because our Lover is imprisoned and our King is not centering our relationships, live out the first statement.

When our Lover is imprisoned by shame, when the King is not operating as powerfully as he needs to, and when our protective Warrior exists in rigid, compensating defensiveness, holding off intimacy that the imprisoned Lover really needs, the Lover will do what any of us would do in a prison cell: turn, however subtly, from his present relationship toward fantasy relationships.

Imprisoned, with no King to help him, our Lover gets lost in his fantasies. Perhaps his fantasies are manifested as obsessions with pornography, or with prostitutes, or with adultery. Perhaps he sees every young woman in the office as a potential conquest. Perhaps, operating out of his fantasies, he says things to women that he finds boldly self-expressive and that they find to be sexual harassment.

Perhaps he watches from within his cell as the Shadow Explorer wanders from relationship to relationship, without real direction. He marries four, five, six times, wandering from one intimacy to another, tossing off the previous intimacy when it no longer meets his fantasy expectations.

Imprisoned, with no King to help him, the Lover perhaps turns to the Shadow Magician, seeking unrealistic love in his long-term or primary relationship. Even a man in a satisfying long-term relationship can be trying to love through the Magician more than he knows. It is one of the traits of an adolescent hero. It is a trait of the Prince, undeveloped in his centeredness. When he hits a midlife crisis, his twenty years of concealed imprisonment finally catch up to him. He yearns for magic to get him out. He throws off his family, thinking they are what imprison him, and seeks magical midlife transformation, often living for another decade without realizing that love depends not on magic, but on realistic self-esteem.

This connection between love and magic appears everywhere in our popular culture and as a theme in our mythology. Nearly every Hollywood movie encourages the idea that love is based in magical transformation. These transformations usually occur very quickly, often as a result of one or two acts on the part of the hero. Suddenly hero and heroine, who formerly disliked each other, are in love. Either she changes or he does. In the fifties John Wayne did some brave thing, and Maureen O'Hara fell in love with him; his courageous deed provided the magic love they needed. Nowadays, Arnold Schwarzenegger or Steven Seagal or Tom Cruise does brave deeds and, to appeal to modern sensibilities, some "sensitive-male" deed as well. Shy, "wimpy" men, like Steve Martin in *L. A. Story*, already "sensitive" but needing more bravery, become more assertive and *voilà*, suddenly he and the maiden are in love. The moment of magic, it seems, is all most lovers are waiting for.

In none of these cases is there any real show of long-term internal change. Tom Cruise's Lover is not liberated in one tender act, nor is Steve Martin's in one assertive act. The man in the shampoo commercial has not set his Lover free by using a new dandruff shampoo, though this supposedly leads to his falling in love suddenly in an elevator. Their Lovers are still in prison; their actions or appearances have changed slightly, and in that slight transformation viewers are taught that love can occur.

This obsession with magic and transformation is not new, just as the imprisonment of the Lover is as old as shame and guilt and pain. The grip of this idea of magical transformation on the way we love our mates and friends has, however, tightened in the last fifty years, due to the plethora of its images in our media-oriented culture. Now realistic self-esteem becomes even harder to acquire because present-day men and women are being told that not only people, and not only mentors and gods, can transform us into great lovers, but practically all consumer products as well.

To explore the Lover within us, we must come to some understanding of our own expectations of magic in love. When in our love relationships do we slip into expecting a fantasy? Are we using that expectation to distance ourselves from real love, from the next passage or stage in our love relationship's maturing? Are we seeking "perfection"—which in itself is a trickster's unrealistic magic potion—and distancing ourselves from what and who we really need?

How did we get so wounded and imprisoned that we try to rely on magic so desperately? How did we give up our own power to love? Let us answer some of these questions carefully, using stories as our guides, so that our meeting with Helen can be a healthy, powerful one.

ARE YOU A FROG PRINCE?

There is a Russian fairy tale many of us were told as kids, a tale called "The Frog Prince." In it the prince is a frog, cursed long ago. A princess is playing with a golden ball her father gave her. She drops it into a pond and cries out for it. The frog presents himself as her rescuer. She thinks he's terribly ugly, but at the same time realizes that he's her only ally. She tells the frog she'll do whatever he asks, if only he'll retrieve her golden ball from the bottom of the pond. He does so and then requests that she take him into her home, feed him, sleep next to him, and kiss him. She tries to run from him, breaking her promise, but finally she is forced to do as he asks. The next morning, she awakens beside a handsome prince, and, of course, they live happily ever after.

Love, in this tale, is based in a woman's magically transforming a man. The man is cursed, unable to transform himself. He is ugly in his curse. Only the princess can make him handsome. Only by doing a brave deed, a deed the princess feels herself unable to do, does he have hopes of getting the princess to remove his curse. She doesn't really want to remove his curse, but she is finally forced to. Of course, when she does, she is pleasantly surprised. And the two fall in love.

For decades women have been reacting against tales of this kind—and for very good reason. The princess is depicted as afraid of the water, weak, deceitful, and completely powerless—going from the golden ball of innocence her father gave her to marriage with the prince, without a life of her own. This story depicts too closely the lives many women are forced to live, in which they must find fulfillment in transforming a man from his curse, rather than in seeking what they themselves need.

Men ought to react to this story as well. Ask yourself if you live this way. Have you been taught that women hold the key to successful intimate relationships? Are you still waiting for women to transform you? Have you asked women to shape you, form you, do their magic on you, free your cursed and imprisoned Lover?

Ask yourself, through the images of this story, how much you require that your intimate partners form your Lover. We'll all always rely on each other to be mirrors for our Lovers, but should we rely on the other to remove our own curses, to heal our own wounds? What happens to the Frog Prince and his Princess after they are married? The story never tells us.

We all know what happens. To the extent that we relied on our falling in love and living with our mate to save us from the curses of our family of origin, we end up one day reactivating the old curses. Things go wrong in our relationships. We end up disappointed, wandering around within ourselves, still waiting for the magical transformation of the kiss to finally work and make us free. And when it does not, we look for that same magical moment with another woman, or our work, or an addiction, still feeling deep within that we're ugly frogs, that one day we'll be found out, that we must avoid having our male curse exposed at all costs.

ARE YOU HUSBAND TO
THE LEOPARD WOMAN?

An African story called "The Leopard Woman" paints a man's story from the other pole of magic. In this story a man and woman and their infant, who is strapped to the woman's back, are walking in a forest. Hungry and tired, they come upon some bush cows.

"You are capable of transformation," the man says to his wife. "I am not. So why don't you transform yourself into a leopard and go kill a cow for our dinner?"

"What shall I do with our child?" she asks. "How can you ask this of me?"

"Just put him here," says the man, "at the bottom of this tree."

She does not want to do what he has asked her, but does. She takes the child off her back and puts it at the base of a huge tree.

Soon the transformation begins. Her hands become claws, and her face becomes hairy and changes in structure; all the while she is glaring at the man. She turns into a growling leopard. When she is fully transformed, she moves to attack her husband and he clambers up the tree. Now she circles around the child, as if to eat it. The man knows he should do something, but he's too frightened.

Finally she goes off and kills one of the bush cows. She drags it back and begins to transform back into a woman. When the transformation is finished, she calls up to her husband, "Come back down. What are you so afraid of?"

"I'm not coming down until you put the child back on your back," he says, trembling. If she puts the child on her back then he knows she won't turn into a leopard again.

She does as he asks and he comes down. She looks him in the eye and says, "Don't you ever ask me to do that again." He resolves not to, and they eat the food.

When we as men do not know what to do, or live in fear of intimacy and ourselves, it is simple to ask the woman to transform herself. Perhaps this is the same woman of whom, when we fell in love with her, we thought, "She is going to be the princess that kisses me and removes my curse." But the years go by, we are with the same woman or a new one, we are still cursed, things aren't changing, and so we wonder if maybe the woman should change.

Yet when she does change, what happens? We are frightened. We have not changed, but she has. We discover she has even more powers than we thought, and we even less.

Are you the husband of the leopard woman?

TASK 1:
TRACING YOUR OWN LOVER'S
PERSONAL HISTORY

As men we are forced by our wounds into desires for transformation that we must become aware of before it is possible for our meeting with Helen—and her revelation of what mature femininity really needs and wants—to be fully empowering. We must understand that we are imprisoned Lovers, relying on tricks and magic, waiting for her to transform herself, or for our own transformation by her kiss.

Making a Map of Your Love Life

Spend some time now doing foundational memory work. This work will help you place who you are now on the map of your past and present.

1. Recall whether and how your parents showed physical affection to each other. Use old photos as a way of spurring memories. Look at the photo of your parent or yourself at a younger age at a picnic or sitting around the house or swimming at the lake. Recall incidents and events. Did your parents hug each other, kiss each other?

2. Recall whether and how your parents showed physical affection to you. Again, turn to pictures to trigger memories.

3. Write a list of the lovers you've had up to this point in your life. For lovers whom you were really using as female mentors, note "female mentor" beside the name. Don't go any deeper into it for now. Make sure to write down every lover's name (if you remember it; if not, note every one of them somehow). Just note names and bare details at this point—something like this:

Grace. Never slept with her but had platonic relationship. I was 23, she was 20, Chicago. She was still in college. She was younger than me, but definitely a female mentor.

Or:

*Liz. Slept with her till we both dropped. I was 20, she was
19. Dallas. 1969. We were drugged out. Sex gets in the way
of my memories. I was clueless about love, though, at
that time in my life. Probably some female mentor there.*

4. Write how you changed in going from one lover to the
   next, if you did change. Concentrate on changes you
   consider deep ones. We all change in many ways, but we
   all know that some changes and growth are abiding,
   while others are not. Concentrate on deep patterns of
   loving. Note how you matured from one lover to the
   next. Be honest and note what patterns stayed the same
   between lovers. Use the terms Female Mentor, Frog
   Prince, and Husband of the Leopard Woman as metaphors to help you, attaching to your writing one of
   these—or some other metaphor of your own that captures your deep relationship patterns and helps you
   work with your Lover.

*Between Toni and Cindy I kind of went underground.
Toni broke my heart so bad I don't think I really gave
much to Cindy. She knew it. She was patient, but then
she left too. I was being a Husband of the Leopard
Woman. If she wanted a relationship with me, she had to
do all the changing. I wasn't going to do any work. Terrible thing was, I really did want a relationship with her.
I missed an opportunity there. I still think about her
a lot.*

Or:

*When I divorced Juli I was so happy at first. I thought I
was saved. But then I rebounded quick with Jaime. A lot
of female mentor there. Jaime taught me to do my own
work. I did some of it, got into therapy. She and I didn't
last but at least I was less of a Frog Prince than before.*

This exercise will take many hours. Include as many details as you can when recording this portion of your Lover's
history.

Constructing a More Detailed History of Your Lover

When you have the list, the brief memories, and the review of your Lover's changes, move forward. I'm now going to assist you in recalling an even more detailed history of your Lover, a history that will go back to your earliest days.

As you are moving chronologically through your life you might have memories of times you have forgotten, perhaps times of sexual abuse you didn't know were there. If one of these moments arises, and if it shocks and overwhelms you, don't be afraid to seek counsel or therapy.

These tasks may take you weeks. Let them.

For each of the time periods provided below, address one or more of the following four ways in which your Lover was negated, wounded, cursed, and imprisoned.

1. In negative interactions with immediate family members (parents, spouse, children) and other relatives. How did abuse from, distance from, or other dysfunctional interactions at the hands of these people shame and imprison your ability to feel absolute delight and unconditional love?

2. In negative modeling from immediate family members and relatives. How did the behaviors you observed in these people who served as models for your own maturity frighten, negatively influence, and imprison your own ability to feel absolute delight and unconditional love?

3. In negative interactions with and modeling in wider environments (neighborhood and neighbors, school and playground, media, workplace, city and town, culture). How did interactions and observations of behavior in these areas shame you, wound you, and force you into imprisoning your own ability to feel love?

4. In inadequate connection to the natural world and ecosystem. The Lover in us is fed and freed by deep interaction with the natural world. In what ways do you and others curtail your activities and interest in connecting with nature, and your undistracted self that is so often revealed in the solitude of nature?

Remember that you are looking for incidents and memories that point to moments in which your Lover was imprisoned. If moments of importance to other archetypes, especially the King, should emerge, note those as well. But keep focused on the shaming, negative modeling, and imprisonment of your own ability to love and feel delight.

Be as detailed as possible as you work with the time periods of your life. Focus on incidents and memories. Use as much of your notebook as you need to. Write the following list of time periods on separate pages of your notebook, filling in memories for each page as they come to you. Perhaps a lot of material will come to you about one time period and nothing about another. Just let come what comes.

1. Birth to Five Years Old

2. Six Years Old to Early Puberty

3. Early Puberty to Early Adulthood (Late Teens)

4. Early Adulthood to Marriage (or First Permanent Partnership)

Focus first on the periods of boyhood, adolescence, and young adulthood. They were the most formative and the time in which patterns of intimacy were established. If you wish, move forward into the next periods, in which patterns of intimacy were manifested.

5. Marriage (Major Loving Partnership) to the Birth of Children

    Whether you have children or not, divide your marriage into time periods that intuitively feel right to you, using milestone events as markers, and trace the patterns of intimacy through incidents and memories of those time periods.

6. Marriage to Divorce (if this applies)

7. Relationships between Divorces (if this applies)

Continue life divisions as necessary until you come to your present age. Modify these divisions as necessary to accommodate the time periods and major events of your Lover's journey in your own love relationships.

Spend time with these passages in your life. At first, the list may seem too daunting to pursue, or too simplistic. If you settle into each time period, however, even dividing it up by single years in your notebook; if you really plumb your memory, focusing on the four ways the Lover is nurtured/imprisoned; and if you do all this focused on your father's way of loving and how it affected you, you will find a lot of grief rising, and also a lot of potential healing and transformation.

Understanding How Your Lover May Still Be Imprisoned

When you have gone through the time periods to your satisfaction, answer these questions honestly:

1. In what ways do I fear intimacy?
2. In what ways do I hold back from deep communication of feeling?
3. Is there a particular kind of behavior in my partner that pushes my buttons and shuts me down?
4. What were *primary* moments of my Lover's imprisonment during my boyhood and adolescence?
5. What were *primary* moments of my father's influence on my fear of intimacy and my Lover's imprisonment?
6. How am I reliving family Lover patterns?
7. Specifically, in what dysfunctional ways am I loving partners the way my father loved my mother?
8. How am I picking partners who will continue the dysfunction of my childhood and will continue to imprison my Lover?
9. What love patterns did I learn from my father that were positive?
10. What positive love patterns did I learn from one or two primary mentors—mentors I identified earlier who taught me pieces of the male mode of feeling?
11. What must I do to free my Lover?
12. What have I already done and what remains to be done?
13. What can a partner do to help me free my Lover?
14. How is my present partner encouraging my imprisonment? Or how did my most recent partner encourage my imprisonment?

When you have answered these questions completely, you'll have a great deal of material. You'll have recalled the chronology of lovers in your life. You'll have noted how you've changed between lovers. You will have traced a great deal of what your mother and father taught you about loving. You'll have touched again, in a different way than you did in chapter 6, what you learned from male mentors about the giving and taking of affection. You'll have traced the wounding of your Lover. You'll have a sense of the work you have left to do as a man in regard to the way you love partners and handle other intimacies.

Honor yourself at this point, before you go on. Do something to celebrate the hard work you've just done. Show pieces of it to your partner or group or to a friend or therapist. Especially appreciate what you've learned about love from strong masculine influences, like your father and mentors. Appreciate the masculine love in you before moving into the tutelage of the feminine.

Recalling a Helen in Your Life

Now that you have gone through your life and traced the way you love, you are better equipped to meet a Helen within you and to recognize a Helen in your own past. You noted earlier which of your lovers served more as female mentors than lovers in equal partnership. You noted earlier how you expressed this giving up of power to the lover—whether by making her kiss you to save you, or by making her transform herself so that you could avoid doing your own work.

Now look back at all your lovers—sexual, platonic, stabilizing, wild, dangerous, intimidating, infatuating. Look back at all your material from the previous sections of this chapter. See if one of the lovers wasn't a Helen. Don't force one of them to be if none were. But if one of them was clearly a female mentor, and clearly helped you transcend some of your own issues about youthful self-confidence and worries about your manhood, she was a Helen. If one of them made you feel like a man at a time in your life when you feared you weren't enough of a man, and if she also somehow sent you off back to your own masculinity for answers, she was a Helen.

Look for someone you related to for, perhaps, less than a year. Look for someone who made you feel strong, someone who loved your young manhood for what it was. Look for someone who gave you shelter, teaching, affirmation. Look for someone secure in her womanhood, who encouraged your masculinity like your male mentors did, but from her feminine position.

Write a long statement about this woman. Recall your relationship with her and honor it. It was imperfect, like all relationships, but concentrate in this statement on the wonders it taught you.

Write, also, where you were in relation to your father during the time you were in a relationship with this Helen. This is crucial. Without your realizing it, you brought your father-son wound to your relationship with Helen. You asked her to help salve that wound by making you feel valuable as a man in a way men (especially your father) were not helping you to feel. Take some time to remember and appreciate that female mentor.

> Jimmy wrote, *I was a junior in high school and she was a senior in college. Kim. She really pursued me. I couldn't understand why, and it scared me at first. I was always embarrassed about myself, like in gym. I hated to be naked. I thought I had a tiny dick and tiny balls. I wasn't much into sports or anything. I wasn't really very smart either. I liked cars a lot. My dad wasn't around much. I hated high school. I'd never do it again. I guess some men peak in high school and want to get back to it all their lives. Not me. I hated it.*
>
> *Anyway, Kim really pursued me. She was the sister of a friend who had a 1956 Chevy convertible she never took good care of. I was great with cars. My dad really taught me cars. That was about the only time we spent together, was working on our old International Harvester.*
>
> *Anyway, I went over to her house to help her with the car. Once I went when my friend wasn't there. I wasn't a virgin. That's not why she made me so nervous. And it wasn't like she was too pretty or anything. But there was something about her. She smoked, I remember that, always smoking and watching me work. She always asked me a lot of questions and looked me right in the eye. Sometimes I trembled when I was around her. She told me later she saw it and that's what made her so attracted to me.*
>
> *Anyway, once I went when my friend wasn't there. I*

*finished doing something, I don't remember what, and I
went in the house to tell her I was leaving. That was the
beginning of it. She just kissed me. I was shaking so much
and she didn't giggle at me. She was always like this, in
the six months we went out. She never laughed at me or
put me down. I guess she was a mentor, she really was.
She really taught me to like myself. I don't think the
lesson lasted too long. I still never really could believe I
was a man, but I remember her so plainly, Kim, and I'm
thankful to her.*

If you cannot recall a Helen in your life, let this piece go.
Whatever your experience of this whole task has been, take a
day or two to relax. Then move on to the next task.

TASK 2:
MEETING YOUR OWN IMPRISONED LOVER

Now let us move from memory of our past into archetypal
imaging of our present life. The following personal ritual takes
you on a journey in which you will meet three figures: your inner mentor, who will appear in this meditation as an embodiment of what older men have taught you about intimacy; your
Queen of Love, who will be a manifestation of the intimate
feminine within; and your imprisoned Lover, who waits to embrace you.

If you were wounded by your father, your Lover is imprisoned, no matter how developed you are. He has no choice but to
be, because your King is not developed enough to help free him
completely. Journey now into the piece of you that is hurting inside, wanting to love better, communicate better, be better at
intimacy and empathy and touch. Your Lover will be naked and
male, though he may have some feminine characteristics.

Find a comfortable position. Quiet your breathing. Enter
your personal ritual of relaxation. Take three deep breaths and
enter the spirit of meditation.

*Bring to mind people in your life, living or dead, whose
Lover energy you have admired and sought to emulate. These
may be parents, teachers, brothers, sisters, friends, cultural
heroes, spouses.*

Now focus on two of them, one male and one female.

In what way did the male figure embody the Lover well? In what way was he capable of trusting the world with his delight and affection? Recall an incident in which this man embodied his Lover. What did you admire about the way this man interacted with others? What did you admire about his interactions with his intimate friends, including you? (Pause)

In what way did the female figure embody the Lover well? In what way was she capable of trusting the world with her delight and affection? Recall an incident in which this woman embodied her Lover. What did you admire about the way this woman interacted with others? What did you admire about her interactions with intimate friends, including you? (Pause)

Now prepare to move into your archetypal wilderness. There is deep affection and openness within you, waiting for you to trust it. Relax and breathe so that your mind's chatter is closed off as much as it can be. Concentrate on the sound and feeling of your own breath as it goes in and out, in and out. Feel your breath begin somewhere down near your navel and travel upward, out your throat, then back in again, downward toward your center.

Begin to imagine yourself becoming smaller. Take a deep breath and imagine yourself at half your present size. Let your breath out. Take a deep breath and imagine yourself at one-quarter your present size. Take a deep breath and imagine yourself so small that you can stand on your own stomach. See yourself there, standing on your stomach, so light your feet leave no imprint.

You are standing at your navel. We all began connected by our navel to life itself. There is still a spiritual cord that is like a tiny tunnel going inward from our navel into our deepest and sacred self. Find your navel, find that magical entrance to your inner life. Climb onto the lip of that entrance. Hang your tiny leg over it. Hang your other leg over. It's frightening to let go. It's frightening to let yourself fall down that tunnel. Push your tiny body a little further, a little further. Let yourself go. Feel the warmth. It's your own body you are moving into.

Come to a soft landing at the bottom of the tunnel. You are in a forest. You are dwarfed by huge trees and vines. Cries of animals are all around you. This is your inner wilderness. You have been here before. Feel at home as you walk in this wilderness.

Walk a few steps toward shadows and light that emanate from behind a mass of trees and vines. Push through vines. Something important sits behind the mass of vines. Sweat rises on you. This pushing through the vines takes a lot of effort, a lot of breath. Feel vines and foliage scratching your skin.

Push through at last to see a tiny open meadow, surrounded by an orderly coppice of trees. You have been to this meadow before. In the center of the tiny space, lit by sunlight and shadow, is a cage. In it is your father. He appears there at any age you suddenly remember, an age in which he taught you something about how to imprison your Lover.

Come to your father's cage. He is bewildered inside the cage. He doesn't know what he is doing here. You may try to calm him down but he will not be able to hear you.

Standing next to your father's cage is a beautiful woman. Speak with her. She is the Queen of Love. She doesn't have the power to transform your father, who wanders dazed and angry in the cage. But she will speak to you. Ask her how your father got there into that cage. Let her tell you what she knows of his life. (Pause)

When there is no more you wish to ask or have answered about your father's imprisonment, the beautiful woman will come to you and take your hand. She will guide you down the path to another meadow. Walk with her now to that meadow. Feel the comfort of her hand in yours.

When you come to the next meadow you'll see another cage. In that cage you will see yourself, at any age you remember when you felt your intimacy imprisoned. See yourself in the cage. Remember that time. Speak to the Queen of Love. Ask her how you got there into that cage. Ask her what part your relationship with your father played in your getting to that cage. Let her tell you what she knows of your life, and your imprisonment.

She cannot transform you into a snake so that you can slither out of that cage, nor can she transform you into a bird. But she can tell you a little of what you must do to get free. (Pause)

Thank the Queen of Love for her insights.

Now let the beautiful woman guide you again down the path. Walk with her. Feel the comfort of her hand in yours. Farther down the path see a masculine figure you have seen before. See your inner Mentor waiting.

Hear the Queen of Love say, "Feminine and masculine together, we guide you to love."

Greet your inner Mentor. Embrace him. Hear him say, "Masculine and feminine together, we guide you to love."

Explain to your inner Mentor what you've just seen. Tell him about the cage of your father and the cage that was your own. He will not seem surprised. He will know of them.

Ask him how your father got to his cage. Ask him how you got to yours. Let your inner Mentor tell you what he knows of your life and your imprisonment. (Pause)

When he is finished, wonder silently over any differences between what he said and what the Queen of Love said. Do not make the two parts of yourself explain themselves. Thank your inner Mentor. If you are not doing so already, stand between your Mentor and the Queen of Love. Walk forward with them as they guide you.

See ahead of you the archway of two huge trees you've seen before. Walk between your Mentor and the Queen of Love under the archway. Walk with them into the meadow.

In the center of the meadow is someone standing, naked, grinning, waiting for you. He is your inner Lover. Here in this meadow he is not imprisoned. Here you can always find him free. Notice the softness of his cheeks and flesh. Notice the passion in his eyes. Notice his energy and warmth. Feel him. Feel everything you can about him. He carries no sword, he wears no armor, no clothes. He is sweet life and delight.

The Queen of Love hangs back now, as you move to the Lover in the center of your meadow. This is as far as she can go. She does not enter the center of the meadow, for that is a masculine center and she respects the masculinity at its core. Your Mentor, too, hangs back, for your encounter with your Lover is meant to be yours alone.

Go up to that Lover, touch him. Touch his hair—what color is it? Touch his eyes—what color are they? Touch his mouth. Touch his chest, his arms, his genitals.

Embrace your inner Lover. You embrace an intimate part of yourself that your busy life rarely allows you to embrace. Hug him.

As the embrace ends, ask your inner Lover to remind you of a time when you loved another in a way that he is capable of—passionately, wonderfully, joyously. Recall that time with your Lover now, whether it was long ago or very recent. (Pause)

Ask your Lover why you feel and know his presence less than you wish. Ask him to suggest ways, changes in your life or attitude, that would make it easier to know him better in your relationships. (Pause)

Ask him what he enjoys the most about your present love relationship. (Pause)

Ask him in what ways he feels you need to work harder in it. (Pause)

Ask him what you need to do in your life to make his embrace a larger part of your life. (Pause)

It may be hard to leave the presence of your inner Lover, yet you must leave. You will see your Lover again. Know this. He is never far from you, walking freely in this meadow, wearing that naive and wonderful grin of pure life on his face.

As you walk away from him and go under the archway you are moving with your Mentor and the Queen of Love toward a huge hole in a huge tree. Big good-bye to the Queen of Love and to your Mentor. Do this in any way comfortable for you.

Enter the hole. You are entering darkness again. Walk up the slippery incline, back up that tiny cord toward your navel.

It's difficult to return to ordinary reality. It's a hard climb. It is difficult to leave your guts and return to the distractions. It's difficult to return to your ordinary size. Yet it must be done.

As you climb, see light above you. Come to the entrance of your navel. Step out into the light. Take one deep breath and find yourself growing in size. Take another deep breath and you have become half your ordinary size. Take a third deep breath and you are now your ordinary size.

Slowly open your eyes.

When you're ready, turn to your journal and record the important moments of this experience. What did your Queen of

Love say to you about the cages? What did your inner Lover tell you? What did this Lover look and feel like to you? When you have written what you need to write, go on to the next section.

SHARING THIS EXPERIENCE WITH OTHERS

If you are currently in a relationship, consider sharing some of what you've been through in this episode with that partner. If you are not currently in a relationship, consider sharing with a friend, therapist, or group. Hear your own voice as it speaks your Lover's dilemmas and beauties. Hear your own voice as it connects problems in your loving with problems around your father.

CLAIMING YOUR SACRED OBJECTS

This episode of your journey is now coming to a close. What objects contain the fruits of this journey for you? Through what objects can you hold the sacredness of your Lover's quest? Is there a picture, a piece of jewelry, a love poem, or something else that encapsulates sacred love for you? Select such an object. Hold it. Put it on your altar.

Sit down to write a letter to your father, which may never be sent. In this letter, tell him about this episode. Concentrate especially on what effect you believe he's had on your Lover and the way you love. Tell him some of why it felt so good to turn to the feminine—to a Queen of Love and to other women in your life—to help you define your masculinity. Honor the benefits of that turn, but also explain to your father where you went too far.

As you settle into writing this, explain to your father how you see him caged. Although you are writing to your father, you are a grown man now and are really writing to your own King, whom your father still represents in you. As you tell your father how he could help you get a foundation for realistic self-esteem in your love relationships, you're also telling your own King how you need him to help you with this. As you tell your father the mistakes you've made in love relationships, you are a Lover

displaying for the King your problems, a display that will ultimately help that King act more powerfully on your behalf as
you continue your journey of Prince to King.

> *Dear Papa,* Vernon wrote, *I never realized until recently
> how lost I felt in my relationships and how much of that
> feeling went back to feeling lost about what a man is. I
> didn't know what a man should be so I turned to women
> to tell me. There was a good side to this, but there was
> also something wrong. I really grieve how little King I got
> from you. I take that tiny King, like a limp dick, into all
> my relationships. It's really like I'm in prison and don't
> have much power to get out.*
>
> *Sally's always saying I don't have any feelings. That's
> bullshit, but that's how it seems to her. Do you remember
> Janice, that woman who lived on 31st? You don't know
> this, but when I was sixteen I lost my virginity with her. I
> was really lost and felt so bad about myself. You never
> knew that I felt bad. Mom knew it a little, but she didn't
> say anything. She just always tried to have her positive
> attitude about things. It was you I wanted to know, but
> you didn't know. I was popular. I was going the college
> and prelaw route you wanted me to go. You were
> satisfied. I felt awful inside.*
>
> *I met Janice and she made me feel good. And I would
> never trade what that woman taught me. She was so gen-
> tle and she thought I was so young and handsome, her
> "young knight." She loved the fact that we were having
> sex on the sly and she loved my sneaking in at night. I
> loved it too. The first time I ever cried with a woman was
> with her. It was one of the last too, unfortunately. I cried
> about you, I remember. You had just yelled at me about
> something and I went to her house and lost it. I was em-
> barrassed at first but she made me feel okay. I really loved
> her a lot.*
>
> *But now I'm coming to realize she made me feel so
> good I just wanted all women to do this for me. I think
> that's what's going on. It has something to do with Mama
> too, I guess, I don't know, I'm in pretty intense therapy
> now and trying to understand it all. I feel so heavy some-
> times when I think about all this. I've spent my life trying
> to make everyone like Janice. I don't know. Help me with
> this, Papa.*

If you never had a Janice in your remembered life, write nonetheless about similar themes—ways in which women mentor to you, and how your father fits into your pain and fear of intimacy.

When you have written your letter, place it on the altar and move forward to the next chapter. In this episode we'll move directly toward confrontation with our fathers.

Descending into the Dark Cave

In the sweat lodge, where it is darker than dark, you will meet evil spirits and you will feel all your life's troubles openly. Where it is darker than dark you will descend into the seventh direction, the Within Direction, and feel from your heart. Inside your deepest self, where it is darker than dark, you will need to be the strongest and the most steadfast, or you will perish.
INSTRUCTION TO BEGIN A SWEAT-LODGE CEREMONY

There is no known culture or mythological tradition in which there is not a journey into the underground, into the dark cave, into the dark center of human life. Something essential to human experience hides in the dark, and we yearn to know it intimately. We sense that our greatest powers come from the dark, and that to know them we must return to the dark.

Our return to the dark is a return to our original nature. "In the beginning," our own Genesis tell us, "the earth was without form, and void; and darkness was upon the face of the deep, and the spirit of God moved upon the face of the dark waters." The Tao Te Ching tells us that the original darkness of existence is "darkness within darkness: the gate to all mystery." Darkness is the dark womb from which we all came, the dark ocean from which our ancestors came, the dark soundlessness before the primal sound.

Human beings were created in a dark pit, according to legends of the Plain Indians. Coyote was carving wood one day and carved a piece into the shape of a man. He carved more and more pieces into the shape, until he got bored and tossed them into a dark pit he had dug out of an anthill the week before. These carvings of wood just lay there until the ants started biting them. As the bites got worse and worse the wooden humans began to quiver. By the next day they were jumping around and crying that it was warm down there and they were being eaten by ants. Coyote let them languish for four days and then pulled them up out of the hole. Born in darkness and pain, they were red from ant bites.

Our return to the dark is a return to our original selves, to the darkness in which our emotions and myths wait to be discovered. Our return to the dark is also a return to our deep fears. We battle them down in the dark. We are either defeated and spiritually die, or we are victorious and find new empowerment.

From Jean-Paul Sartre's *nothingness*, which grounds existence, to Buddhism's *void*, which unites existence, darkness is portrayed as the center of what we are. No wonder, then, that in all mythological systems, heroes and princes find themselves confronting their demons, dragons, and enemies in the bellies of whales, in caves, in labyrinths, in the bottoms of wells, in holes, underground in Hades, in the remembered childhood closet of the boogeyman, in the basement where a horde of spiders lie in wait, at the bottom of the sea, in hell, in dark prison cells, in darkness at noon, in long, endless nights.

No wonder, also, that in so many sacred ceremonies dark space is essential for creating the safe space in which a man's heart can open. Among the Hopi, the initiation of boys into men is marked by a boy's long stay in a kiva, an underground ceremonial hole. The sweat-lodge ceremony is the world's oldest practiced cleansing ceremony. The sweat lodge is a small hut covered by skins, blankets, mattresses, or whatever works to cut out light entirely. If there is any light at all, it is faint, from the red glow of the rocks burning in a pit at the center of the lodge.

"In here, in this darkness," the ceremonial elder will tell the men, "you'll need to be open and strong, for in here you are doing battle with the demons in your own heart."

KATABASIS: A DESCENT IN THREE STAGES

The descent into the darkness was called *katabasis* by the Greeks. Every man in any age must do katabasis, the Greeks believed. The Greeks recognized two ways of doing katabasis that resemble two ways of being initiated into manhood: by default, without seeing it coming; or consciously, with guidance. And we know from our own lives, whichever way you do katabasis, no man can avoid the descent into the darkness in his life. No man. Many of us try, but the dark will find us.

A divorce we have not seen coming, an addiction to work, booze, drugs, or gambling, a midlife crisis that shocks us to the core, a sudden change in our economic situation, a sudden death of our spouse or child—all of these will cause us to descend. All of these will *force us* to go down into hell, where it really hurts to be who we are. How will we respond to the darkness? Some of us will be depressed for a while and then return to our old patterns, unchanged. We'll go down into the dark by default and have a few insights and return to a life by default.

Some of us will do more: some of us will take the opportunity to do important emotional and spiritual work in the face of the divorce, the addiction, the lost job or child. Some of us will use the initiation by fate and crisis to start a journey of self-discovery. We will not just glance sidelong at our demons who hide in the dark; we will confront them. We will make katabasis conscious, a part of our conscious autobiography. We will confront the addictions, feelings of inadequacy, fears of death, and we will confront them with grief and honor. Robert Bly writes in *Iron John:*

> One has the sense that some power in the psyche arranges a severe katabasis if the man does not know enough to go down on his own. Depression usually surprises us by its arrival and its departure. In depression, we refuse to go down, and so a hand comes up and pulls us down. In grief we *choose* to go down.
>
> With initiators gone from our culture, we do not receive instruction on how to go down on our own. . . .

As boys and adolescents, we were not initiated into our sacred selves, selves that know the honor there is in making the dark and painful visionquest, selves that know the honor there is in feeling grief. Uninitiated, we grew up without the capacity to know that darkness and grief are to be used by men for a sacred purpose.

A man I was working with recently talked about his marital situation. He and his wife had three children. They had been married fifteen years. They were getting ready to break up. Their situation had been bad for almost a year. Over the last two months he had moved down into the basement. He wanted to do his part to save his marriage. He wanted to understand why he was so unhappy and why his marriage was so unhappy.

"I'm trying," he said. "I know I need to grieve, especially my relationship with my abusive father. But I just sit in my basement. I read. I listen to tapes and keep my journal. I'm becoming attached to the basement."

At first, he was just becoming accustomed to the space down there. But as the months passed, he did a great deal of work down there. He was in a men's group; he was in a twelve-step group. He read everything on men. He contacted his father, tried to talk to him. He kept a journal. Always he returned to his dark basement, journaling, crying, confronting his demons, growing.

One day, almost a year after I first met him, he said to me, "I've moved back upstairs. Shirley and I are working things out. Something has happened to me." On his face was the kind of glow that comes only after a prolonged period of paleness in the dark. "The basement," he said, smiling with the insight of it. "I was literally going down, wasn't I? I was going into the cave."

His katabasis was represented in his descent into his basement. Down there he made the journey through his father, his marriage, his angers, his wounds, and his grief. He descended, like Dante, into hell. All his problems were not now solved. But because he had "lived in his basement" and lived in it consciously, doing hard work down there, he had confronted many of his demons. Now he was a changed man. He had gone through what medieval Christians called "the dark night of the soul," and he was now a different man.

There are three stages of katabasis, with a great deal happening in each. The emotion that sparks katabasis and follows a man through the three-stage descent is *grief*. In the first stage the grief itself and the object of the grief are discovered. In the second stage they are *confronted*. In the third stage the object is integrated into the psyche, or *forgiven*.

Over the last few years we have done a lot as men to recognize our need to grieve, and to recognize objects of male grief: the way our ancestors have treated women; the way our own emotions have been squashed over the generations; the way we treat our planet; our distance from other men, especially our fathers. In the process you have joined thus far, the object of grief was identified from the beginning to be your relationship with your father.

The book you are holding is designed to help you grieve. During the experiential journey of this process, you've been searching especially for a vision of your father, and so you have been grieving, especially, the wounds of your father and his distance from you.

In this chapter I will ask you to take further steps toward *confronting* the source of the grief, your father. Strong Hans, you'll remember, had to go down into the cave a second time during his adulthood. The cave he descended in his adulthood resembled the cave he lived in during his boyhood years. In the same way, the cave we descend when we join a process of deep self-discovery resembles the darkness we lived in during our troubled and difficult times in our families of origin. For men who had disengaged fathers, the cave we enter as adults is the cave our fathers brought us up in when we were boys.

This is the place where you must go now to confront your demons, your dragons, your angry giants, your father. There will be time later for forgiveness. In this dark place you will be guided to experience the kind of spiritual death and rebirth that a hero experiences in his confrontation with his demons.

No hero on a spiritual quest, says Indian scholar Ananda Coomaraswamy, can reach the next spiritual resting point until he or she has ceased to exist. The previous self must be "killed" and the new self given room to emerge. In the dark, your very existence will be challenged and you'll have to withstand that attack. Perhaps you have been withstanding it throughout your life in an aching, unconscious way. Now you join the confrontation in a conscious way. You have discovered an inner mentor to help you. And I will be helping you. You will not face the darkness alone. If you can share the work you're doing in this chapter and the next with trusted male friends, that work in the darkness will take on added richness and power.

In this chapter, you'll also discover the Warrior within yourself, whose energy, strength, and discipline are tested and strengthened in the dark confrontation. Enduring your journey into the dark cave requires a strong, well-disciplined Warrior. Getting what you need out of your encounters in the cave requires a sacred, enlightened Warrior.

Each man needs one thing most of all in the confrontations of the cave: he needs to know and feel his own stamina, power, and self-discipline. If his Warrior is not activated appropriately, he will either be consumed by the dark and its many demons (in prolonged depression and perhaps suicide) or turn immediately away from the dark (in avoidance, grandiosity, and denial). After you have been led to select a safe, dark place for your confrontation, you will be led to meet your inner Warrior.

TASK 1:
FINDING A DARK CAVE

While most of your work up to this point may have been done in any space you've chosen, this and the next episode, in which you confront your father, will be more powerful if done in a physical space that resembles the dark underground. Even if you only dim the lights in your room and make it dark, try to approximate the darkness a Greek hero experienced in Hades when he descended to a major confrontation, or Strong Hans experienced in the cave when he met the brutal dwarf, or a Native American man experiences in the sweat lodge or on his vision-quest.

Find a place in the basement of your house that you can use. Or find a place in the woods private enough to do the tasks and rituals, a place capable of being used, without distractions, at night. Wait until nighttime to do the tasks and rituals, perhaps fasting for a day and staying up all night. Or find a cave in a mountainside near you. Scout out these places now, getting a sense of their physical space. Put a candle or two in the space, no more—just enough to create dragonlike shadows. If you are doing these tasks in a group, find a way to cut out much of the light in your group meeting place. Or integrate the tasks with a sweat ceremony, using the sweat lodge as your dark place.

The space a man chooses for his sacred rituals is important to the outcome of those rituals. It is an act of self-empowerment for a man to choose a sacred space. Take some time to find a space appropriate to your descent. When you have found and sanctified the space, move on to the next task, your first in the dark cave.

TASK 2:
MEETING YOUR INNER WARRIOR:
ACTIVATING YOUR STRENGTHS

The Warrior's Dance of Swords

All of us live at times from the negative side of the Warrior; all of us feel the Shadow Warrior driving us to rages and abuses. Don't think of those rages and abuses now. At this point, we want to concentrate on the Warrior's positive aspects. We know the Warrior within ourselves better than we realize. Especially in the workplace, men see themselves as warriors. We fight for personal safety and family security. We do battle for advancement and gain. We conquer competitors for profit and reputation. We know we need the Warrior to survive out there. Much of our success and failure as men in our society and relationships depends on the Warrior in us.

What we also know is that the Warrior is often not integrated into the whole man. It often takes over. Especially in the last few decades, men have been encouraged to disavow it altogether. How shall we integrate the Warrior? That is an essential question.

Before proceeding further, review the material in the Appendix on the Warrior archetype. There, his dance of swords is introduced. After you've made that review, get something in your hand that resembles a sword—a sword itself, a long kitchen knife, a long stick or staff. Hold it out as if it were a sword. Feel it as if were a sword. Put your sword in its sheath. Draw it out and raise it. Hold it pointed outward toward the opponent. Do this until the movement is very smooth, like an Oriental *kata*, an exercise in body harmony, a tai chi dance. What does it feel like to wield a sword? What we described in the Appendix as the dance of swords we will now feel in our bodies. To do this it is essential you be in your safe, sacred space. If anyone not privy to your process saw you doing this, it would be embarrassing and misunderstood.

Do the dance of swords. Feel the power rise up from your guts. Jump around, this way and that, like a warrior being attacked, guarding boundaries. See enemies coming toward you. Fight them. Recall your boyhood—when holding a sword in your hand, even if it was a twig, seemed like the greatest feeling of all. Dance around with this sword, like a Teenage Mutant Ninja Turtle, like a knight in a tournament. Dramatize the Warrior within you. If you are working with another man or a group, do the dance with a partner, banging your sword or stick against his. Dance this way until you are breathless.

When you have become tired of the dance of swords, put your sword down. Return to your notebook. You may do the dance of the sword whenever you want, and as often—with men in men's groups, with your child. It's an eternal dance.

In your notebook, recall an incident during the last month, in your home or workplace or anywhere significant to you, in which you have done the dance of swords in relating to another. You'll recall many negative times, when you cut and "killed" others unnecessarily, and you'll remember other times when you turned away in fear of your own Warrior, or theirs. Often, when you turned away in fear, you were stabbed in the back. Let these negative times come into your mind and then let them fade away.

Right now, remember an incident—perhaps it happened just yesterday—wherein your Warrior did the dance of swords very well. If you can't think of one for this month, go back a month, and back another till you do. Perhaps a coworker was trying to backstab you and you confronted him. Or your friend didn't respect your feelings and you confronted him. Your spouse attacked and you defended yourself well. Or you started in on her and both of you danced a strong, revitalizing confrontation.

Recall the incident on paper, in sections pertaining directly to the positions of the sword. Recall what you said and felt as you reached your hand toward your sword in its sheath. Did you start the confrontation? If so, your hand went to your sword first. Or did he/she start the confrontation? If so, his or her hand pulled out the sword first. Let's look at an example of a dance in which someone else started the fight and you were put on the defensive.

"We need to talk," a spouse or partner said, "about what you've been doing . . ." In her tone you heard danger; your hand went to your sword.

Recall her next parry and your next response: the raising of your sword in defense. She said something accusingly and your sword came up: "No," you said, "that's not what happened. I will explain it to you."

Recall her next thrust. She became angrier, didn't believe you, and you put your sword out, metal hitting her metal. "Now listen to me," you said, "here is what happened!" You persisted, parrying with her until she did listen.

Recall the verbal jabs that reflect the warrior dance between you. You knew, unconsciously, that her sword was out and that your warrior dance—your strength and discipline— was interwoven with hers. It was a terrible argument but you stayed strong and so, probably, did she. Neither of you dropped the sword or let the other kill; neither of you took the quick, enraged way out.

When the argument was over, the dance was done. Swords were dropped in a mutual way, with scratches and wounds still hurting, but none fatal. The dance finished with swords returned to their sheaths. You made up in whatever way you two make up.

Was there a winner or loser to this fight? Maybe, maybe not. Because the encounter was a dance, the winner or loser matters less than the dance itself. This is the difference between seeing warriors as deadly competitors—a popular misconception—and seeing warriors as spiritual dancers. Except when survival is at stake—as in an actual time of physical threat or war—warriors dance rather than conquer. Even in basketball, football, racquetball, or any sport that is based on competitiveness, the loser of this week's game may be the winner next time. Losing hurts and winning feels great, but most of us know that the game is for discipline, excellence, and fun. In close love relationships, we know that the game, the warrior dance, is for working out differences and engaging in healthy confrontation.

In more starkly spiritual terms, this is also the message of advanced martial arts: body, mind, spirit, and soul are brought into balance by self-discipline and by the testing of that self-discipline in a dance with another. Only in extreme cases are death, conquest, and terrible wounding the necessary outcome of martial arts. Just as, in our relationships, while the relationship cannot grow without testing, prodding, dancing, and confrontation, conquest is not necessary at all.

It is the dancing warrior we seek in ourselves as we seek to activate the Sacred Warrior within. It is this essential, spiritually empowering part of yourself I invite you to recognize as you recall an incident of your own Warrior at work. Whatever your incident was, write it, and see it as a dance of swords. Attach verbal jabs to each internal jab of your Warrior's sword. See your strength, your perseverance, your courage, and your decisiveness. See, too, your self-control, your respect for the other warrior.

As you confront your father, you'll often need to invoke the strength of the Warrior. Your boundaries of safety will be challenged. You'll face terrible obstacles and difficulties. Even the act of writing itself—even writing no more than a letter to your father—requires Warrior strength: endurance, self-discipline, decisiveness. You need to invoke the Warrior strength within you to do surgery on your wounds. You need to do the dance of swords with your father and strike out at the old wounds with healing strokes of your sword. Let us go, then, to the next ritual step in this quest. In this guided meditation, you'll get a deeper sense of your strength, your Warrior.

Meeting Your Inner Warrior

In this personal ritual you'll meet an imaginative representation of your warrior energy. For some of you this warrior will be in armor, for others in loincloth. He will be a samurai or biblical David or man in soldier's uniform. For some of you this warrior might be an old man, for others a young man. There is no right or wrong warrior. The warrior you meet will be right for you because it will rise from you. Your meeting with this inner Warrior will be an important moment in your life. You'll see a piece of yourself from the inside out. You'll also be able to converse with a part of your hidden, deepest self. As you meet this Warrior, notice surroundings, costume, tools. In the future you will be able to call on this Warrior again.

Find a comfortable position. Quiet your breathing. Enter your personal ritual of relaxation. Take three deep breaths. By the third breath, concentrate only on the breathing, only on the movement of your breath in and out.

Bring to mind people in your life, living or dead, whose warrior energy you have admired and sought to emulate. These may be parents, teachers, brothers, sisters, friends, cultural heroes, spouses. Call out their names into your sacred space.

As the space still echoes with their names, focus on one of them. In what way did this person embody the warrior? Recall an incident in which this person used his or her Sacred Warrior well. What warrior tools did this person employ? What did you admire about the way this warrior handled enemies and friends? What boundaries was this warrior protecting? (Pause)

Call out this person's name into the space. (Pause)

See yourself standing in front of a wall-sized mirror. Stand and look at yourself a moment. As you are gazing at your body and your face and into your own eyes, begin to see standing behind you people from your own past and present, from history and contemporary society, and from literature and culture, who have taught you important, positive lessons about the Warrior within you. Let these people crowd behind you in a semicircle, each of them putting his or her hands on your body, your shoulders, your arms, your head. Feel the energy of their warriors melting into yours. Who is standing behind and beside you? Some of them you'll consciously recognize; others will rise up from your unconscious and surprise you. Take a second to acknowledge each one in the mirror. (Pause)

Now prepare to move toward your own inner Warrior. You who are standing at the mirror must now close your eyes. Feel the people who have touched you return to their own space, their hands moving away. Let go even of your need for the mirror. You are moving into a deeper place. There is deep strength within, waiting for you. Concentrate again on the sound and feeling of your own breath as it goes in and out, in and out. Feel your breath being somewhere down near your navel and travel upward, out your throat, then back in again, downward toward your navel. When a warrior holds his sword its butt pushes there, at the navel. Open your inner eyes now, finding mirror and people gone, and finding yourself getting smaller.

Take a deep breath and find yourself becoming half your present size. Let your breath out. Take a deep breath and become one-quarter your present size. Take a deep breath and now imagine yourself so small that you can stand on your own stomach. See yourself there, standing on your stomach, so light your feet leave no imprint.

You are standing at your navel. We all began at a navel. Our cord was cut when we were born, but there is a spiritual cord that is like a tiny tunnel going inward from our navel into our deepest and sacred self. Find your navel, find that magical entrance to your inner life. Climb onto the lip of that entrance. Hang your tiny leg over it. Hang your other leg over. Push your tiny body a little further, a little further. Let yourself go.

Slide down the tunnel. Slide . . .

Feel the warmth. It is your own body you are moving into.

Come to a soft landing at the bottom of the tunnel. Feel your feet hit the earth.

Walk forward now. You are walking inside a cave. Feel what it feels like to be walking in this dark cave, alone, vulnerable, full of wonder. Call out softly to the cave, "Who holds my sword?" Call it out a little louder: "Who holds my sword?"

Come to the cave's entrance and find yourself in a forest, the forest you have been in before. You are dwarfed by huge trees and vines. Cries of animals are all around you. This is your inner wilderness. Find in it animals, people, things that you imagine live in your inner wilderness. Feel at home as you walk in this wilderness. Ask, "Who holds my sword?"

Walk a few steps toward shadows and light that emanate from behind a mass of trees and vines. Push through vines. Something important sits behind the mass of vines. Sweat rises on you. This takes a lot of effort, a lot of breath. Notice scratches on your skin.

Push through and at last see a tiny open meadow, surrounded by an orderly coppice of trees. In the center of the tiny space, lit by sunlight and shadow, are huge carved stones, jutting upward. On each one is a picture and under the picture, some writing.

Come to the first one. On it is a picture of your mother. It is a picture of her at an age you suddenly remember, an age when she taught you something about being a warrior. It was something that you have used in health throughout your life, or it was something that has haunted you throughout your life, something that has weakened your ability to protect your boundaries and be decisive and strong. It was either positive or negative. It has lingered in you powerfully.

Underneath her picture is a statement carved into stone, a statement in her words of this thing she taught you.

Walk up to the monument. Touch her face. Run your hands on the carved words. What are the words? See the memory again. (Pause)

When you are finished here, move to the next monument. On it is a picture of your father. It is a picture of him at an age you suddenly remember, an age when he taught you something about being a warrior. It was something that you have used in health throughout your life, or it was something that has haunted you throughout your life, something that has weakened your ability to protect your boundaries and be decisive and strong. Positive or negative, it has lingered with you.

Underneath your father's picture is a statement carved into stone, a statement in his words of this thing he taught you.

Walk up to the monument. Touch his face. Run your hands on the carved words. What are the words? See the memory again. (Pause)

Move to the next monument. On it is a picture of some-one else who was and has been important in your maturing. It is a picture of this person at an age you remember, an age when this person taught you something about being a war-rior. It was something that you have used in health through-out your life, or it was something that has haunted you throughout your life, something that has weakened your abil-ity to protect your boundaries and be decisive and strong. Positive or negative, it has lingered in you.

Underneath the picture is a statement carved into stone, a statement that embodies this thing taught to you by this person.

Walk up to the monument. Touch the face there. Run your hands on the carved words. What are the words? See the memory again. (Pause)

Spend whatever time you need in this place of monu-ments. Maybe you see a line of many more monuments. Ap-proach the picture on each, see the statement, follow the rit-ual of touching the face and the words. There may be too many monuments here for you to know them all. That is all right. You can always come back to this place. (Pause)

Walk beyond the last monument. A path continues past the last monument. The forest is huge and singing. Before you are two huge trees. Their branches form an archway. Whisper to the wilderness, "Who holds my sword?"

Walk toward the archway. Walk under it. You are coming to another meadow. Walk forward along the path into this meadow. In it are no lifeless monuments. There is a figure standing in the center of the meadow. The figure is human or animal, well known to you or just discovered. This is your in-ner Warrior.

Look at this Warrior for a moment. Notice the clothing, the etchings on the sword, the stance, the lines on the face, the veins on the hand. This is the part of you that holds your sword—that holds your power of discipline and confron-tation.

Look into your Warrior's eyes. Ask, "Are you the one who holds my sword?"

Hear the Warrior reply, "I am your Warrior. Are you ready to receive your sword?"

It is a beautiful and meaningful question. Are you ready

to admit this sacred strength within yourself? Say yes. Even if it feels awkward. Even if your Warrior is still vague to you, say, "Yes, I am ready."

Let your Warrior hand you your sword. Feel the sword's weight. Hold it in both hands. Feel the sword. Move with it if you wish, dancing in the meadow as if shadow fighting. (Pause)

When you know the feeling of the sword in your palms, turn back to the Warrior. Say to your Warrior, "I will use this sword to protect my boundaries and to assert my worth."

Hear your Warrior answer, "If ever you are unsure of its use, come back to this place and you will find me here. I know that sword very well."

Let your Warrior hand you his sheath. Strap it on. Slide the sword into it and feel its calming weight at your side. You shall never be unprotected again. When you are attacked, you shall have this sword. You know the Warrior is right—you will have to come back here to continue learning the dance of swords—but know also that you are a warrior.

Thank your inner Warrior. Your thanks may be verbal or silent. Your best thanks to your inner Warrior will come as you tell this warrior some terrible secret, some terrible feeling or circumstance that you can rectify in your life now that you carry your sword. Is there something going on right now in your immediate life that your sword and your knowledge of the dance of swords can rectify? Speak to your inner Warrior. Perhaps he will have something to say about this. (Pause)

Embrace your inner Warrior. In the embrace of your Warrior's body, feel power and strength. As you finish the embrace, ask the Warrior what you can do to confront your father with positive results. Hear his wisdom. (Pause)

When you have spoken enough, for now, to your inner Warrior, feel your sword by your side and turn back up the path. See the monuments and the pictures and the words as you pass them. Walk back through the vines, more easily parted now that you have your sword. Walk back to the cave's entrance. Enter the cave and again enter darkness. As you come to the tunnel, walk up the slippery incline. It is difficult to return to ordinary reality. It's a hard climb. It's difficult to leave your guts and return to the distractions. It is difficult to return to your ordinary size. Yet it must be done.

As you climb, see light above you. Come to the entrance of your navel.

Step out into the light. Take one deep breath and find yourself growing in size.

Take another deep breath and you have become half your ordinary size.

Take a third deep breath and you are now your ordinary size.

Slowly open your eyes. Cover them for a moment with your palms.

When you're ready, turn to your journal and record the important moments of this experience. What did your inner Warrior say to you? What did this Warrior look and feel like to you? What advice did he give you about confronting your father?

What teachings did you remember from your mother, father, and mentors? What figures stood behind and beside you in the mirror? Was it embarrassing to dance with the sword? Does your own power sometimes embarrass you?

When you have written what you need to write, go on to the next task.

TASK 3:
YOUR WARRIOR IN THE CAVE:
RECALLING YOUR SACRED WOUNDS

One of the primary ways you learned how to be a warrior was in your father's act of giving you sacred wounds. Before moving into this task, familiarize yourself with the material on sacred wounds in chapter 1. Recall the story of the African boy, the rat, and the ax handle.

Recall the sacred wounds your father gave you. In giving you these wounds he was teaching you a lot about responsibility, self-discipline, and your own physical and mental strength—all qualities of the warrior. As you attempt to recall these sacred wounds, don't be surprised if only a few come into memory. As I've helped men do this task over the years, I've found that most men can recall only one or a few vividly. Sons of absent, distant, or abusive fathers, we didn't live in an intimate relationship with our fathers; thus most of the wounds we got from him did not feel very sacred. And if he was gone most of the time, there simply was no opportunity for him to give us many sacred wounds.

Now is the time, however, to recall at least one of these wounds and to record it in your journal. As you record it, note how it helped you develop your Warrior. Note first how your father wounded you, second how he helped you to understand the meaning of the wound (or how you yourself understood it), and third how he accepted you back to his side.

I have a vivid recollection of a sacred wound I received from my father. I was seventeen. I had received six speeding tickets. After my seventh, my father and I were called in to the magistrate. The magistrate told us I had to go to disciplinary driving classes. He also told my father that he would suspend my license or not, depending on my father's wishes. I remember vividly watching the two older men, these two kings, deciding my life.

My father told the magistrate to take my license away. You know how much a car means to a seventeen-year-old, so you can imagine how angry I was. As we left the court, my father told me exactly where he stood on the issue. If I didn't get a substantial punishment from the law, he figured I would probably kill myself in an accident. I told him I hated him. I bitched, but he stood his ground, and there was nothing to be done.

As we drove home, my father made a gesture that I will never forget. He stopped at the Dairy Queen and invited me to order anything I wanted. Gone for a conspiratorial second was our family's usual obsession with pinching pennies. Gone too, for a second, was our family's usual avoidance of sugar products, which my mother often tended to preach against. My father knew somehow that to buy me ice cream was a gesture that would help me see myself in some light other than the shame I was feeling at losing my license. Through the ice cream he accepted me, even in my embarrassment and anger.

Think back to incidents in your own boyhood and adolescence. Perhaps some of these incidents involved abusive spankings or beatings. Make sure, if they did, that they were in fact sacred wounds, not routine beatings. Trace the wound from the hurting process to the understanding process to the reacceptance process. Perhaps some of these wounds involved no physical touch. Perhaps some of them, as mine, were coadminis-tered, by mother and father or by father and another male or female in a position of strength and authority.

The recollection of some of these sacred wounds is a re-collection of moments of healthy initiation into manhood. As you are searching back for these wounds, you'll remember shadow wounds as well—times when you were beaten by a parent just because he or she wanted to strike out at the weak in the world, shamed in a locker room just because you were different. Note these moments here. Note the time your father said he was disappointed in you in such a way and followed this by a week-long silence that led you to believe you'd never regain his affection.

Many times in this journey to kingship, shadow wounds will rise up and must be counted. Note that they were not sacred—that they were missing one or more of the three sacred steps in the wounding process. Note that they were toxic, sham-ing, and abusive.

Note them but do not linger on them. Move again to recall-ing the sacred wounds, the wounds that helped you become an initiated, healthy warrior. It is that healthy strength you'll need as you go deeper into the cave.

TASK 4:
YOUR WARRIOR IN THE CAVE:
RE-EXPERIENCING YOUR PAIN AND GRIEF

We have said that when our fathers, our Kings, don't fulfill their sacred duties our Prince feels abandoned and cannot become a whole King himself. Abandonment is a source of pain and of grief. It is like experiencing a death. Before we move to the next chapter, in which we will deliberately and specifically feel the pain of confronting our fathers, let's take a moment to center ourselves in pain and in grief.

You have met your inner Warrior and activated that part of your psyche. You and he are joined, and you are capable of reex-periencing your pain without turning away from it, without falling apart. If at all possible, do this task in the presence of a group, trusted friend, or therapist. They will give you support and hear you. If your dark cave is in a place away from these people, put the following four-stage ritual on tape as you go through it, and play it back for them to hear later.

1. If you are not now in your dark cave, go to it. Get comfortable. Let the dark space of your cave remind you for a moment of the darkness that frightened you as a child. Try to remember closets, corners, places under the bed, forests at night, that frightened you. When I was a boy I stopped three feet away from my bed and jumped up into it, convinced that criminals lived under my bed. I wouldn't even dangle my feet over the bed for fear that the murderers would slash my ankles with their knives.

Recall your own version of darkness and fear *out loud*, whether you are with others or alone. Claim that earlier dark place in your life, your childhood fear of it, your own shame about that fear, and the pain that shame caused you. Now, perhaps, that childhood time seems no more than entertaining. Enjoy looking back on it. It was a time of pain and fear that you transcended. Jot some notes down about this experience *after* you've spoken it out loud.

2. Now recall a time of pain and fear in your adolescent life. This may be associated with a dark place. Perhaps your fear of losing your virginity came out one night, full-fledged, in the dark backseat of your car; maybe you were sixteen and so scared you couldn't perform.

Or this adolescent experience of pain may not have taken place in or been associated with a literal dark place. Perhaps you feared going out for the varsity team and failing. Or maybe you did something morally repugnant, something even to this day you've told no one about, something that still haunts you. Whatever you recall from adolescence, the darkness will probably be associated in some way with failure or your fear of failing.

Speak *out loud* what that pain was like. Describe it and describe the incident or incidents. Claim that earlier darkness in your life. If you have transcended it, enjoy that. If pieces of it still manifest themselves in your life, see them clearly. After you have spoken this pain aloud and let yourself grieve it as much as you can, jot down some notes about it so it will not be forgotten.

3. Now recall a dark night of the soul that may have lasted months or years in your adult life. This may have been an experience similar to that of the man who lived in his basement. Your dark night may have been a divorce, a separation, a painful midlife crisis, a death of someone you loved. It could have been a time in which you felt abandoned, rejected, hurt. Your dark night might have been a time in which you felt depressed, angry, grief stricken—and not just for an hour or a day. As you recall this time, recall how painful it was.

Recall issues that came up for you during this time, issues about your own emotional legacies and character defects, issues and people and pain from your past that you had to confront. Celebrate your stamina, your endurance. Celebrate the fact that you came through it, that you had what every man needs to have if he is to be whole—a dark time to confront demons.

Recall your pain and speak *out loud* what that pain was like. Describe it and describe the incident or incidents surrounding it. Claim that earlier darkness in your life. If you have transcended it, enjoy that. If pieces of it still manifest themselves in your life, see them clearly. If you are currently living in this dark time, feeling lost right now in a midlife crisis or separation, feeling depressed and inadequate, describe your pain now. After you have spoken your pain aloud and let yourself grieve it as much as you can, write some notes down about it in your journal so it will not be forgotten.

4. Now answer this question: *What is the most painful wound a man has given me in my life?* Answer the question honestly, focusing on an incident or incidents in which a man has hurt you to the core. Did it occur in your childhood home, in adolescence, in early adulthood, more recently? Did the infliction of pain occur over a period of years or months or days? One man answered the question this way:

> *A man named Jack Slieter, a competitor in my business. I was wounded by my father worse than by any other man in my life, but somehow it's Jack who comes into me when I think about this question. He tried to destroy me. I still to this day don't understand why.*
>
> *We used to be friends. That's what hurt so bad. We*

went to college together. Something happened between us. I don't know what it was. Something happened that he never told me, something I'm not aware of. Did I do something? Sometimes I want to ask him but then I don't get up the guts. I know if I do ask him he'll just find a way to make me feel ashamed.

This has been going on for ten years. He tries to destroy my reputation, making my work out to be shoddy to my competitors. I only hear a year later what he said about some previous project of mine. I've survived what he's thrown at me but sometimes he'll just show up in my head and I'll feel like I'm exploding, I don't know with what—rage or anger or just flat-out confusion and darkness and pain. I can't seem to even get close to understanding what happened between us, or how to resolve it, and when I see him at a restaurant or some meeting my stomach knots up and I feel like the walking wounded.

Recall your own pain. Speak this pain aloud, then write it down. Describe the wound this man gave you. Recall the place, the man, how he hurt you, why he hurt you so much, how you dealt with the pain. Grieve this wound now. Hear your own pain.

5. If the man who hurt you was not your father, ask the same question of your father. *What is the most painful wound my father has given me in my life?* This wound will not be a sacred wound. This wound will be one founded in toxic shame. Touch this wound. Speak it aloud, then write it down. Recall the places and times the wound was inflicted. Recall how you dealt with the pain. Speak out loud. Hear your own pain.

This is how one man spoke of this pain.

I remember a lot of bad times. I remember him not talking to me for days and I didn't know why. I remember him beating me when I messed up in Little League. Everyone was scared of my dad, even my coach.

I remember a time he told me to stand up on the mantel above the fireplace. I was maybe five or six. He told me to jump into his arms. I was really scared to do it but he put me up there and I had to jump. So I closed my eyes and jumped. At the last moment he stepped away, letting me fall flat onto the floor. My knees and wrists hurt like hell. I wailed. I thought I had broken them. He told me this was a lesson. Don't ever trust anybody. That's what he said.

I went crying to my room and hid under the covers in the dark, afraid my father would come in. But he didn't. I finally fell asleep. Don't ever trust anybody, nobody at all. How could I forget that? I couldn't. That's how I've lived my life.

In these moments of reexperienced pain, there will probably be pieces and places of darkness that you can remember. As you remember your father beating you or turning away from you when you needed him most, there will probably be a dark place to which you ran for womblike comfort and private sobbing. Places of darkness surround our pain, challenging it, comforting it, giving it back to us to honor.

CLAIMING AND CREATING YOUR SACRED OBJECTS

You have begun the descent into the dark cave. Claim a sacred object now that holds the sacred energy of that descent. Perhaps you'll claim the stick you used as a sword for your dance of swords. Perhaps you will claim another object that was given to you by someone who taught you a lot about being a warrior. Perhaps, if you had battlefield experience, now is the time to claim as sacred an object from that experience.

Create, also, a scroll that makes holy this episode of your journey, a letter that captures the energy of the cave. Write a letter to your father, one like the others, a letter you may not send, in which you describe one or two of your important experiences in this chapter.

Perhaps you will want to recall for him the sacred wounds he gave you, and also those he did not. Perhaps you'll want to recall the shadow wounds you have suffered at his hands or at the hands of other men. Perhaps you will want to describe yourself to him as a warrior. Perhaps you'll recognize in him

negative aspects of the warrior that you work to transcend in
your own personality and behavior.

Write to your father whatever you need to write concerning the warrior and the cave.

> Frank wrote, *Dear Pop, I never saw myself as a "warrior"
> until recently. At first I didn't know why not. Now I'm
> realizing more and more what happened.*
>
> *I mean, not only was it about my not going to Viet-
> nam. That wasn't it altogether. It was about my seeing
> men who were kind of crushed by the system and by
> women.*
>
> *Like you. I don't think you taught me how to be a war-
> rior very well, Pop. I really don't. I'm sorry to say it, but
> I'm beginning to realize it now.*
>
> *You did what your boss told you and what Mom told
> you. You hardly fought anything.*
>
> *I'm 48 and I've been so dense all these years not to
> realize that a son might turn out a little like his father.*
>
> *You're dead but I know your spirit is reading this. I
> know deep inside you was a warrior. I think since I'm
> even embarrassed about mine, maybe you were embar-
> rassed about yours. Maybe that's why you just got into a
> rut where you never could really show it.*

> Lacy wrote, *Dear Daddy, I have been working to under-
> stand the warrior inside me. This warrior knows how to
> assert its needs and feel honest anger and protect its
> boundaries. But there's another side to it. He also has a
> shadow side. He sometimes gets too aggressive. He gets
> enraged and destroys needlessly. He protects his bound-
> aries much too much, not letting other people in.*
>
> *That's how you were, Daddy. At least that's how I see
> you now. I'm on a journey to make peace with you. I'm
> learning how to be my own warrior in my own way. Wish
> me luck. I'm not there yet. But I'm getting there. The first
> time, I couldn't hold it and I just smashed Linda in the
> face. After that I've gotten help. I've never done it again.
> Swear to God. Never. It scared me how much I was get-
> ting like you. I never thought of it in terms like the "war-
> rior" before, but that's just the right term for it. I like
> being a warrior, but I can't be like you, not in the bad
> ways at least.*

Claim and create your sacred objects. Feel a stick or other symbol of your Warrior in your hands. Feel it, if only figuratively, when you go into *any* confrontational situation. Make your own statement about your Warrior, about your ability to protect your boundaries and assert your needs. Feel your own strength as, in the next episode of your quest, you go deeper into the cave.

Confronting
Your Father

I am thy father's spirit,
Doomed for a certain term to walk the night,
And for the day confined to fast in fires,
Till the foul sins done in my days of nature
Are burnt and purged away.

WILLIAM SHAKESPEARE

Like Hamlet, we stand in the presence of the ghost of our father. That ghost is with us more than we can begin to count or explain. He is with us in the way we love and work and live. His ghost helps us much of the time; and much of the time his ghost, by its very presence within us, keeps us living in the wounds we received from him years ago.

To grow toward fullness and to heal his wounds, a man must confront his dragons, his demons, his enemies—he must face his deepest wounds and fears. If we do not, if we avoid slaying our dragons, we will slay ourselves.

There's a Grimms' tale called "The Gnome" in which a man goes down into a cave and has to fight three dragons, one with three heads, then one with six heads, then one with nine heads. And even after he has slain them, scalded by their fiery breath and wounded by their claws and teeth, he must still stay down in the bottom of the pit, walking the ground smooth, until he is ready—emotionally stable and self-knowing—to come up. And after all this his rising back up is still a wounding process, for the thousand dwarves that help him each take one strand of his hair, pulling him up that painful way. But when he does rise back up to the top he is self-knowing, transformed, and empowered. He has faced his dragons and demons and come through.

The slaying of dragons, giants, and demons occurs in all cultures in similar ways. The man goes into a place of conflict and is tested. The confrontation with his dragon, his giant, or his demon is a huge, prolonged moment of wounding, stamina, and initiation.

In countless myths around the world, the confrontation a man has in the cave or other place of conflict is a conflict with his father. In fact, the most common male Hero's Journey in world cultures is the journey of initiation toward and then through the Great Father. It's as if mythology is telling us that to be a man, you must face your father. Joseph Campbell writes:

> The ogre-father breaks us, but the hero, the fit candidate, undergoes the initiation "like a man"; and behold, it was the father: we in Him and He in us. The dear, protecting mother of our body could not defend us from the Great Father Serpent; the mortal, tangible body that she gave us was delivered into his frightening power. But death was not the end. New life, new birth, new knowledge of existence was given us. That father was himself the womb . . . the second birth.

Confrontation with the father in the dark cave, in the womb of our second birth, takes us forward in a man's sacred journey to the second step of the katabatic descent: confrontation with the object of our grief. Confrontation with the father in the dark cave is a part of becoming ourselves, and we have come to this point now in our journey. To discover our own King we must confront the King of our childhoods.

We have arrived at this episode in our quest by acknowledging that our fathers were abusive or distant; that we, therefore, acquired a dark hole within, a place filled with demons; and that we live too much as adult Princes, too little as whole Kings. We have arrived here well prepared by trusted, supportive mentors. We have arrived here knowing how to invoke our strengths. We have the steady feel of a strong sword in our hands. We are stronger now than we were at any other time in our lives when we struggled to confront our demons, our dragons, our father.

Often I hear men say, "I don't need to confront my father. I just need to turn away from him. Look at me. I'm doing fine; my life's okay." And so it is. Yet what is that dark hand that comes up from within and pulls the man into alienation and despair, especially as he nears middle age? It is many hands from many dragon claws blended into one; and it is, more than he realizes, the hand of his father. To gain our own birthright and to discover a masculine spiritual ground, we must now go down into the cave and fight the Great Father Serpent, the Outlaw Father, the father's ghost, deep in our archetypal imaginations. We must now surpass him within ourselves.

TASK 1:
CONFRONTING YOUR LIVING FATHER

If your father is dead, answer the questions in this task as you think he might have answered them at your age. Imagine him sitting in the room with you. Talk to him. If your father is alive, try to talk to him personally.

Call your father or write him. Don't be surprised if this task requires a series of conversations and encounters. If at all possible go see him, or talk to him directly. Ask him questions—like the ones suggested below—about himself, about his role as your father, about how he saw you. Ask him specific questions in the language you have been learning, questions about your initiation, your birthright, your wounding at his hand, your spiritual ground. Focus his memory on the years during which you lived with him. It is more important for you, at this point, to learn his point of view during your first two decades of life than his present point of view.

Within your family system and your relationship with him, certain questions may be too painful, too likely to cause upheaval in the relationship. Pick and choose your questions carefully. Be as nonthreatening as you can be. Talk to him with as much steady emotion as you can, keeping your sword up and letting it protect you from the bad or empty memories that will arise as you talk to him. Tell your father about the journey you are on. Help him to understand that it is not a journey of blame. Begin your conversation with positive statements about him, his influence on you, and his fathering. With that positive connection made, proceed to the more painful topics.

Questions about How Your Father Saw His Own Manhood

1. How did you feel about yourself as a man?
2. What were you taught were your duties as a man?
3. Who taught you these duties?
4. What sense of the divine did you have?
5. When you were hurting, what did you do?
6. What was the most painful time in your life?
7. What was the most pleasurable time in your life?
8. How do you feel you were treated by society?
9. Were you able to share your deepest feelings with another man? If so, with whom?
10. Did you like being a father?

Questions about How Your Father Saw His Relationship with You

1. In your mind, what are the characteristics of a good father?
2. Do you feel you possessed these characteristics?
3. Why did you . . .? (Recall incidents from childhood in which he hurt you.)
4. What expectations did you have of me as I was growing up?
5. In what ways did you try to get me to fulfill your own dreams?
6. How did you help me learn a spiritual ground?
7. Do you remember sacred wounds you gave me? (Describe sacred wounds to him, perhaps telling him the African story of the father, the boy, and the rat.)
8. What did you do during my childhood to help me grow to healthy manhood?

9. What did you do during my adolescence to initiate me
   into manhood?

10. How did you help me learn my lineage and birthright?

Questions about How Your Father Saw You

1. Were you proud of me? What about me made you
   proud?

2. What most angered you about me?

3. What about me gave you the most pleasure?

4. What was I like as an adolescent?

5. I remember a time (recall a negative time still vivid in
   your memory, a time of great fear for you as a boy).
   What did you see during this time as you looked at
   me?

6. I remember a time (recall a positive time, still vivid, of
   great triumph for you as a boy). What did you see during this time as you looked at me?

7. I remember a time (recall a negative time during your
   adolescence). What did you see as you looked at me?

8. I remember a time (recall a positive time during your
   adolescence). What did you see as you looked at me?

9. What was a good son in your mind?

10. Was I a good son?

Handle this confrontation in whatever way you can and
without expectations. Just try to get to know your father better,
armed with the questions and feelings this journey has evoked
thus far. Be as nonjudgmental and noncritical in your question-
ing as you can. Write out questions ahead of time that you want
and need to ask him.

Perhaps you won't be able to contain your anger. Perhaps
the confrontation will get out of hand. Go into it knowing that
this potential exists. Go into it knowing the consequences—
whatever they will be for your family. If you know you cannot
hold your temper, and if you know that the consequences will
be dire, forgo this task.

If you do go through with it, remember that you are confronting him not to change him and not for his sake. You are

confronting him, at this point in your life, solely for your own benefit. Try not to let him push the buttons in you that will strip and gouge you in order to fill his needs. Stay focused on what *you* need.

You may feel guilty about being hard on your father after talking to him. You may realize he had hard times you didn't know about and "good reasons" for being abusive and distant and absent. Sit with that knowledge and those feelings. But don't let your guilt rule you. It's an important and honorable feeling. It is easier to see his point of view and sympathize with his defects as a father if you have children of your own. To heal yourself, however, you must move back into your own pain and your own wound. Whether or not your father had good reasons for doing what he did, he left your Prince wounded and stunted. Reasons don't change the wound itself. Honor his reasons in your heart, without disempowering your own psychological growth.

Whether the confrontation with your living father leads to little growth but merely silence, or goes very well and leads to some healing and peacemaking, proceed when you are ready to the inner work that follows. The journey you are on asks you to confront demons outwardly when they arise in the world. But since our worst demons are always within, it is within that we must go for the ultimate confrontation.

TASK 2:
CONFRONTING YOUR FATHER WITHIN

Two rituals of confrontation follow. Do the first. Then wait a few days before doing the second. Your memory and your emotions need time to regroup. You'll also need time to write after each one. In the writing will be a lot of healing. To rush the rituals is to deny yourself their deepest content.

In doing these rituals, your memory needs to be open and active. You will be asked to recall painful incidents, when your father called you "stupid," or made fun of you, when he pushed you out of his life, when he hit others around you, when he self-destructed, or committed suicide. Let your memories flow.

If your father is dead, imagine in these rituals that he is

alive. If you had both a father and a stepfather, do each of these
rituals for each man. If your father left and you had no father for
many years, let your imagination do what it wants as it con-
fronts that time in your life. If you are adopted, do the rituals for
your adoptive father and for your biological father, even if you
never knew him. You still have mythology in your imagination
about him. Some of your King passed into you through this
mythology.

Meeting Your Father Again

Get comfortable in your chair. Undo tight clothing. Close your
eyes. Stiffen all your muscles, then relax them.

Take three deep breaths. Continue through your rituals of
meditation and relaxation.

*When you are relaxed, imagine yourself in a hospital
room. Your father is pale and thin, lying on the bed. Tubes are
moving through him. There is the hum of machines. The door
is closed but you hear a phone ring, muffled, down the hall.
The wing is relatively quiet. In the room is the smell of hospital sheets and antiseptic.*

*You are sitting at your father's bed, holding his hand. He
has been comatose for two months. The doctors say it is time
to take him off the machines. They are planning to do this tomorrow. You can feel the bed pressed against the side of your
leg. You feel the cold boniness of his hand in yours. You have
been grieving his loss for two months and now you feel even
more pain and grief, for now you know that his death is immi-
nent. Tomorrow, he will be gone.*

*There are things you want to say to him. You want to
speak to him. Few men get this chance. He may not acknowledge you, but you know he will hear you. You know that when
he dies he will be within you in memory. You want him to enjoy his life inside you. You want to be able to enjoy him inside
you. You don't want him to be an alien living inside you, always stopping you from living your own life. What do you
want to say to your father?*

*Start with your earliest childhood. You are less than five
years old. Recall an incident in your childhood in which your*

father did something that hurt you, someone else, or himself terribly.

Was it something he did directly to you? Was it something he did to himself? Was it something he did to your mother? Was it something he did to a sibling of yours? Was it something he did to a relative or friend?

When he hurt himself, another person, or you in this terrible way, it opened a channel of distrust in you, a channel that kept widening through other incidents of this kind. His shaming, his distancing, his absence—they made you distrust him and, because you were his son, yourself.

See this incident from your earliest childhood as in a dream. Linger in it as you hold your father's hand. (Pause)

Keep your heart's eye in early childhood. See now the same incident or another in which your father did something to you that directly hurt you and hurt you terribly. You were scared of something but he forced you not to cry. You messed up at something and he shamed you for it.

Where did this incident happen? See the furniture of the house or the trees in the woods. See the inside of the car or the building or supermarket. Keep looking at that incident and memory. How did you respond to being distrusted? Did you cry? How did he respond to your crying? Were there others around who watched it happening? How did they respond to what your father did, and to how you felt? (Pause)

Now move a few years forward. You are five, six, seven years old. You're in school by now. Recall an incident in which your father did something that hurt you, someone else, or himself terribly.

Was it something he did directly to you? Was it something he did to himself? Was it something he did to your mother? Was it something he did to a sibling of yours? Was it something he did to a relative or friend?

See this incident from your earliest childhood as in a dream. Linger in it as you hold your father's hand. (Pause)

Now move forward to that strange time around ten, eleven, twelve, thirteen—the time of late childhood and early adolescence, the time when your body and voice were changing or, if not yours, then the bodies and voices of your brothers and friends and school enemies.

Recall an incident in this time in which your father did something that hurt another, or you, or himself. Was it something he did directly to you? Was it something he did to your mother? Was it something he did to a sibling of yours? Was it something he did to a relative or friend? Was it something he did to himself?

Where did the incident happen? See the ball field, the house, the woods. What did he do or say to you that shamed you or another to the core? How did you or the other person respond to being distrusted in that way? Did you cry? Were there others around who watched it happening? How did they respond to what your father did?

See the incident as if in a dream. See it again now and linger in it as you hold your father's hand. (Pause)

Continue later into your adolescence. You have pubic hair now. You are growing too fast and in confusion. You want girls all the time and you're scared of the wanting. You want to be a man. You are fifteen, sixteen, seventeen.

Recall an incident in this time in which your father did something that hurt you, another, or himself terribly. Was it something he did directly to you? Was it something he did to your mother? Was it something he did to a sibling of yours? Was it something he did to a relative or friend? Was it something he did to himself?

See the incident as if in a dream. You were a young man. There have been so many of these kinds of incidents—so much absence, shame, and distance already—that by now your trust in your father, and in yourself, is badly wounded. Your normal teenage rebellion is mixed with a deeper, more painful sense of paternal abandonment. See the incident from your adolescence. Feel it and linger in it as you hold your father's hand. (Pause)

Now enter your late teens, your early twenties. You may have moved out of the house by now. You have been thrust into a man's world. You may have had sex for the first time by now, or many times. You are beginning to see the future, still in confusion, but with sublime moments of clarity. Your dreams are big, and the world may not realize it yet, but you are the one it has been waiting for. Recall that time and that feeling.

Now recall an incident in this time in which your father

did something that hurt another, you, or himself terribly. Was it something he did directly to you? Was it something he did to your mother? Was it something he did to a sibling of yours? Was it something he did to your partner or spouse? Was it something he did to a relative or friend? Was it something he did to himself?

See the incident as if in a dream. See it again now and linger in it as you hold your father's hand. (Pause)

Keep your heart's eye in this time of early adulthood. Stay there. See the same incident or another in which your father did something directly to you that hurt you terribly. How did he shame you? How did he abandon you? As you live in this incident, can you feel all the previous years of shame, distance, and abandonment circling around it? Don't take your heart's eye off the incident and memory. Feel your pain as you linger in it, holding your father's hand. (Pause)

Now see yourself in your present age. You are sitting with your father in the hospital room. Recently you have been involved in a difficult time with your father. It happened last week or last month or last year. It happened directly with him, or you are not in contact with him but it keeps happening in your memory. You keep remembering bad times with him. You feel him working inside you, hurting you, distrusting you.

In what way does your father still feel or act untrustworthy and abandoning to you? What does he still do that makes you unable to trust that he loves you with all his heart? Remember incidents, memories, conversations. Let them flow through you. Feel now how you are becoming his son in your own patterns of behavior with your spouse, friends, children. You have resisted many of his negative patterns—you have revised many of his negative myths of manhood—but still you are his son. (Pause)

As you sit at his bedside, holding his dying hand, in what ways do you distrust yourself? Recall a recent incident to your father aloud. Perhaps it is a fight with your partner or spouse in which you should have raised your sword but you did not. Perhaps you made a decision concerning your work or livelihood that you regret now, a decision you would not have made if you trusted yourself.

You know that a man's lack of self-trust manifests itself

*in his fear of taking risks. As you recall your recent incident
you will notice that there were risks you should have taken
and did not. Grieve that incident. Grieve your lack of self-
trust. Grieve it now as you hold your father's dying hand.
(Pause)*

*When you have finished telling your father how you feel,
look into his closed eyes and say good-bye to him. Come back
to this room when you wish to do so.*

Write in your journal whatever feels important about the
experience you've just had. Don't try to write everything, just
what struck you the most. If the experience of early childhood,
for instance, was most powerful, linger there in words; write
whatever you can. Perhaps that will be the place you'll go back
to with most power as you continue your epic story later. Whatever you write at this point, write about your relationship with
your father—memories, teachings, shame, grief.

Becoming Your Father

Before doing this ritual, recall the incidents of the previous ritual in which your father hurt others, himself, and you: incidents from early childhood, middle childhood, early adolescence, late adolescence, early adulthood. You may have more
incidents than these locked in your memory and your journal.
If so, you can extend this ritual to include all of them.

For this ritual, you need to stand up and have a few feet of
uninterrupted space around you. Undo tight clothing. Close
your eyes. Stiffen all your muscles, then relax them.

Take three deep breaths. Continue through your rituals of
meditation and relaxation.

*When you are relaxed and ready, recall the first incident,
the incident from your earliest memories of boyhood. See
your father clearly. See his face and posture; maybe you see his
arm raised to hit you; maybe you see his back as he turns
away from you, leaving you feeling unloved. See him as your
memory still sees him from your boyhood vision. Freeze the
picture in your mind.*

Now change your point of view. See your spirit step out of your boyhood body and step into your father's body. Make a sound like your father made when you were a boy, some sound you remember. Maybe he used to wheeze from asthma or burp or grunt or laugh from his belly. Use any sound he made. Take on his posture. Go into his body and go behind his eyes. Go into your father.

See his fingernails. They are your fingernails now. What do they look like? What kind of shoes are you wearing? Even if you can't remember, let your imagination show you. Your imagination holds all the imagery. What kind of clothes are you wearing? How old are you? Do you have a beard? Is there anything on your breath—booze, tobacco, garlic? How tall are you? How does it feel to scratch your balls? These are your father's balls so they are big! Are your arms large, small, in between? Do something as you become your father that your father always used to do, some idiosyncratic gesture.

Now speak. You have become your father. Say something in your father's voice. Hear yourself talk. Say something your father always used to say. Look around. Take in the room, the car, the outdoors, wherever you are standing. Perhaps say something about that place.

Now return to the picture you froze moments ago. You are no longer the boy in that picture—you are no longer yourself. You are now your father, the man in that picture. You are doing something to that boy. Unfreeze the frame and do that thing now. (Pause)

What are you feeling as the father of that boy? That boy has done or said something you are now hurting him for. Or perhaps he has done nothing. Perhaps you are simply angry or afraid and he is nearby. Be honest with yourself, as honest as you can be. Feel your rage, your anger, your embarrassment, your shame, your fear, your grief. Lash out at the boy in whatever way you have chosen—by hitting him or crushing him with words or denying him and turning away.

Linger in this body, your father's body, even after he does the thing to that boy. Don't leave, no matter how painful it is to do the thing this body has done to that boy. Linger in this body even after it has finished with the boy and gone somewhere else. Linger in this body even as its hands put the belt back on the pants or your wife goes to comfort the boy. Linger in this man's body as his hands shake with rage and confusion. You will be staying in this body awhile.

Let some time pass. The incident is over. The emotion of the moment is over. What emotions fill the new space? Feel those emotions. You have become your father. What do you feel as your father? You are in his body. Can you feel his pain and his grief? You are in his body. Can you feel his shame? He was wrong to do what he did. He was cursed and he cursed his boy. Feel what it feels like to be in that body at that time in that man's life. (Pause)

Move forward now to the next incident, one that occurred in the boy's middle childhood. See the whole picture again. Play out the action of that picture. You are still your father. You are still in his body.

Now do that thing to that boy, that thing he will remember so many years later when he is a man. What are you feeling as you hurt that boy? Be honest with yourself, as honest as you can be. Feel your rage, your anger, your embarrassment, your shame, your fear, your grief. Lash out at the boy in whatever way you have chosen—by hitting him or crushing him with words or denying him and turning away.

Let some time pass. The incident is over. The emotion of the moment is over. You feel many things. You are that boy's father and you hurt him. You wish you hadn't hurt that boy, but one day that boy will feel what it feels like to be in your body at this time in your life and only then will he see what life's about. You hope life will be easier for your boy. You wish it with all your heart. You don't mean to curse him. If only he knew. (Pause)

Move forward now to the next terrible incident, one that occurred in that boy's early adolescence. See the whole picture again. Play out the action of that picture. Do that thing to that boy, that terrible thing he will remember so many years later when he is a man. Lash out at him, hurt him, turn away from him as you did then.

What are you feeling as you do that thing to that son? Be honest with yourself, as honest as you can be. Feel your rage, your anger, your embarrassment, your shame, your fear, your grief. Lash out at the boy in whatever way you have chosen.

Now the incident is over. You are walking away from it. As you walk you are rationalizing. It's good for him, you are thinking to yourself. What I said to him was good for him. What I did to him was good for him. Your hands are shaking with rage and confusion, but the shaking is ebbing.

Let some time pass. The incident is over. You hope life will be easier for your boy. You wish it with all your heart. You don't mean to curse him. If only he knew. What you wish is for him to grow into a healthy man. Look at him. He's wanting to shave already. All you want is for him to grow to be a decent man. Yet you hurt him. Why? (Pause)

Move forward now to the next painful incident, one that occurred in that boy's late adolescence. See the whole picture again. This son of yours thinks he's a man. And hell, look at him. He almost is. Play out the action of that picture. Do that thing to that young man, that thing he will remember so many years later when he is a man.

Your son has done or said something you are now hurting him for. All he does these days is rebel. He's asking for trouble. He has not lived up to an expectation of yours, or he has surpassed you too quickly. Or perhaps he has done nothing. Perhaps you are simply angry or afraid and he is nearby.

Be honest with yourself, as honest as you can be. Feel your rage, your anger, your embarrassment, your shame, your fear, your grief. Lash out at him in whatever way you have chosen. Your lashing out may be to distance yourself from him, to turn away from him when he needs you most.

Let some time pass. The incident is over. All you want is for him to grow to be a decent man. Yet you hurt him. Why? (Pause)

Move forward now to the next incident, one that occurred in your son's early adulthood. See the whole picture again. This son of yours thinks he's a man. And hell, look at him. He is. Play out the action of that picture. Do that thing to your son, that painful thing he will remember so many years later.

What are you feeling as his father? What are you feeling as you do that thing to your grown son? Maybe it is a repeat of something you did when he was a boy, the same pattern. Your son has not lived up to an expectation of yours, or he has surpassed you too quickly, competing all the time. Or perhaps he has done nothing. Perhaps you are simply angry or afraid and he is nearby. What is this new refrain of his these days? That I'm not a good father. I've done my best. No wonder I get mad at him. He provokes me. Even if he's not saying it to me, I know that's what he thinks. Let him think it, the damn kid.

Be honest with yourself, as honest as you can be. What are you feeling as you do what you do to your son? What do you feel about that young man who stands before you? Feel your rage, your anger, your embarrassment, your shame, your fear, your pride, your grief. Lash out at him in whatever way you have chosen—by rushing him with words or denying him and turning away. That son is your own self, Father, in your own wounded manhood. Do you see that? (Pause)

Now the incident is over. You are walking away from it. As you walk you are rationalizing. It's good for him, you are thinking to yourself. What I said to him was good for him. Your hands are shaking with rage and confusion, but the shaking is ebbing.

Let some time pass. The incident is over. The emotion of the moment is over. What emotions fill the new space? Feel those emotions. Feel your distrust, your shame and grief. You don't mean to curse him. If only he knew. What you wish is for him to raise a healthy family and have a good life. Look at him. All you want is for him to grow to be a decent man. Yet you hurt him. Why? (Pause)

Move forward now to the last time you saw your son. See the place. Stand or sit in it, or lie in it, if it is the time you died. This is the last chance you have had to be with your son and communicate to him what it has felt like to be his father. What was raising him like for you? Talk to your son awhile about what you really thought of him, deep down, beyond all the mistakes and all the hurt. (Pause)

Now move to a time that probably has not existed between your son and yourself. It is the most recent time in his life when he needed to take a hard risk, the most recent time when he needed to trust his manhood to carry him through. See him in this time of decision and sit with him. Hold his hand. Feel the sweat in your son's palm. Feel his anxiety.

What would be the most helpful thing you could tell him

at this time of risk and trust? Even if you disapprove of what his heart tells him to do, support him as best you can. Stretch the limits of your emotions and your fatherhood. This may be your only chance to do it. Even if you are a ghost now—even if you are dead during this time of your son's most recent risk— stand or sit by him and hold him. Take your hand out of his hand and raise it to embrace his shoulders. Embrace your son. Do and say what you must to show this son that, after all those incidents of anger and hurt, there is still within you the core of every father's being, the center of a man who loves his son dearly. (Pause)

It is time to return now from your father's body into your own. Take time to do this. You may find you miss his body a little. You may feel disoriented. Feel his body movements and idiosyncrasies give way to your own. Shake your arms and feel the manhood in them.

With your eyes still closed, run your fingers through your hair. Scratch your mustache, your beard, or your shaved face. Touch your chest and feel your muscles, your ribs. Perhaps reach in and feel your hair, if you have hair on your chest. Touch the hair on your arms. Your hair carries a lot of the wildness of your manhood. Scratch your balls, reach down your legs toward your feet, feeling the stretch in your hamstrings and lower back. This is your body, this is a man's body, this body began in your father's body and in the body of all the men of your lineage, but now it is yours.

When you feel ready, open your eyes. Look around your room, your house. There are ways in which your room and house, or the woods you are in now, resemble your father's world. There are ways in which you and your vision resemble his. But this is your own world and you are the man of this world. You are its King.

Write in your journal whatever feels important about the experience you've just had. Don't try to write everything, just what struck you the most. If the experience of early childhood, for instance, was most powerful, linger there in words and write whatever you can. Perhaps that will be the place you'll go back to with most power as you continue your epic story.

Writing Your Father's Story

Having done these guided meditations as many times as you
need and want to, sit down with your journal or at your compu-
ter and begin a letter to your father, a letter in which you tell
him the story of his life *as you see it*. What was your father's
side of the story as he was wounding you? Much of the material
for this letter you will find in your journal response to the previous guided meditation.

Always remember that it's not important whether you
send the letter. There is no critic, editor, or judging father who
will come around and review it. Your open heart and memory
are all the letter needs.

Free-write the letter, without going back and erasing or
correcting grammar. Follow your father's feelings through the
incidents in which he hurt himself, others, and you. Focus on
those that stand out for you.

> *Dad, I understand you so much better,* Robert wrote. *You
> were so cruel to yourself, like your father was cruel to you,
> like you were cruel to me. When you told me you never
> wanted to see me again that time when you caught me
> masturbating, you were so fucking homophobic. I never
> realized it before. You were so scared I would become a
> homosexual. God you were scared.*

Focus on incidents and answer some questions:

- What was your father feeling as he did terrible things
  to people?
- What of his own past was operating through him?
- What of his own father, specifically, was operating
  through him as he hurt you, himself, and others?
- What did your father's body feel like as he hurt you,
  himself, and others?
- How has your father suffered for having hurt himself,
  you, and others in the ways he has?

Let memories, imagined memories, feelings, and thoughts
flow. Close out other distractions. Stay in your dark cave, or at

least remain in the safe place you've established for the writing rituals of this book. Sit there and, if you are inside the house, turn off the phone.

ISOLATING YOUR MOST DAMAGING
MALE MYTHS AND LEGACIES

Having written your father's story, sit again completely in your own body and feel your own most damaging myths and legacies in his shadow. Go back to the important incidents you remember and ask what messages and patterns they taught you and passed down to you—what legacies your father gave you. Address these legacies to your father.

> *Daddy, every time you hit me,* Peter wrote, *I thought it was okay to be hit. I've allowed other people, men and women, to hit me in various ways, and I haven't stood up for myself. Even my kids hit me, especially Andy* [Peter's adolescent son]. *You've seen it. You told me I should be harder on him. How can I be? I'm afraid of becoming you.*

Peter ended up with seven legacies of this kind. Some men have had more, others less. There is no right number. Whatever is right for you is right.

As you write these legacies, give yourself time. You may need days to recall, process, and distill your most compelling inheritances from your father-son wound. Go over what you've written, not as an editor of form but as a magician, trying to bring out hidden things that did not come out before.

For this writing ritual to be most valuable, it must not be considered complete until you are capable of looking at your own son (real, imagined, or anticipated) and speaking your legacies in a comprehensible, moving, proud way. If you are to break the chain of the dysfunction you inherited in your childhood with your father, you must linger in it awhile.

At some point, you might show some of this work to your son, if you have one and if you feel he is at an appropriate age to understand. Or you might imagine a son in the room and tell him aloud which of the legacies you are trying to heal and transcend.

For some of you, one compelling myth or legacy might seem to loom over all the others. Don't be surprised if you discover in your list of legacies this single, dominant myth. One myth many men acknowledge as most damaging is inadequacy. This makes sense in the context of searching for the King, for the King is the man's root of a sense of adequacy in the world.

"I have a terrible secret," Sam, a very successful lawyer, once told me. "It's a secret I keep thinking my wife, my kids, my clients, and my colleagues will find out any day.

"I feel like a failure. I do everything I can to make like a success, but I always feel like I'm on the edge of failing." This very successful man did not trust himself to make big decisions in his family's life. He was in full possession of his warrior powers in the courtroom. He felt comfortable in that professional container. But in his personal life, where there was no such container, he felt inadequate. His father, he realized, felt the same way.

Our psychological fears—fear of rejection, fear of success, fear of failure, fear of intimacy—have their roots in the fear of inadequacy. It is often a root fear clutching at an adult Prince and keeping him from becoming King. The fear of inadequacy and the legacies that feed that lack can rot the core of a man. If they are rotting your core, admit it now.

When you have spent enough time on this task, move out of your dark cave and rejoin the world. As you go about your life, live in what you've written and are writing. Talk about what you've experienced and written, even to your father if he'll listen. Talk about it with your friends, spouse, therapist, men's group. If you have isolated a single myth within you, a single secret or painful theme of your life, work with that theme in therapy or in your group.

CLAIMING AND CREATING
YOUR SACRED OBJECTS

As you come to the end of this confrontation with your father and as you move out of the dark cave back into your everyday world, claim a sacred object for your altar. Perhaps now is a time to put a photograph of your father or letters from your father on the altar. Or if there is some other physical object that fits this episode of your journey, add it to your sacred space. Let it be an object that represents an underlying sense of successful confrontation with your father. You are less scared of your father now than you were before. You have become him for a while. You know him better. You know your own wound better. And you are stronger and more able to heal it. Claim an object that holds your strength in its container.

You have done a great deal of writing in this episode that might be your sacred scroll. See if the letter you wrote feels to you like it is this scroll. Place it on your altar.

If you should choose to create a new scroll, write a new letter to your father (one that you may never send) that represents your confrontation with him. In it, refer to incidents and vivid memories. If appropriate, refer to a time when that confrontation led to a darker future and more pain.

Relate to your father important moments in this episode of your inward journey toward your King. If you were able to contact him in the first task, relate important things he said. Relate your feelings as he said these things. Stay with incidents, memories, pieces of conversation, and your feelings.

Whether or not you were able to contact him, relate your feelings as you went through the meditations. Tell him what it was like to hold his hand at his deathbed. Tell him what it was like to become him for a time and see yourself, a young boy, in his kingdom.

Write this letter with passion and feeling. Throughout the tasks of this episode, you have been guided toward specific questions and incidents. Sometimes that much guidance can limit and close off pieces of feeling that need to rise. Use the space of this letter now to open those feelings. If you find yourself writing something over and over, let it come. If this sacred object of your confrontation is an outpouring of grief, let it come that way. If this letter takes the form of a direct confrontation with your father—a yelling at him, a rage at him—let that come. Send this letter if you believe it will be helpful, knowing that your father may feel hurt by the letter and that your relationship, while it may ultimately grow, may also suffer for a while. Al wrote and sent this letter of confrontation to his living father:

Dad, this is kind of a continuation of what we discussed on the phone. As I told you, I'm going through a thing where I'm confronting what happened between you and me. I appreciate that you've been okay about it. I know you've done a lot of growing over the years. You've inspired me to do a lot. Like I said before, I'm not going through this to yell and scream at you. At least I'm trying to stay pretty even. I'm trying to understand what happened to me back when I lived with you. I'm really nervous writing you, just like I was when I called.

There's something that happened between us almost fifteen years ago. I need to know about it. I need to know if some memories I'm having are true. I did a thing where I sort of became you and tried to see myself. I had a very strange memory suddenly. You were doing something to me. I was eleven or twelve. You were teaching me how to masturbate. You were holding onto my penis and rubbing it and showing me.

Is this true? I see it so clearly. I'm asking for your help, Dad. I'm asking you, between you and me. No one else will know. Did more happen? Did things happen between us? I have to know. Is this why I don't remember that time in my life? Did I block it all out? I don't want to blow anything out of proportion. I don't really know what I want. I'm going to go find a professional counselor and talk to him about this. But I've got to know, Dad. What do you remember? . . .

Al's letter involved an allegation of sexual abuse. Al's father wrote back that Al's allegation was true. This letter began, for Al, a long journey to come to terms with that abuse, a journey that took him into anger and grief he could not have imagined in this early letter.

Jonathon, whose father is dead, wrote his letter in tears, confronting his inner father about a time in his life when he wished he had been able to confront his father with his real feelings:

I hurt, I hurt. Dad you hurt me, I hurt myself. I went to Vietnam because you wanted me to and I got hurt and it was always like you were hurting me, hurting me. I did it to make you proud goddamnit to make you proud and you kept writing you were proud of what I was doing "over there" and I can't explain it but that hurt me even more because I wasn't proud. I wasn't proud. I hated myself for what I was doing, killing the gook women and children. You loved it and I hated it and I can't explain it but it hurt me that you liked what I was doing. I couldn't explain to you how bad I felt. What was I to you, just an extension, like an arm of yours or a leg of yours, no feelings just feeling nerves and pain! I was like a part of you fighting the war you once fought and were too old to fight again. That's it, right, that's it. I was like your arm out there fighting but you couldn't hear my pain, not for a minute you were so proud. . . .

Jonathon's letter was very long—an outpouring, he told me, like nothing he had felt free enough to do before.

When you have finished this episode in your journey, move forward to the next chapter, in which you will learn where your wounds and scars are, and say good-bye, for now, to the mentors who have helped you.

ELEVEN

Bidding Your
Mentors Good-bye

The pupil will throw off his mentor like a lion, only to find
him again in unexpected places.
                    WORDS ATTRIBUTED TO THE BUDDHA

As the work with your father sits in you, it is time to bid good-bye to both your living mentors and your inner mentor.

You have had different teachers during this inward journey, and more will probably appear before the journey is over. But you've had one primary male mentor, he who walked with you. The act of leaving that mentor is an important part of developing your King. In this journey, that male mentor played the part of your inner Magician. The Magician is responsible for a large chunk of the initiation of the young man—especially for bringing the young man to the place and time of confrontation in the cave. When he has fulfilled these responsibilities, his role is temporarily finished. He will return later, in a different role, but for now you must break with him; if you do not you cannot fully become your own King. Once you know your own King within, you will call the mentor back as vizier or adviser. You don't lose the mentor; he changes roles from substitute father to trusted brother.

If you review your own life, especially your adolescence and early adulthood, you'll recall breaks and good-byes with many mentors. Perhaps it was a high-school coach, a man who taught you a craft, an uncle, a college professor, a friend of the family who used to take you hunting. Sometimes your breaks with these men were amicable, sometimes nasty. Sometimes the man sent you on your way into the next episode of your journey to your own kingship with his blessing. Sometimes he tried to overwhelm you and convert you to his way of life, and you rebelled and spurned him.

As full-grown adults, the way we feel about male authority figures is often tied as much to how we were mentored by men as to how we were fathered. If we had traumatic relationships with mentors, or very few significant mentors, we tend not to trust male authority figures. We tend to feel our own sense of inadequacy every time they give us an order. Mentors can wound us to the core, so breaks with mentors must be accomplished very carefully.

As your work with your father sits in you, this chapter gives you an opportunity to recall your mentors and how you grew beyond them. It also gives you an opportunity to do some healing work with your mentors. And as you work with the mentor, he will continue helping you make further steps in healing your father-son wound.

Male mentors can never become wholly separate in our psyches from our fathers. Both father and mentor are responsible for giving the Prince sacred wounds—the father being more responsible through adolescence, the mentor more responsible in late adolescence and early adulthood. In that way the mentor is a sort of continuation of the father. Later, as a Prince prepares to leave his mentors and move toward kingship, the mentor—in a last action before bidding farewell—is in the best position to help the Prince understand where his scars are, especially those concerning his father.

You may recall that as you left some of your mentors, they didn't hesitate to tell you what work you had left to do. They congratulated you on how far you had come, and encouraged you to go further in certain directions. What they were doing is exactly what mentors and magicians in the sacred realm do in relation to sacred wounds and sacred scars. If those mentors were therapists or trusted friends who knew your family situation, they may even have given you advice about what you still had to do concerning your family of origin and your father.

THE WOUND LOVES A SCAR

The wound is for men a kind of male womb. Men give birth to who they are through their wounds. As we suggested earlier, the woman's wound (her womb), which bleeds every month, gives birth not only to a child but also to a large portion of her sacred identity. Men rely on ritual and sacred wounds to help them bleed, learn their own strength, and thereby give birth to large parts of their mature selves.

In earlier episodes you were led to recall some of your childhood and adolescent wounds. You explored sacred wounds your father gave you, as well as shadow wounds your father and other men gave you. As you move forward in this episode, move back in your journal at any time to review what happened during those stages of the journey.

Wounds become scars, and scars become a source of pride and confidence in men. Of course, scars can become trophies of the Shadow Warrior, worn to show off brute strength and to scare others, like the stereotypical scar across the face that's used to make a pirate captain's or an ex-convict's face look villainous in Hollywood's vision of the world. But in the sacred realm the scar indicates more than sinister hypermasculinity; it indicates the scarred man's very identity.

Such is the case with Odysseus when he returns after his twenty-year journey to Ithaca. He has not revealed who he is yet, still looking around and figuring out a strategy for removing the outlaw suitors from his castle. One of the women who looks after his wife, an old woman who also happens to have been his nurse when he was a boy, is given the job of bathing his feet. He has many scars, but one in particular suddenly worries him—one he received on his thigh when, during his boyhood, a boar attacked him. The nurse would recognize this scar, so he tries to hide it. Too late: as the story goes, "the nurse touched him with the palm of her hand and felt the scar. She knew him and dropped the leg, which fell in the basin with a clang, so that all the water was spilt." Her voice choked with joy, she embraces him, and he swears her to secrecy.

The wound was in the thigh. In Greek mythology, as in Hebrew mythology and so many other mythological clusters, the thigh implies the genitals and often represents the very identity of a man. The thigh connects the man's male identity, his genitals, to the journey he makes in this life, his legs. A wound in the thigh is a wound in his identity as well as in the journey he must make to understand and live in that identity.

The thigh wound becomes, then, symbolic of a man whose identity was once nearly lost, and whose ability to journey was nearly lamed as well. But Odysseus killed the boar and the wound healed and became a scar. By that scar Odysseus became known as more of a man than he was before. He persevered beyond his fears and gained a deeper measure of manhood—in his own eyes, and in the eyes of others. This scar is how he first becomes known upon his return to his castle, his home. By this scar he is no longer a stranger there.

So too in our own lives our scars, most of them emotional, become a way to feel the honor and identity of our own manhood and our own journey. Significant emotional wounds—significant shame and abuse and distance and absence we suffered at the hands of our fathers—bleed in our thighs. As wounds, they threaten our male identity as well as our powers to journey forward. As we heal the wounds, they become scars on our thighs that by healing become as empowering as the wounds were lethal. Now that they are scars they are a source of pride and honor in a way that an open wound cannot be. For even though the open wound honors us, it weakens us, too.

The father-son wound is a wound to our thighs. We have honored that thigh wound throughout this book and worked to understand it, to grieve it, to heal it. By now it should be scarring up a bit more than it was before this journey began.

In this chapter, you'll be guided toward a leave-taking with your mentor, which itself will follow an inventory, in your mentor's presence, of your scars. The mentor stands before you and can often see your scars better than you can. Sometimes he'll see scars already forming where we think we are still languishing in wound. He may also guide us to another place where we did not even realize we were wounded, and where now we have work to do.

TASK 1:
CONTACTING YOUR LIVING MENTORS

Take some time now to contact mentors from earlier in your life who are still alive. Before contacting them, take some steps to

assure that you choose those mentors who would be most useful at this time in your journey. Before contacting them, read
through all of the steps suggested here.

Recalling Your Mentors

Review the material you generated in response to questions
about mentors in chapter 6. Review especially the mentors
whose names you starred.

Choosing Mentors to Contact

Pick one or two of these names to concentrate on. These men
will rise up in your mind's eye, imposing figures from the past.
If suddenly you remember another mentor, concentrate on him
as well.

Follow your guts as you pick these names. Which of these
people do you feel, in the context of your journey, would be
most helpful to you? Which ones do you most want to contact?
In chapter 6 you concentrated on one male mentor in particular,
one man whom you considered, at that point in your journey,
your most significant male mentor. Perhaps he will be one of
the men you'll want to contact now.

"I wonder what old Mr. Tourtellotte is doing right now,"
you might say. Or "I haven't talked to Professor Johns in twenty
years." Or "Weinstein must be seventy by now." Or "Coach
Walker sure put me through hell."

Recalling Each Separation

After you've decided on the chosen mentors, write their names
in your journal. Then write an entry for each man. In this entry
you won't need to repeat work you did in chapter 6—what life
skills and modes of feeling the mentor taught you. Rather,
you'll need to concentrate on recalling your separation experience from this mentor. Was it a painful break? Was it ritualized
in some way? Did you two just drift apart?

Recall how you separated. Tell the story of your separations. Recall the places, the times, the conversations—even the
arguments, the yelling, the bitterness. Recall how you felt afterward and have felt since those breaks.

Perhaps a graduation ceremony was a ritual separation. Or
perhaps your professor came to your apartment for a graduation

party and a farewell. Or perhaps you saw your mentor for lunch every month or so after you had seemed to separate, then just drifted away from each other. Be specific about when, where, and how the separations took place.

Recalling Bitter Breaks

If there is a mentor with whom you had a bitter break, about whom you still feel painful, unresolved emotion, write down everything you can about how you felt during the break, and what part you played in the bitterness. Honor who you were at the time of the break, even if you did and said some things you wish you hadn't. Maybe your mentor just seemed to be too controlling. Maybe you just rebelled, rationalizing at the time that he was too controlling. Maybe now you can see more clearly what was really happening.

Remember that no matter how your separation from a mentor went, it was probably meant to be that way, given your personality and his at the time. A young man must separate from the mentor, and sometimes it just doesn't go easily.

Contacting Your Living Mentors

Get on the phone and call, write letters to, or go visit the mentors you've chosen to concentrate on. Take the mentor to lunch. Take a walk with him. If a mentor is dead, write him a letter anyway. Perhaps try to find this mentor's grave and place the letter on it, or burn the letter in some ritual way in your own ritual space.

These visits, phone calls, and letters are deeply empowering to your King. They help you make separations, no matter how old you are, with male figures whose shadow and power over you still inhibit your own King.

Honor these mentors as you talk to them. You are well prepared to do this because, in having written and recalled all that you have, you're probably better equipped to remember your time with them than they are. Tell them what they gave you and how significant they were in your life. Recall for yourself and express to them what they passed on to you, whether it was helping you see your own gifts and talents and skills, or whether it was teaching you more than your father did about a healthy male mode of feeling.

In talking to each living mentor, ask him how he *saw* you. Tell him how you *saw* him. Tell him how you trusted him. Ask him how he trusted you. Tell him how much you appreciated him. It is a very powerful thing to reconnect with the purpose of celebrating his sacred role as the man who activated a significant portion of your own Magician.

When you're finished having lunch with, visiting, talking to, or writing to each mentor, say a very conscious good-bye to him. Tell him that that is what you are doing.

"You meant this and this to me," you've been saying. Now say, in some tactful way, "I see you differently now. I see you as a wonderful equal now. I need to see you this way. I need to let go of you."

Contacting the Mentor with Whom You Had a Bitter Break

Try to contact a mentor with whom you had a bitter break. There is anxiety in reapproaching any mentor with an open heart. We have the sense that we were so young back then, and we're a little ashamed. There is a special anxiety about contacting a mentor with whom we had an angry break. It is useful, however, to go through this. The break with a significant mentor can leave a profound wound, and that wound must become a scar. Contacting the man who wounded us (or whom we wounded) can help form the scar.

So try to approach the man or woman with whom you had a difficult and terrible break. If you contact that person with some thoughts and memories already written down (as described above), you'll have something to hold on to as you speak. Perhaps contacting the mentor again will give you moments of regression, when you'll feel you have to go back into the role of submissive pupil or angry rebel.

Yet in most cases you will find that the mentor does respect you as an adult man, does not require submission, and really wants to see you confident, strong, and powerful.

Making an Inventory of Your Scars

While writing about and contacting your mentors, take an inventory of what emotional scars you see in yourself.

"I used to roll up into a ball when a woman rejected me," you might recall, "but now I just move on to a new relationship."

"Early in our marriage I responded with aggression to anything my wife asked me to do," you might recall, "but now I know how to handle it."

There have been times when your wounds were so naked you had little choice but to be depressed, or go into denial, or become hypersensitive and angry. Now many scars have formed over these wounds.

Make a list in your journal of each wound or scar. Do not hesitate to number them. Or you can draw a body on a large piece of art paper, a physical body that represents your emotional body. Put xs at any point on the body that represents an emotional wound or scar. This is an imaginative exercise in body memory—the idea being that a lot of emotional wounds still act physically in the body. Back pain, for instance, is often a result of emotional pain carried in the body. By drawing a picture of your body and associating wounds with parts of it, you can reconstruct some of this body memory.

Though you are being led to focus on emotional traumas, your actual physical scars have stories to tell as well. As a way of preparing your imagination and psyche to inventory your emotional scars, you might stand naked in front of a mirror and try to remember the story of each physical scar you see on your body.

Getting Help from Your Mentors in Doing Your Inventory

As you recontact your mentors, ask them in what ways they used to see you as wounded. Then look at yourself honestly now. Are you still wounded in that way, or has that wound become a scar? Ask them to help you with your inventory, if this is the kind of task they would understand and not shame.

"You're so well put together now," a mentor might say after a lunch together. Or "You just seem so much more centered now." Any comment like this is powerful to hear and to feel. Press the subject. Ask what the mentor means specifically. How were you less put together back then? Mentors can often say amazingly wise and perceptive things, things you could not recognize as well alone.

As you take an inventory of your scars and wounds, you may think something is healed up and scarred, only to find two months later that a fight with a partner or spouse suddenly brings the old wound back up again. This inventory does not exist as a final document of who you are. It exists as a way of separating what in you still needs significant work and what work you've already accomplished and probably honored too little.

Mentors are not the only people who can mirror you in this inventory. Friends, spouses, even children can see how you've changed over the years and can help you celebrate your growth and healing. Mentors will, however, because of the special relationship they had with you years ago, give you special insight into your scars and wounds. This act of returning to them for help is a transitional act in your relationship with them. It asks them to mentor to you just a little bit more after all these years. At the same time, you are no longer a pupil. You are asking them, from a position of adult strength, for the kind of wisdom a Magician gives the King. The mentor is standing beside you now as adviser and brother, not ritual initiator.

Connecting Your Inventory to Your Father

As you ask your mentors about your scars and take an inventory of your scars yourself, spend time on the scars and wounds you've received in your relationship with your father. Though you may make some errors in this—blaming your father-son relationship for felt inadequacies that might have origins elsewhere—you'll also make a lot of very surprising, exhilarating, and beneficial connections.

Put a star or other symbol you consider sacred next to wounds and scars that you feel have origins in your father-son relationship. You may want to open more space in your journal to explain why you've put that symbol there and how you believe that wound or scar relates to your father. One man I worked with did not remember, until he connected his inventory to his father, how much he yearned for his father to help him understand his sexuality, and how completely unavailable his father was to help him. His own adolescent phobia of sexual contact, scarred over in his much healthier middle age, came partially from his spurned attempts to discuss sexuality with his father. Small and large connections will occur as you connect your inventory to your relationship with your father.

After you have recalled and contacted some of your mentors, and worked through your inventory of scars and wounds, take a day or two to review the material you have worked with. Sit with it as long as you need to. When you are ready, go on to the guided meditation.

TASK 2:
BIDDING YOUR INNER MENTOR
FAREWELL

Find a comfortable position. Quiet your breathing. Enter your personal ritual of relaxation.

When you are relaxed and ready, see in your mind's eye the landscape of your journey, filled with its forests, oceans, mountain tops. Step out onto the path that you know leads to the meadow. You are dwarfed by huge trees and vines. Cries of animals are all around you. You are not afraid. You recognize this place. You have been here before. There is the archway of the two trees. See your Mentor standing under the archway. Go up to him. Greet him. If he does not appear at first, wait for him to appear.

Let your Mentor guide you under the archway and into the meadow. This meadow is the safe place inside you that no one but you can ever quite know. This is your place of sacred retreat.

Enjoy the meadow as you have before. Hear the song of birds around you, the soft purling of creek water somewhere nearby. Sit on the ground with your Mentor and talk with him. You have just confronted your father. Tell your Mentor what you need to say. Express the power of the experience. Hear your Mentor celebrate your stamina and ingenuity as you went through the confrontation in the dark place. Your Mentor admires you. You can see that in his face and feel it in his warmth.

Feel how absolutely this Mentor believes in your worthiness. Feel worthy of that affection from another man. (Pause)

When you have finished expressing the experience in the dark place, talk to your Mentor about your wounds and your scars. Ask him to help you understand where you are still wounded, and where you should celebrate your scars. Express to him that you feel blind sometimes when you try to see your own wounds and scars. Ask him to guide you toward incidents and memories that display the receiving of wounds and the healing of wounds.

Out of a hidden place on his person, your Mentor will pull out red ribbons, ribbons the color of blood. He will ask you to take off your clothes and stand naked before him. Both of you will stand up.

Once you are naked, he will tie the blood-red ribbons onto your body, in any place where you have been wounded by your father. Sometimes he will tie them to a place you consider strange for that wound, but he will explain why he does that. (Pause)

After he has tied all the ribbons on your body, and after he has explained each one, he will pull off the ones that represent healed wounds. Everywhere that he has pulled off a ribbon, you will now see a scar. Let him explain to you why he believes it is now a scar and no longer an open wound. (Pause)

When he has finished this ritual, run your fingers over the scars. Leave the wound ribbons intact, touching them but not pulling them off. Concentrate your fingers on the rough edges of scars. Enjoy the scars on your nakedness. Express to your Mentor any feelings you have, any memories surrounding these scars. (Pause)

When enough words have passed between you, put your clothing back on, letting it cover both the scars and the red ribbons that remain. Now sit in silence with your Mentor. Look at your Mentor, touch him if you need to, embrace him. Do it silently. (Pause)

Hear your Mentor say at last, "Now it is time for me to leave you."

Express to him how his leaving makes you feel. Ask him how you can find him again. (Pause)

In conjunction with your Mentor, stand up. Hear him say, "When I see you again, I will be your brother." Embrace your Mentor. Embrace him hard, for there is great love between you. You are embracing strong male energy as you need to embrace it, with trust.

When the embrace is over, walk with your Mentor to the meadow's edge. He will leave first through the archway of trees. Watch him go until you can see him no longer. (Pause)

Wait a moment or two and then follow him. Walk back under the archway of trees and up a path through the forest. Some paths have monuments, some do not. One path leads back to the dark place. The one you are on now does not. As you leave the meadow, know that there are many paths to and from the meadow, but there is only one meadow. It is your sacred place. You will not be gone from it for long.

From that forest slowly return to the world of your ordinary life. Take three deep breaths. Open your eyes. As you open them cover them for a moment with your palms.

When you have returned, write what you need to write in your journal. Describe your experience with the ribbons. Where were your scars? Where were your wounds? Don't try to write everything down. Concentrate on just a few important scars and wounds. Concentrate especially on the scars and wounds that connect with your father.

Write your experience as you left your Mentor. What feelings arose for you? Write what you need to write.

CLAIMING AND CREATING
YOUR SACRED OBJECTS

It is time now to claim an object sacred to a relationship with a mentor. Perhaps that object will be a picture of yourself and your mentor together. Perhaps that object will be a picture only of yourself dressed in a uniform of the sport your mentor coached. Perhaps that object will be a letter your mentor wrote you long ago, or something you wrote under his tutelage. Perhaps it will be a tool, a wrench or hunting rifle, he gave you back then. Perhaps it will be something he recently gave you, or a picture you took when you saw each other again all these years later. Or perhaps it will be a strand of red ribbon that reminds you of the blood-red ribbon and the scars.

When you have chosen the sacred object, put it on your altar.

Write, also, a letter that becomes a sacred object of this episode. I've suggested that previous letters be written to your father. This one might be written to him as well. In it you might tell him about the scars and the wounds. You might tell him about your breaks with your mentors. You might connect your feelings about his authority with your feelings about theirs. You might tell him what all this means to you now, years later.

This letter, on the other hand, might be written to one of your mentors. Perhaps it is written to a mentor with whom you had a bitter break—a bitterness you try to resolve in the letter. Or perhaps it is written to a significant mentor who is dead. Perhaps only its ashes will be put on your altar. Perhaps it is written in joy to a mentor who lives thousands of miles away, too far to visit, but not too far to contact by letter. Or perhaps it is written to a mentor who lives near you, a letter you may never send.

> Gerald, whose father and mentor were both singers, wrote as follows: *Dear Dad, I guess I have to admit how hazy things get when I try to remember back and separate how I felt about Mr. Cane, my voice teacher in college, and you. I just called him, because it was part of some work I'm doing, and because I just wanted to. I had a great talk with him. He told me something I didn't remember at all. He told me I kept saying to him, "But that's not the way Dad taught me to do it. Dad did it this way." It was like I was confusing the two of you together. I was substituting him for you or something. But I really wanted you, I guess, and that's why I kept trying to correct him with your way.*
>
> *It was hard talking to Mr. Cane. But in another way it was easy. I felt so much better about myself than I thought I would. I was nervous at first, but then we got to talking and I thought, "He's just a guy like anyone else." I asked him if he thought it was weird, me contacting him after all these years. He didn't think so at all. He said he was delighted. I remembered how much he used to say, "We will all be delighted if Gerald will get on key."*
>
> *You know, Dad, I've spent so much time looking back at my youth, thinking it was a terrible time. But talking to Mr. Cane I remembered a lot of good times. So much of living in the present is about remembering the whole*

past. I've been going through a ritual to see how wounds in me have turned to scars—I'll explain that later. The thing is, what I've been seeing is that I kind of misinformationed the past, if that's a word. Talking to Mr. Cane I kind of felt like I've spent a lot of time spreading misinformation inside me about the past, like what foreign spies supposedly do. I was seeing darkness and distortion everywhere when it wasn't always there.

Then it hit me. I thought, Jesus Christ, that's Dad, that's Dad, that's what Dad was like. That's how you felt, wasn't it! While I was growing up you always seemed so sad. Everything seemed so negative to you. You always said everything was terrible in your past, too. I thought, Jesus Christ, how had this happened! How had I become my father! And what was so weird was that I've spent my adult life not wanting to become you, and I'm proud of how I do some things so differently. But this piece was so sad, so much like your sadness. I'm glad Mr. Cane was there for me. . . .

When you have claimed and created your sacred objects, and when you feel ready, move forward for a reunion with your father.

Forgiving Your Father

For the son who has grown really to know the father, the
agonies of the ordeal are readily borne. . . . He beholds the
face of the father, understands—and the two are atoned.
JOSEPH CAMPBELL

The third step of katabasis is what Joseph Campbell calls "atonement with the father." I call it forgiving the father.

From mercy comes courage, says the Tao Te Ching. The wounded man cannot ultimately be whole without showing mercy to the one who caused the wound. This does not mean the wounded man forgets what the other did to him—in fact, just the opposite. In remembering, there is power. But he does forgive. As Charles de Gaulle said of the wounds Europe experienced in World War II: "Forgive, don't forget."

In the psychology of fathers and sons, as in the mythology of princes and kings, the resolution between father and son occurs after confrontation with the dragons and demons and Great Father Serpent. It also occurs after the parting with the mentor. The prince-hero has been on a journey, faced danger, and then is reunited with the king and father. In most of the Grimms' tales, like "Strong Hans," the prince or young man gains his kingship by reuniting or uniting with a king and marrying that king's daughter.

In Homer's *Odyssey*, the reunion occurs when Odysseus finally returns from his twenty years of travels, dispatching the outlaw suitors with his sword and Telemachus's help. Odysseus shows great affection for Telemachus and Telemachus for him. And just as Telemachus is reunited with Odysseus, so too is Odysseus reunited with his own aged father, Laertes. Resolution between Prince and King, reunion between father and son, mythology teaches us, comes after painful, sometimes near-fatal confrontation. But it does come, and it is essential.

In the archetypal reunion with the father, we see our fathers as separate beings whom we now approach as our equals, not our superiors. We see both the dignity and the fragility of our fathers. We see their strengths and weaknesses. We see them as mortal men who, like the king who promises his kingdom to the young man who rescues his daughters, are ready to give up their dominance and allow us our own power. Confrontation with the darkness, with the shadow, with the dragon is unresolved if we don't have ceremonial and ritualized passing of kingship from father to son.

What this means in terms of our inner journey is that we won't be able to accept the throne from our fathers until we take steps toward forgiving our fathers. As men we have felt this when we have had children of our own or become adults. We begin to hear ourselves say things like, "I understand Dad a little better now, now that I'm going through some of the same things." Or "Some of the things Papa did weren't so way-out after all." Or even, in some cases, "Some of the things Dad did that I thought were wrong and hurtful were right after all." We feel this as we ourselves move into adult male roles and feel the natural midlife urge to reunite with our fathers before they die.

In chapter 10, as you confronted your father, you took steps toward forgiving him. In this chapter, we'll refer back to that moment and suggest ways to further extend this forgiveness. Forgiveness is not something that can be forced. It is not something that comes easily. Yet it is something we can move toward. If this chapter functions only to start you on a path of reunion with what is best and most loving in your father, it will be a step in forgiving yourself and your own masculinity for the curses and wounds it has both inflicted and endured.

REUNION WITH YOUR FATHER

The letter I suggest writing now is the only letter I'll suggest actually sending to your father. If he is dead, consider putting it on his grave. If he's been cremated, consider taking this letter to the resting place of his ashes, burning it, and joining it with those ashes. If you feel you cannot send this letter to him, or if there is no practical way to join it with his dead body or being, find some other way of ritualizing and ceremonializing this letter's existence, and its connection to your father.

The previous episodes of confrontation may have been exhausting. Take some time to recover from those rituals. Take some time to let some of the feelings that arose in them blend into your everyday life. Don't begin this letter until you have lived in the confrontation for days, weeks, even months and have felt the anger ebbing, the confusion and even ecstatic epiphanies contracting again to your normal life rhythm. When you can begin this letter with some feeling of freed spirit, sit down and write.

TASK 1:
WRITING TO YOUR FATHER, PART 1

Here are some of the areas to cover in the first part of your letter.

1. Begin the letter by explaining to your father what you've been through in trying to heal your wound with him. Include episodes you've experienced in this book that moved you.

Here is a piece of what one man wrote:

> Pop, I've been going through this process of trying to heal my wound with you. It's been very painful because I never admitted before that I had a wound. I just did what you did, closing off my feelings. When I went to the workshop and heard about this I said, "No way, my dad was just fine as a father." But the thing is, you were gone so much I grew up feeling really empty.
>
> I really love you and I know you love me, but I just kind of grew up with a sadness I didn't know I had. It was when I was doing this meditation of confronting my image of you that I really started to cry. I just couldn't hold it in. I'm going to send you the meditation I did so you'll see what I mean. I had to become you during the meditation, and when I became you I got the feeling from you that you were lonely. Were you lonely while I was growing up? I love you. I hope you'll talk to me about this meditation.

2. Tell your father about the journey you've made thus far in your male life. Talk to him specifically about what your accomplishments have been. What birthright are you yourself forming through your own deeds, a birthright you will hand on?

Here is a piece of what one man wrote:

> *Grandpa Hector talked about Spain all the time. He talked about coming over here from Barcelona. About always missing Spain. Remember you never wanted to go back there. Never. So I went back. You never stood in my way but I'm just realizing now that I always felt confusion about going back. Like you didn't want me to go. Like there was some shame in you about our Spanish birthright. It wasn't Spain you didn't like. I understand it now. Grandpa had such a bad temper. You never got along with him. In your head he was Spain to you. I wished I realized this before.*
>
> *I don't blame you for anything, but I am happy now that I went back to Spain. I wish you were feeling well enough to go. I would take you. I have a pretty bad temper too. You never did have a bad temper. Maybe I take out my temper on you like Grandpa did. I'm sorry I do that.*

3. If you have children, write to your father about your own fathering. How have you changed his destructive fathering patterns? How have you instituted his healthy fathering patterns? If you have no children, look to relationships in which you mentor young people. You can write this section by looking there.

One man wrote:

> *For a long time I said I wouldn't do anything like you did it with me. But now I'm seeing things differently. I'm becoming like you. And it's not so bad. I think I tried to hold on to my rebelliousness too long, even into my forties, I don't know. But now when I see you with Jimmy I see a lot to like in the way you treat him and I see that even though I hated being your son back when I was a boy, maybe there's a lot to like there too. . . .*

Since you are writing this letter with the intention of sending it, it can't be as free-written as the others. It cannot rage in the same way the others might have. It needs to be tempered. It needs to be written with a respect for the king who reared you, even if you still feel anger, even rage, even fear of him. It should also be written with an equal respect for your own King, even if you still feel some distrust of yourself, some fear of your own inadequacy. Your life is not miraculously cured of its ills, but your being is filled with more power than it had before you began this journey.

After you have written to your father what you need to write about the history of your quest, skip two spaces and start a new section of the letter.

TASK 2:
WRITING TO YOUR FATHER, PART 2

1. In this section, write sentences beginning with your father's appellation (for example, "Dad") and continuing with "I forgive you for . . ." Some of these sentences will become paragraphs.

What do you need to forgive your father for? Write these things even if you don't feel you forgive him for each one. Write them even if there is still anger or if there are unresolved issues for you surrounding many of them. Look back at what happened in previous chapters. Look back at the childhood, adolescent, and adult incidents. What events in those periods do you need to forgive your father for? What lessons did he teach you that you now know were wrong and hurtful?

> "Father, I forgive you for the times you beat me without any good reason. By beating me like this you taught me to be violent and to stuff my feelings . . ."
>
> "Daddy, I forgive you for your inability to hold me and hug and really talk to me . . ."
>
> "Dad, I forgive you for making me go to the college you went to, not letting me make an independent decision . . ."
>
> "Pop, I forgive you for the way you treated Mom during those years you were drinking so much. You taught me to mistreat women, and you taught me to blame them for my troubles . . ."

As you write this, your power comes in separating yourself from your father. Your power comes from saying, "I am a man in my own right, as capable as you to sit in the center of my being and judge what's right and wrong. I've got to tell you that that thing you taught me was wrong. I forgive you for teaching me that, I forgive you for doing that to me. I won't forget it, but I forgive you." One of the great powers of the King is to bless the kingdom. Part of blessing is forgiving, even forgiving former enemies, mending fences, making alliances.

As you bless your father by forgiving him, remember that your father is now part of *your* kingdom. For your childhood and large chunks of your adulthood, you have been a part, a Prince, of his. But now you are asserting that your father is a part of yours, that now in your manhood *your* kingdom and the way *you* need to live your inner and outer lives are of utmost importance. Your acts of forgiveness toward him are acts that a King can make. A Prince isn't capable of that kind of self-confidence yet.

Write "I forgive you . . ." and tell him everything you forgive him for. Keep writing until you've told him everything.

2. When you are finished, go back over the letter and read each item again. Identify those items that you really feel, in your deep heart's core, you can forgive him for. Run your fingers along these sentences, as you would if they were words carved onto the monuments in the meadow of your inner wilderness. Celebrate how far you've come over the years, the months, the days—how much healthier you are now than you may have been years ago, how much more easily you can forgive these things.

Then identify the things your father did that you don't yet feel you can forgive. Feel your own anger, even sadness, as you run your fingers over these, and remember the incidents described by the words you've written. Honor these. Honor the fact that you're trying to forgive your father for these, but that you have more work to do. You'll come back to them. You'll be watchful in your own life not to repeat them. You are a King, and you are ordering and blessing your kingdom. But some of your wounds from a previous attack on your kingdom are still tender.

When you feel ready, finish off the letter in any way you feel is right.

I asked you to write this letter as if you were really going to send it. I asked this because writing it with some temperance and some real respect, and in a voice your father would be able to handle, was a way for you, in the solitude of your own sacred space, to reunite with him. Actually sending the letter would be a further step of reunion. This will never be a perfect resolution; unresolved issues will still remain, and more may rise up when he receives it. But it is an act of reunion.

If you feel you cannot send the letter as written, see if there's any part of it you can send.

If you feel you can send none of it, if you feel that sending it will just damage your relationship with your father all the more, hold on to the letter. You've made a powerful act of re-union within yourself just by writing it. Now all you can do is try to live that act when you see him or, if you never see him, when next you remember him and think about him.

Whatever decision you make about this letter, make it from the vantage point of the King, your father's equal. You are a man who is surpassing your father in some emotional and spiritual ways that he may never understand. This is something you must do in the sacred journey of manhood, and you are doing it with honor.

If you feel you can share the letter with a spouse, friend, or men's group, do so; you will feel strengthened by sharing it. You will feel the King in yourself having the inner power to share the letter and say boldly who you are at this time in your life.

CLAIMING AND CREATING
YOUR SACRED OBJECTS

By now, you have an altar full of sacred objects. Claim another one now—perhaps the pen you wrote this letter with, or a stick or stone or anything else you associate with the place, time, and feeling in which you took this step of reuniting with your father. Claim this object from your journey.

As you decide which scroll to create for this episode, consider including the letter you have written. Perhaps you can make a copy of it and put that on your altar. If it is possible to share the letter with others besides your father, and if there is emotional value to you in doing so, pursue that sharing. Share it in your men's group or with a spouse or friend or even with your own son, if you think he's at an age when he would understand. You may find that by now, as you come close to finishing your journey, enough of your own issues are moving toward resolution that sharing some of what you've been through with your son (and/or daughter) might feel all right. Your children will certainly benefit from that sharing.

If you should choose to create another scroll that captures your forgiving your father, consider writing a poem or some other written form that concerns your sense of reunion.

Dan, a newspaper reporter, had this piece published in his paper on Father's Day. He begins by describing his cluttered attic and a packet of his father's letters hidden away up there, dated May 18 through September 12, 1967, which was during the time Dan was in basic training and going to Vietnam. Dan describes his troubled relationship with his father, his sense that his father, a hard, difficult man, never approved of him.

"There is an old saying," Dan writes, "that a father is someone who expects his son to be as good a man as he himself meant to be. I felt crushed by that pressure."

Dan is much older now and has been through a lot around his father. Things are changing between him and his father. His article continues with text from some of his father's letters—text that, even in retrospect, surprises him:

> *May 18*—*"It seems strange to be writing to my son, inasmuch as I have never had the occasion to do so before. Rest assured that you are in my heart and mind all the time. Although at times I may seem gruff and mean, I am as pleased and proud as punch of you, even more for what you're doing now. Love, Dad."*
>
> *June 6*—*"Keep the letters coming even if they are just short notes. We all wait for the mailman each day to hear from you. Your letters are a thrill to us all. I'll do the same because I know what a word from home means. I used to get so homesick I could bawl. But most of the time I was too busy to think about it. Love, Dad."*
>
> *Sept. 12*—*"Don't get discouraged, son. If the Army*

gets you down, remember, it won't last forever. Your Dad's been in the Navy for 25 years now and after a while you get used to it. So cheer up, keep smiling, and make the most of the three years. After it's all over, you will look back and have some good laughs. Love, Dad."

There's more, much of it mixed with family gossip, all of it in the same vein.

I don't remember how I felt about my Dad's words then. I may not have trusted the emotions I encountered there. Avoiding intimacy, for me, has been a lifelong game of tag.

But I trust them now. My Dad and I have grown closer over the years. I'm 42 and a father myself, so these words hold a special meaning for me on this Father's Day. I can finally see what they say.

I wasn't a disappointment after all.

When you have claimed and created your sacred objects, go on to the next chapter. In this final episode of your journey you will stand in the sun and say who you are. You will claim your King.

THIRTEEN

Standing in the Sun and Saying Who You Are

. . . I am here . . . myself, the same as before, yet
unaccountably new.

D. H. LAWRENCE

You have been through a long journey. Whenever a man goes
down into the dark to confront his demons and their sources
within him, it's as if he has died for a moment down there.
When he returns to his former life, he is changed; he is unaccountably new.

The journey you have made has followed the ageless archetypal pattern of the prince's journey toward his father and his
own kingship. You have asserted that you were wounded, that
you needed medicine for your wounds. You have found some of
that medicine within yourself, using mythology as a guide.

You stand now with the triumph of life in you. You stand
in the sun, ready to say who you have now become and will be.
In ancient Greek tradition, a man's statement after his ordeal,
sung in poetry and song, was given before the sun. The sun was
the sun god, Apollo, whose golden eye watched over men as they
traveled, whose radiance admired their triumph. In Native
American Vision Quest traditions, a man's statement after his
ordeal is often given before the sun. The sun is Father Sky, il-
luminating the man who has just come out of the dark ordeal of
his Vision Quest.

You, too, can participate in this long tradition. You, too,
can sing a song that tells the sun that you have come through
the hard time; that you know what sunlight is now and feel its
warmth in a way you had not before; that the sunlight that

passed from the Sacred King, the god of the sun, to the heads and hearts of your ancestral kings, then to your father, has now passed to you. You are capable now of functioning with the energy of the Sacred King in your own inner life and in your relationships with men, women, sons, and daughters, in a way you were not before.

You have now reached the point in your journey where you make a statement of this new power to the sun, to the Sacred King who watches you from the sacred realm. If you don't feel ready to make this statement—if you are still *in* the work of the previous chapters—go back to that work. Don't read on. Hold off on this chapter until you have confronted and forgiven your father. Wait until you feel ready to ascend to your own throne and to cut the strings to your father's shadow. If you were brought up by some form of the disengaged father, you'll probably never feel that your masculinity is *completely* severed from your father's shadow and the shadow of abandonment in which you were raised. But at this point in your journey, you need to say honestly that some very strong cords have been cut, that some wounds have become proud scars. You must be able to say that you are stepping up to your own throne.

TASK 1:
SURPASSING YOUR FATHER: ACCEPTING YOUR OWN SACRED ASCENSION

It is time to create your own script for your ascension to kingship, just as kings throughout history have held a sceptre and received a crown when they've ascended to the throne. Their sceptre and crown, and even scrolls on which were written certain regal duties, all represented a script for their ascension, a statement of the pride, honor, and responsibility they now had as ascended kings. In a similar way, you are gaining inner power and need a script for how you'll use that power. Without a sacred object or scroll to which you can return for grounding and empowerment in the future, you'll all the more easily fall into the shadow patterns of domination and distance that kings risk falling into all the time.

In your journal, write responses to the statements and

questions that follow. You'll recognize these as statements and questions that were formerly asked of your father, and now are asked of you.

As you respond to some of these statements and questions, you may want to say, "I'll just do things the way I do them now." If you feel honestly that you would not change something you are doing now, celebrate that status quo. Celebrate the fact that in that particular part of your life you are already existing as a powerful King. As you come to statements and questions that you feel you must honestly respond to by saying, "I will change the way I do that," celebrate the change also, for it represents your new power.

Will I Be Known as a Man Who Orders His World in a Healthy Way?

The King orders his world and guides others toward fullness in it.

1. In what ways will I order my life differently?
2. In what ways will I take more time to stay connected and grounded with my sacred center?
3. What rituals will I establish for myself, my family, and society that will bring my own immediate surroundings closer to fullness?
4. In what ways will I take on the responsibility of giving sacred wounds?

Will I Be Known as a Man of Personal Honesty and Integrity?

The King exudes integration and integrity as a man.

1. In what ways will I exist with more integrity than I have in my dealings with my family and my community?
2. In what ways will I take a leadership role in fostering integrity in young people around me?
3. What people must I seek out to get help and advice in fostering my own wholeness?
4. What people must I let go of in order to avoid being drawn into situations of personal and emotional dishonesty?

Will I Be Known as a Man Who Stands Strong at the Center of the Storm?

The King stabilizes chaotic emotion and out-of-control behaviors. He brings maintenance and balance.

1. In what ways will I encourage more stability in my own emotions?
2. In what ways will I encourage more stability in the lives of my family members?
3. In what ways will I take a leadership role in calming others who are in crisis?
4. In what ways will I increase my ability to *listen* to others in crisis?

Will I Be Known as a Man of Passion and Joy?

In his fertilizing and centeredness, the King embodies vitality, life force, and joy.

1. In what ways will I bless and fertilize my own gifts?
2. Which of my accomplishments will I now look on with confidence and admiration, rather than fears of imperfection?
3. In what ways, and with what rituals, will I make the world a place where others are safe to feel joy?
4. What activities will I avoid, and encourage others to avoid, that contract our ability to feel passion and joy?

Will I Be Known as a Man of Gentleness and Discipline?

The King looks upon the world with a firm but kindly eye.

1. In what ways will I try to be a little kinder to myself and others?
2. To whom in particular should I be a little kinder, and how?
3. In what ways will I be firmer in my own resolves?
4. In what ways will I be firmer with others?

Will I Be Known as a Man Who Values Himself and Others?

The King sees others in all their weaknesses and in all their talent and worth. He honors them and promotes them.

1. In what ways will I honor and respect others more than I have?
2. Who in particular deserves more showing of my love and respect?
3. How will I work to promote others' talents in the world?
4. Who in particular deserves more of my loving attention?

Will I Be Known as a Man Who Accepts Himself?

The King is not envious or covetous. He is secure in himself.

1. Whom do I envy, and what must I now do to quiet my envy?
2. What rituals can I establish for myself that will strengthen me when I am feeling envy and help me to respond to envy with a return to inner power?
3. What behaviors must I encourage in myself in order to experience my sacred powers in equal portion to the powers of others in the world?
4. What dreams must I pursue during the remaining portion of my life if I am to feel comfortable with my own limitations?

After you have completed this part of the ritual, take a day or two before moving on to the next. Live with your responses for a while. Perhaps share them with the people they may touch in the future. Work especially for a few days on developing rituals that will help you feel and promote the King within you.

Perhaps writing a journal beyond the auspices of this book will become a sacred ritual. Perhaps a daily or weekly walk outdoors will become a sacred ritual. Perhaps increasing your sacred time with your spouse, partner, and/or children will become a sacred ritual. Perhaps cutting out something unnecessary in your family routine and substituting quality time.

Perhaps joining a men's group or other self-honoring activity.
Return to the questions and your responses at later intervals in
your life. See how you are doing.

When you have answered the questions to your satisfaction, move on to the next task.

TASK 2:
FINDING YOUR INNER KING AND HIS
KINGDOM

What follows is the last guided meditation of this journey. This
one is like the others—something you may want to experience a
number of times, until you meet the archetypes within you that
feel absolutely right to you. When at some future time you feel
yourself to be out of balance in your life, you may want to return to these guided meditations, in which you meet your inner
archetypes. They may have new wisdom and feeling for you at
that time. If issues with your father return, you may want to explore parts of this journey again.

For now, however, we will close the journey in the same
manner in which journeys of mythic sons close: with a final vision of integration and an ascension to kingship.

Find a comfortable position. Quiet your breathing. Enter
your personal ritual of relaxation. Take three deep breaths, concentrating in the last one on nothing but your own breathing.

*When you are relaxed and ready, see in your mind's eye
your ancient landscape. Feel yourself floating above it, as if in
a chariot. Float for a while, enjoying your chariot, your magic
carpet, your ability to fly.*

*Bring yourself down to the forest floor, landing at the
archway of two trees. Drift down slowly. Land smoothly.*

*Now on the forest floor, as you've been at previous times
in this place, you're dwarfed by huge trees and vines. Cries of
animals are all around you. This is your inner wilderness and
you know this place. Recall it from previous visits. Look at the
archway of two trees and recall the archway. Recall your feeling of safety here. See beyond the archway a small meadow.
You want to go into the meadow but something holds you
back. What is it? It is something behind you.*

Turn and see your father standing behind you. See him at your age now. He is bewildered, nervous, looking around. Who has called him suddenly into this wilderness? How did he get here?

Go up to him and embrace him. Even if this makes him more nervous—even if he stiffens—embrace him. Even if this embrace makes you uncomfortable, hold him tight. Embrace your father here, in your inner wilderness, where you are safe.

When you let him go, ask him to say to you whatever he needs to say about the life you and he have had together. Ask him what sacred words he needs to tell you at this moment in your life, as you ascend to your own power. Ask him to express his love for you. (Pause)

What do you need to tell your father at this moment in your life, as you prepare to turn toward the meadow and find your own spiritual center? In a moment, he'll turn away and be gone. In a moment, the father will be a spiritual brother to you, not a superior. How do you feel about this change within you? Speak to your father. Tell him about your nervousness, your fears, your pride, your joy. (Pause)

When you and your father have spoken what you need to say, ask him for his blessing. Let him bless you in any way he chooses. No matter if the blessing is tinged with his own old angers or fears—no matter how the blessing comes out—accept it, for this is your father's blessing. Its sacred feelings can add to the deep well of sacredness within you. Its shadow feelings cannot harm you here in your sacred inner world. (Pause)

When your father has blessed you, say good-bye to him. Shake his hand or embrace him or nod or let him turn away. Do whatever you and your father always do when you say good-bye. After you have said good-bye, wait for him to turn. Wait for him to walk away down the path before him. Don't move until you can no longer see his back. (Pause)

Turn back toward the archway of trees. If you look through the archway you'll see a male figure you didn't see before. You cannot see him clearly. You are too far away. But someone is there. Wait until you can see someone there before you move.

Now move under the archway. Walk into the meadow. Walk toward the figure. Can you see him more clearly? How is he dressed? He is holding something in his hand, a scroll of some kind. Study his face. Who is he? Does he remind you of someone? Is he totally new to you? Who is the man or god who stands at the center of your being? Who is this sacred male whom your imagination has conjured to represent the sacred masculine energy that grounds and centers your existence upon this earth? This figure is your inner King.

Let him open his arms to you. Stop a few feet from him. Let him come to you. Let him embrace you. This King comes to meet you from the deepest region of yourself. This King cares for you. Embrace him. For a moment be in total physical connection. Celebrate this moment. Feel how absolutely your inner King knows your integrity and power. Feel your inner King's strength and wisdom. (Pause)

Hear your King speak: "I am the center of being. I am immovably strong. I am a man of honor. I am the sacred father within you who orders all being. And you and I are one."

With your embrace of the inner King you embrace the cosmos. Through these words and other sacred words and silences in your life you connect with the ground of all being. With the masculinity of this King within you, you know yourself as a strong, balanced, respectful, and honorable man.

Speak to this King. Ask him what you need to ask. Ask him any of the questions from the previous task that you had trouble answering, or whose answers still feel incomplete to you. What advice does this King have about how to bring sacredness into your everyday life? (Pause)

When you have spoken enough for this moment, hear a rustling behind you. See coming under the archway the archetypal figures you have met on your journey. See them circle the King and thus encircle you. Your Magician is walking in. Your inner Warrior is walking in. Your inner Lover walks in. And a figure completely new to you, your inner Explorer, walks in last. What does he look like? He has been with you, invisibly, throughout this journey of exploration. His energy has been in your journal and in your stories and in your search.

These figures and any others who walk into the meadow now encircle you and the King. Let them join hands around you. Let them rotate around you and the King in a quiet dance. Watch them. Follow one of them with your eyes as he makes the whole circle. Standing in place, follow each of them with your eyes as they dance around you. They admire you and care for you. They will never again be far away. You will always be in their circle. (Pause)

Notice a change in your own dress and your own posture. What is happening? You are wearing the clothes your inner King was wearing. You are standing as he stood. Where has he gone? Look at the spot he was standing in. Look outside the dancing circle. You will not find him anywhere but in you now.

Touch your new clothing. Hold the scroll the King was holding. Follow the dancing circle with your eyes. Feel the power of standing in the center of that circle. Feel the power of being he who centers the world. (Pause)

When you are ready, ask the dancers to stop. Look at each of them. Speak to them as a King speaks. Tell each one what you want of him as you become the King. Speak with the spiritual power of the sacred fathers. Speak with the power to order chaos. Speak with the power to bless each part of yourself equally. Speak and hear and enjoy your power. This is sacred power. This is not the power of oppression. This is the power you have yearned for all your life. (Pause)

When you have said what you need to say, close your eyes. You will return to ordinary reality from this King's body so that you'll remember yourself in it from now on. Take three deep breaths and slowly return to the outer world, retaining the feel of the clothes, the scroll or other sacred object in your hand. Sit with the feeling for a while. Come back into the outer world slowly.

When you feel ready, record this experience on paper or on tape. Describe the feelings of power, the archetypes you met— anything you need to write. You are continuing to write the scroll that records your journey to a new sense of manhood, to a sense of yourself as King of your life, connected to the sacred and ordering the ordinary.

CLAIMING AND CREATING
YOUR SACRED OBJECTS

As your journey ends, what sacred objects represent that closure? Do you have a photograph of yourself, sitting or doing some activity that shows you in comfort and strength? If you don't, have someone take a photograph of you doing something that blesses you. Perhaps it will be a photograph of you and your family. Pick whatever object feels at this point like an outward expression of yourself as King. Place it on your altar.

Once you have done this, it's time for you to make a statement of what you have learned and experienced, a kind of proclamation of who you are, now that you have arrived at the end of this journey. It's time for you to stand in the sun, feeling Apollo's admiration, and "sing" who you are.

In this song you'll want to tell what you need to tell as you ask your supportive community to accept and respect you. Tell some of what you have gone through and are going through; some of what you have learned; how you feel connected to the sacred. Engage the great themes as you speak—love, a man's work, children, death, human transformation. If you wish, review your wounds and scars. Honor major life events and your stamina in living. Honor your birthright and spiritual ground. If there has been healing between yourself and your father, now or at any point in your life, speak to that. Speak in any way you choose—in poetry, in prose, in a song you decide to write and put on tape. Speak it privately in your journal or publicly in your men's group or with another audience.

Louis wrote this brief statement and repeated it aloud for one month. He had to get up early to go to work, so he repeated it every morning at dawn—his way of standing in the sun.

> There is room for me in the kingdom of the world.
>
> What my father has cursed, I can bless.
> There is room for me in the world.
>
> What my father left undone, I mourn,
> But now I'll do it.
>
> What my father could not feel, I grieve
> But I will no longer give up those feelings.
>
> I am returning from exile and claiming my strength.
> There is room for me in the world.

Your own statement can be of any length. Its length will depend somewhat on inspiration and somewhat on how long you take to write it.

Dan, who wrote of his Vietnam experience earlier, spoke on a very sunny Father's Day in a church service about fathers. Instead of making a formal statement, he told a story about the partial healing of his relationship with his father. Here are pieces of his story. As he began talking, he recalled that he had just returned from a trip to Nicaragua; that his father was a career military man; that as a boy Dan learned to spit-shine his shoes, to check for dust on door jambs, to be perfect.

> *The problem was that hardly any of this was by choice. The fact was that my father was unable to turn off his military gruffness when he came home. And so our relationship was set early: he was my-father-the-commanding-officer, I was his-son-who-followed-orders-or-else. The or-else part resulted in a regular session with a coiled belt, the sharp pain of which I can feel to this day. Along with many lessons in military procedure, I also learned to equate fatherhood with force and punishment. There was very little room left for love and forgiveness. There was only room for anger . . . .*

As Dan grew up, he rebelled against his father. His father seemed disappointed in him and the two were estranged. His father supported the war and Dan went on peace marches. His father wanted blind obedience. He and his father were still living in patterns of anger and estrangement. The son still felt he was a disappointment.

But over the years, as Dan gained his own profession and family, things began to change. His father mellowed some and Dan matured. Both father and son did some of the work they needed to do. Dan worked with his grief and pain around his father, and joined a men's group. His father, after retiring, got a college degree, bought a motorbike, and let his hair grow out. Son and father started trying to really communicate. It was difficult for a long time, but things began to change.

> *And slowly, we gravitated toward each other. When he was stricken by a kidney-stone attack, I spent several hours with him in the lonely halls of a hospital corridor discussing the meaning of life. We began talking for long periods on the phone. We began to see that the twenty-four-*

year difference in our ages was not as wide a gap as it once
had been. Before we were even aware of it, we'd become
more than father and son. We'd become actual friends . . . .

There was no greater test of this friendship, earned by hard
personal work and years of maturing, than Dan's visit to Nicaragua. His father had always represented the American govern-
ment as correct in all things. Dan was going to Nicaragua without
such a belief.

To Dan's surprise, his father did not lambast him for going.
He supported him.

I couldn't help but be dumbfounded. I still am. This man
whom I feared for so many years, whom I resented and
who I believed was disappointed in what his oldest son
had become, was saying things to me I never dreamed I
would one day hear. He had been transformed from a
mere father figure of distant power into a true father of
gentleness and understanding. It's that father whom I cel-
ebrate today. And I light this candle in his honor, and in
honor of all of our fathers, in the hope that each finds his
own way to become the gentle source of understanding
that all children need—no matter what our age.

In Dan's standing in the sun is a public statement of grief
and transformation, a relationship between father and son that
moved from anger and disappointment to friendship. Dan
gained his King by a hard route, and in the process he also
gained back his father.

When you make your statement in the sun, you join a
group of men who have done a special kind of work, the work of
surpassing their fathers, surpassing the outlaw or diminished
men who once ruled their kingdoms.

Michael Blumenthal published a song in *The Nation*
about surpassing his father and about standing in the sun,
"Poem for My Father at 85 after Cross-Country Skiing with My
Nephew, Marlon, Age 7":

It is as the Good Book says: he whom the gods love,
they correct, so, amid spruce, fir, and pine
dusted with snow, we set out, he in his blue down suit
and the fiberfill gloves I bought him for Christmas,
I in my dark blue vest and red hat, pushing off

like two birds into the hills, gliding up and down
the deeply grooved tracks the others have left for us,
as I call out to him: Suis-moi, mon ami, and he follows,
imitating me, and I am part ache, part happiness
as he glides with such perfect, self-congratulatory delight,
down the hill after me, and two beautiful women turn in
        their tracks to watch, thinking I am his father,
loving the brisk, initiatory glee of it: this young boy
following an older man like an imprinted duck,
waving his arms wildly into the air, bending his knees,
as I fill the white, wintry woods with applause,
calling out Très bon, Marlon, Magnifique! Champion!
Then his cheeks grow pink with contentment and cold,
as we stop at a stump bathed in a tent of clear light,
where I help him off with his skis and we share a banana,
and now we are two men, full of our bodies and winter
and the half-jesting mockery of women, and now it is I,
father, who am an older man, and like all men
raging to repeat themselves, shimmy only half-blessed
toward my own bettering, as I brush the snow
from this fatherless boy, all laughter now,
who must issue nearly alone into the half-lit,
half-darkening world of his own manhood, and then
we are done eating and a white sootfall of flakes
begins again, and I say: On doit retourner.
Les autres attendent, and we start back down the hill,
along the river's trickling glassflow, where I show him
les feuilles mortes de l'année passée, and then
I am thinking, again, of you, with whom I could never
have done this, and, next thing I know, we arrive,
in the brilliant, January light, at the waiting arms
of his mother, and my wife, and he looks back,
this boy who is now leading me out of the woods,
and cries out: Nous arrivons! And I half-weep
my way into their arms, these beautiful women,
pushing one foot in front of the other, planting
my poles like canes, loving what little I can,
turning my face toward the sun, correcting the world.

Make your own statement, in your journal or on tape, in your men's group or before another audience, in which you tell the world about your relationship with your father, how you are surpassing its dysfunction and finding its sacredness. Sing to the world that you are a King, a new man.

Epilogue

We have followed in the discovery of our own King the long and ancient tradition of prince-king mythology. Using the father-son myth contained in Homer's *Odyssey* as our frame, we have gone through the moments in what Joseph Campbell has generally marked as the Hero's Journey. We have seen it more specifically as "the Prince's journey to kingship." We are different men than we were when we went in. We are initiated in a way we were not before we began the quest.

We have been on a visionquest in an inner wilderness. We have met mentors, learned warrior skills, confronted our fathers. We have sought answers to questions of love and relationship. We have learned, as all heroes and men learn, that the great obstacles and the great triumphs lie first and foremost within.

It has been a long journey, sometimes joyful, sometimes painful. It has pushed our boundaries, alerted our defenses, taught us more about who we are, and brought us closer to others. Now the journey is, for this moment in our lives, completed—perhaps to our great relief!

But of course the journey continues. Life itself is meant to be lived as a hero's journey, as a man's visionquest toward the truth. And the truth is not an abstract principle; the truth is self-knowledge. The accuracy of this is clear when we look at the lives of boys and men, and the deepest questions that haunt us.

When an adolescent in search of the true way asks his father, other men, himself, his friends, his mother, and his culture, "How should I know a man?" he will often hear principles in response: "A man knows how to love. A man knows how to shut off his feelings. A man feeds his family. A man is good at sports. A man is wild and crazy. A man changes diapers. A man goes to war." On and on. Some of the responses will be down-right unhealthy. Most will be somewhat helpful. But none will give the young man the truth. None will truly answer the question. We realize this when we become adult males and still are not sure how to answer the question.

The only answer that will give us the truth, the only answer that will satisfy, is, "To know what a man should be, you must know yourself." There is a double message in that answer. On the surface the answer says that you can't discover your manhood without learning what's going on inside you. And underneath the surface the answer says that when you do discover what's going on inside you, you will see how clearly and wonderfully and painfully you are a man.

When a boy asks his father how he should know a man, the father's life must say to the boy, "Know me first, as you seek your manhood. Know me well. Then, when you are of age, know yourself well. Thus you will know what a man is, and live a man's life. And when, later, other boys ask you, 'How should I know a man?' you will answer them, 'Know me well, boy, as you seek your manhood. Then, when you are of age, know yourself.'"

How should we know a man? By claiming our own maleness. Thank you for allowing this book to be a part of your life-long journey of spiritual consciousness. May we meet someday, and meet as Kings.

Appendix

Here is a brief description of each male archetype discussed in this book, its shadow manifestation, and its relationship with the other archetypes. Before we go into new material on the King it is important we have a clear understanding of these archetypes, because in a man they act in relationship with each other and around the man's King. It is important, also, to note that these are not the only archetypes, masculine or feminine, in a man; and that each of these has feminine aspects as well as masculine.

THE WARRIOR

The Warrior is that part of ourselves that protects emotional boundaries and asserts our needs in the world. Where exactly it should stand to protect our boundaries depends on where the King tells it to stand. First a mentor initiates it, as a drill sergeant is the first initiator of the young soldier. But then the King initiates it, gives it a cause, a mission—as a general gives the soldier his mission.

The Warrior serves the King and follows the King's instructions to the letter. Key words to describe the Warrior are *duty, honor, loyalty, discipline, boundaries.* The Warrior's tool is the sword (or any equivalent weapon of protection and assertion, including, in martial arts, the human body).

There is a dance to fencing or sword fighting that dramatizes the Warrior's role. You have danced it in your life without realizing it. We all carry a sword (or its equivalent) in a sheath at our belt, even if we never identify that that is what protects us.

And we manifest that dance in many more ways than the physical. The dance is internal, hidden behind many of our interactions.

Think of yourself at work or playing sports or even in times of physical danger. It is the warrior in you that pushes you further and further in productivity and competition and self-protection. Your sword is in its sheath much of the time. But when you face a challenge from an opponent—your boss, a mugger—the sword comes out. You do battle, fighting against the opponent. You find a powerful solution to the intellectual problem or obstacle in your profession. You protect yourself against the mugger physically attacking you. You compete with the opponent in the game, you shape the task with your sword, you survive the attacker. If you had no sword and knew no dance of swords you would be powerless to compete, to transcend obstacles, to protect yourself. You would simply stand there, numb, without drawing your sword, without showing your power by raising the sword, without exercising your power by parrying the other's sword, and without closing off the dance by returning the sword to its sheath and moving on.

In close human relationships, the dance of swords is essential. Generally in healthy love relationships (and in parent-child relationships), the sword manifests itself verbally. An argument with a spouse, partner, or lover begins with swords in sheaths and ends with verbal jabs that wound. Usually, when the fight is over, both swords go back in their sheaths. Sometimes the dance ends in the death of the relationship. One of you may say, "That's it, you're nothing. I never loved you anyway," and the words wound so terribly that the break in the relationship becomes irreparable. Sometimes the heart is strong; it may take five or ten of these stabs before it "breaks."

The warrior is master of this dance of swords. Within your psyche is a Warrior who knows this dance. If he is well initiated by the King and by mentors, he has discipline. He knows when to go for the kill—and this will be rare, especially in love relationships. More often, he knows when just raising his sword is enough. He does not flail the sword wildly, yelling, "You bitch, I hate you" every time he feels like it. He does not pick unnecessary fights, coming down on his wife or kids for small things that don't really need the showing of his sword. He asserts and protects, always keeping in mind that he is a servant of a higher purpose, a sacred purpose: the life of the King, who is the moral and psychological center of the man's psyche, the holder of the man's knowledge as to what his most important missions and needs are.

When a man kills for no reason, we say his Warrior is in shadow. The Shadow Warrior asserts his sword for his own entertainment, or for ill-conceived gains. Each of us has had moments when we've done something we regretted. We have become enraged and hurt someone in a way we didn't want to. There is Shadow Warrior in all of us, and there always will be. Shadow Warriors in geopolitics often ascend to kingship (to presidency or dictatorship) and take a whole nation into a needless, brutal war.

Because the Shadow Warrior has done so much damage in the world, many people have confused it with the Warrior, asserting that we need to get rid of the Warrior within us altogether.

Accomplishing this is impossible and dangerous. The Warrior is archetypal and essential to our survival and to our growth. As long as fate, crisis, and other obstacles and challenges exist—that is to say, as long as we are alive—we need the Warrior. What we need to work toward, mythology teaches us, is a healthy, *initiated* Warrior, and a Warrior so well taught and disciplined by a healthy King that it knows how to control its own shadow aspect. Often we discover that men who are overly aggressive have come from homes of fathers who taught them to be so—that is, from homes of abusive fathers—or from homes in which the father did not initiate them in any substantial healthy way. The son does not learn control of his shadow in either of these homes.

The Warrior is projected by us as young children onto parents, older brothers, powerful friends, and figures from popular culture. When we are little, the Warrior is still out there. We experiment with it, fighting other boys with swords, but when push comes to shove most of us run away from fights, expecting our elders to come into the fray and save us.

We learn the strengths of our own inner Warrior as we individuate; we start defending ourselves and, especially in adolescence, start asserting our own needs whenever possible. In the sacred realm, rituals and ceremonies of adolescence are set up as rites of passage in which sacred wounds are inflicted by fathers and other men, wounds by which we taste our own blood and know our own strengths.

The Warrior, then, is that part of ourselves that guards our boundaries and asserts our needs. It is activated throughout childhood and especially in adolescence. If Kings and Magicians in our lives don't do a good job, our Warrior will be activated in its shadow aspect, falling easily to rages and bullying; or it will barely be activated at all.

THE MAGICIAN

You are five years old. Your bike is broken. You know there is nothing you can do to fix it. Your father comes home. Using a few tools, he fixes it as good as new. Magic!

A clown comes to your eighth birthday party and does magic tricks. He pulls handkerchiefs out of his arm, then shoves them in his hat, then says some magic words and, *voilà*, out comes a live bird!

You are twelve years old and an uncle teaches you how to drive an old tractor that once seemed too huge for you ever to negotiate. A mystery has been revealed to your young mind and body!

You are twenty and a college professor blows your mind with her ideas!

All of these external manifestations of magic reflect an archetype within us that we call the Magician. The Magician holds our power to transform things. The Magician knows the mysteries and uses them to alter life. When we watch it we are amazed at his powers. When we truly know it in ourselves, life becomes a richer experience than we can imagine. We become empowered to know mystery, to transform the world, and to transform ourselves.

As we grow up and individuate, the Magician that was our father and our uncle and our college professor and the clown is discovered within us. We become able to do magic tricks and fix bikes and drive tractors and even rockets. We begin to blow

others' minds. We get initiated by these elder magicians into
our own abilities as Magician.

For healthy manhood to be ours, even deeper initiations by
magicians need to occur. We need to be spiritually initiated into
the mysteries that sacred space and ritual can reveal within us.
Elder magicians need to initiate us into the transformative
powers in our sacred selves. This is what we were getting at in
chapter 2; a large part of a boy's separation from boyhood and
arrival in manhood is ritual initiation into life-the-mystery,
and into his own powers to transform his inner world as it faces
the mystery. Our culture initiates young men very well into
outer mysteries and technologies—tractors and molecular biology—but does not initiate us very well in the inner mysteries.

Shadow manifestations of the Magician are the destructive trickster and the false shaman. In our culture, a culture
dominated by barely initiated men, we are overwhelmed by
tricksters, especially in the guise of politicians and inside
traders and commercial advertisers, who get what they want
through tricks of image or word, tricks that deceive, rob, and ultimately destroy self-image. In response to a popular culture
seemingly ruled by tricksters, our culture also breeds a false
shaman a minute. Everywhere there is someone with the key to
life who will save us from all the other false, inauthentic, ma-
nipulative money magicians. Usually this false shaman takes
us back to "simpler values." Usually this false shaman promises
to reveal mystery altogether. You know a shaman is false when
he or she pretends to reveal mystery altogether.

Deep within each of us is a trickster and a false shaman.
Our own capacity to lie and shroud the truth has even saved us
heartache here and there. What the trickster and false shaman
can't give us is authentic self-transformation. Truth cannot be
revealed through theft. We must each get to know the mysteries
of our psyches and of the sacred realm within us so that our
own Magician can teach us transformation, and so that we do
not have to rely on false shamans without.

Primary in the Magician's relationship with other archetypes are (1) his role as initiator of and mentor to the Warrior,
noted above, and (2) his essential role in relation to the King: he
tends to sit close to the King, "at his right hand," a vizier, an adviser, a trusted brother. The Magician acts the role of initiator
in the development of the boy, then acts the role of trusted ally

to the adult man. In your own life perhaps you have experienced how men who were mentors to you when you were a boy have become trusted advisers now that you are a man. So it is within you. The center of your masculinity, the King, is advised by the Magician as to the powers available to transform the world and the psyche.

If you think about kings in mythology, you will recall that a king always had a trusted adviser, sometimes a technician who only knew the mysteries of political intrigue, but more often a priest or a Merlin who knew the sacred mysteries and helped the king feel connected to Godhead.

Sometimes within a psyche, as also happens in our outer worlds, a hard break with a mentor will occur. Sometimes we will have spent years connected to a certain vision of sacred mysteries and then find that something explodes within us. We can no longer believe in that Christian or Jewish or Hindu view anymore. Our psyche may sometimes throw out that Magician and start seeking another. Soon a new Magician will appear who knows the mysteries and brings new powers of transformation to the kingdom. Or perhaps this new Magician is not new at all. Rather, it is our Magician in a new guise. The King, strong in his center, will enjoy this new power and insight, accepting the new way of mystery from the Magician.

THE LOVER

The Lover is perhaps the most misunderstood and unexpressed part of the male psyche. The Lover in the male, as in the female, is the part of ourselves that feels absolute delight in the world and unconditional love. The Lover's arms are always open. The Lover has no boundaries of its own. All other parts of the psyche tell it what to do and where to do it. Meanwhile, it just strives to do whatever is emotive and passionate and loving. It is activated by beauty, sensuality, children, sex, relationship, nature.

When you are sitting out by the river and see the sunlight glimmer in the water in a certain way, and you are filled with a sudden and absolute delight, that's your Lover rising up for a moment, enjoying the world. The great moment of sexual union activates the Lover. Deep and abiding love for another human being is the Lover giving unconditional love and taking absolute delight in the body and spirit of another. Tears of joy when watching your child perform in a school play are the Lover taking absolute delight. If you recall moments of joy, of sensual delight, of unfettered emotional intimacy, you are recalling moments when the Lover was activated in your psyche.

The Lover is the first archetype within us to emerge in our lives. When we are first wrenched from the womb, we might say the Warrior cry rises up to tell the world we are angry as hell at all this damn fluorescent light. But very soon it is the Lover that our parents' affections activate. The Lover cuddles, coos, sings. We are tiny infants, with very little King, Magician, Warrior, or Explorer. Throughout our infancy, the Lover is open, arms wide, seeking attention and affection all the time. Soon our Explorer begins to search through the world. Then we develop our Warrior, we seek to become little Magicians, and we follow the Queen and King around, seeking our own Great Feminine and Great Masculine selves. But early on we are the naked Lover.

What happens to this Lover? Where does it go? Why do men and women both complain at every adult turn that men are "bad at relationships," "don't have feelings," "can't open up," "can't communicate loving emotion?" Where does the male Lover disappear to?

Robin Norwood's book *Women Who Love Too Much*, subtitled *When You Keep Wishing and Hoping He'll Change*, makes the argument that women seem to have too much Lover and men seem to have very little. Women are put in the position of being responsible for the love relationship. They end up opening their hearts with the often-unrequited hope that men will open theirs. Men remain closed.

This dynamic has been the starting point of books on the subject by men as well, such as Herb Goldberg's *The New Male* and his *The New Male-Female Relationship*. Women are trained to be "in relationship." Men are trained to compete, and thus to be against close relationship. The Lover in men somehow becomes imprisoned in a dungeon, often never to be freed. It becomes so paralyzed that a man once said in a men's group, "I want to feel things, I really do, but I just can't."

Most of us, as boys, found the Lover within us shamed from very early on. We were taught not to cry, not to feel unconditional love or absolute delight. We were taught to develop the Warrior as quickly as we were able. At five years old we were already told, "Be a man, dammit!" Often there was a battle within our families over this: our mothers kept trying to activate the Lover in us; our fathers kept trying to shut it down. Our mothers kept saying it's all right for us to cry; our fathers kept saying it's not. Or even if our mothers and fathers both supported the continued activation of our Lover, even if both of them said, "Go ahead and cry, go ahead and cuddle and give hugs, be sensitive and open," the culture around us—television, magazines, peer pressure, and school—taught boys to curtail the Lover, to curtail their tears and honest emotion, and to develop their competitive spirit, their "warrior."

For decades men and women have argued that this approach toward male development has curtailed the feminine in men. These thinkers, even including Carl Jung, associate emotion with women and reason with men. Thus, it has been argued, men have lost their feminine side when they are shamed into losing their ability to feel deep and fragile emotion.

I believe this is a dangerous misconception. It proposes that there is less capacity to love within the male spirit than within the female. It proposes that to learn to love, men must become more like women. This is a convenient stereotype, but is disempowering for men. What instead must happen is that men must become more like men.

In the process of boys and men being taught to hide and in fact deny emotion, the Lover within men has become imprisoned deep in the self, forced there by the Shadow King (or Prince) who, viewing the world, sees that gentle and passionate emotion in a man is dangerous to the survival of the psyche, and by the Warrior, who is ordered to keep the Lover, for the Lover's own good, imprisoned.

They are not just throwing the feminine in prison; they are throwing the masculine archetype of the Lover in prison. It is this masculine Lover that empowered women want. I do not believe empowered women are pleading with men to bring out their feminine; that is just a convenient label. They are pleading with men to bring out the healthy, empowered masculine Lover who will give them, as women, the empowerment of partnership between opposite sexes, not just the boring comfort of married life between two feminine elements. A woman who is empowered wants a man who is empowered. She does not (unless that is her psychosexual preference) want a partner ruled by the femininity in which she is already immersed. If she did want that, the masculine within her would never be activated by her partner, and she could not be whole.

George Taylor, a men's group leader in the San Francisco area, once said, "It's not that men don't know how to feel; it's that they don't have a safe place to feel in." This is key, I believe, to understanding what happens to men and love. Men do not feel safe anywhere in the world to let this masculine Lover out of prison. Thus even men join the chorus of disempowerment that sings that for men to love they must "bring out their feminine," and "become more like women."

Even as men sing this chorus, the masculine Lover remains in prison. He will continue to have moments of escape, loving in spurts, infatuations, fantasies. He will continue to become addicted to the spurts, the little escapes. Even his escapes will continue to be short spurts, because the Shadow King or the immature Prince within us, sitting at our center, will order him back to prison, and the Warrior, following orders, will continue to bring the Lover back just as soon as he is discovered missing.

Feminine elements of the male self do certainly get imprisoned in a man. But they are not all that the man must free. It is especially the pattern of archetypal imprisonment of the masculine Lover that we can and must take experiential steps toward changing. In Part II of this book we take some of those experiential steps. We explore what a masculine Lover looks and feels like within us. We learn from our feminine elements, but we have the task, ultimately, or reclaiming our masculine Lover.

THE EXPLORER

As with the other four archetypes, the Explorer begins in our childhood as a projection onto our mother and father, who leave the house and then come back bearing gifts and stories—especially onto our father, who usually leaves home more than our mother. The Explorer is also projected onto relatives, family friends, and guests who come into the house with various stories to tell. Like the other four archetypes, it moves inward as we grow older, as we are initiated by ritual explorers (our parents, our older siblings, our friends), and we form the inner Explorer.

To see this Explorer clearly in a child, think of yourself as a young boy who has just learned to walk. Picture your father sitting on the front steps and you, fifteen months old, running across the yard, ready to step down into the street. You are exploring in any and all directions. Your father, like a King, seeks to order your boy's world. "Don't go out there," your father says, "it's dangerous." And perhaps you don't go out, at least not until Dad's not looking.

In a few years, your boundaries of exploration will not be the street; they will be the town or the state. And you will keep exploring, in books, in cars, in boats, in foreign lands.

The Explorer is the archetype within us that is curious. We have all felt this part of ourselves as we have developed, the part that embodies wonder. No matter how confined we are, whether in family responsibilities or physically in a wheelchair, the urge to explore often supplants every other urge. In our spiritual and emotional life we are always exploring new ways to see ourselves, new ways to understand the world. When our Explorer is activated, our vehicle might be our car or a television set or a new idea that takes hold of us.

The Explorer is a scout for all the other archetypes. The King, the Magician, the Lover, the Warrior—all will send the Explorer out to see what's around the next corner. In love relationships this is subtly clear to us. Before we reveal our whole Lover to someone else, we explore that person, we send out feelers, we get to know her. Our Explorer mediates between our Lover and hers.

The Explorer is the least bound within the constellation of archetypes. He is not, like the King, sitting in the center of the kingdom, nor, like the Magician, on the King's right hand; nor, like the Warrior, is he stationed at the boundaries, nor, like the Lover, naked and vulnerable and therefore protected deep within the kingdom. Yet he is bound, as all the others are, by the King, who centers and orders everything and who gives him instructions. Like explorers of Spain and Holland and England and France in the fifteenth and sixteenth centuries, the inner

Explorer needs instructions and blessing before he sets out on his next search.

The Explorer's tool is the map. We are always making maps—both before we explore and afterward. Whether we are Amerigo Vespucci or Vasco da Gama or Lewis and Clark or a man preparing for a family vacation, the Explorer within us loves maps in the same way the Warrior knows the world in his sword, the Magician through his magic, the Lover through his senses.

When the Explorer is in shadow, he wanders too much. The man who is existing in his Shadow Explorer cannot settle down, is never content or satisfied, believes the grass is always greener somewhere else, and acts on it by giving up the stability and security he has achieved. As with all the other archetypes, the Explorer's shadow aspect often relates to the King; if a man does not have a strong center and does not feel spiritually and emotionally grounded in this center, he becomes lax in controlling his Warrior, he allows the Magician's magic to tantalize him into moments of ecstatic blindness, he does not aid the Lover's journey, he does not give his Explorer specific and sacred missions. Thus the Explorer, eternally dissatisfied, takes over the psyche.

Some amount of dissatisfaction is built into manhood. As Goethe said, "It is impossible to satisfy a man." But too much dissatisfaction indicates that a man is allowing his love of exploration to become an addiction to wandering.

It is your Explorer who is constant in the search for betterment. It is therefore your inner Explorer who has begun your journey in this book, and who brought you to many other self-initiations over the years. It is this Explorer who will introduce you to your inner Prince. It is this Explorer who is right now studying the map of this book and this journey.

We are wounded sons seeking healthy personal power, a sense of a strong male center, a King that we cannot find if we remain wounded sons, undeveloped Princes. One of the most inhibiting qualities of our wounds is that we are so isolated from our deepest feelings, our secret inner life, that we cannot immediately discover these feelings and damaging myths. We cannot, with the snap of our fingers, know the wounded Prince inside us. We need to set out on the Explorer's chariot for a while, getting a sense of the landscape, of the past, of the terrible pain and the powerful tools that linger within.

The Explorer helps us scout out and get comfortable with the wilderness. Especially in part I of this book, we let the Explorer sift through information. In part II, we move to activate other archetypes. We walk more deeply in the wounded Prince's body. Because the Explorer has done his mapping in part I, we are ready for pain, joy, and grief in part II. We will not cow from our wounds.

THE KING

Though the King is developed in depth in chapter 1, a special note must be made here to the debt I owe to the work of Sir James Frazer, John Weir Perry, Joseph Campbell, Geoffrey Ashe, Robert Bly, and Robert Moore and Douglas Gillette. Moore and Gillette's *King, Warrior, Magician, Lover* provided me with updated information and inspiration on masculine archetypes, especially the King.

Selected Reading

Roger D. Abrahams. *African Folktales*. New York: Pantheon Books, 1983.

Aleksandr Afanasev. *Russian Fairy Tales*. New York: Pantheon Books, 1945.

Geoffrey Ashe. *The Discovery of King Arthur*. London: Guild Publishing, 1985.

Morris Berman. *The Reenchantment of the World*. Ithaca, NY: Cornell University Press, 1981.

Bruno Bettelheim. *The Uses of Enchantment*. New York: Vintage Books, 1977.

Robert Bly. *Iron John*. Reading, MA: Addison-Wesley, 1990.

_____. *What Stories Do We Need?* Audiotape. New York: ARC Audio.

Jean Shinoda Bolen. *Gods in Everyman*. New York: Harper & Row, 1990.

John Bradshaw. *Healing the Shame That Binds You*. Deerfield Beach, FL: Health Communications, 1988.

_____. *Homecoming*. New York: Bantam Books, 1990.

Joseph Campbell. *The Hero with a Thousand Faces*. 2nd ed. Princeton, NJ: Princeton University Press, 1968.

_____. *Historical Atlas of World Mythology*. New York: Harper & Row, 1983.

_____. *Myths We Live By*. New York: Bantam Books, 1988.

Joseph Campbell, commentator. *The Complete Grimm's Fairy Tales*. New York: Pantheon Books, 1972.

Allan Chinen. *In the Ever After: Fairy Tales and the Second Half of Life*. New York: Chiron, 1989.

Robert Coles. *The Call of Stories*. New York: Houghton Mifflin, 1989.

Mircea Eliade. *Rites and Symbols of Initiation*. New York: Harper & Row, 1975.

Richard Erdoes and Alfonso Ortiz. *American Indian Myths and Legends.* New York: Pantheon Books, 1984.

David Feinstein and Stanley Krippner. *Personal Mythology.* Los Angeles: Jeremy P. Tarcher, 1988.

James Frazer. *The Golden Bough.* New York: Macmillan, 1907.

Herb Goldberg. *The New Male.* New York: Signet Books, 1979.

Stanislav Grof. *The Adventure of Self-Discovery.* Albany: State University of New York Press, 1988.

Michael Gurian. *The Odyssey of Telemachus.* San Francisco: Swallow Song Press, 1990.

Mark Helprin. *A Soldier of the Great War.* New York: Harcourt Brace Jovanovich, 1991.

Gilbert H. Herdt, ed. *Rituals of Manhood: Male Initiation in Papua New Guinea.* Berkeley: University of California Press, 1982.

James Hillman. *Revisioning Psychology.* New York: Harper & Row, 1975.

Jean Houston. *The Search for the Beloved: Journeys in Sacred Psychology.* Los Angeles: Jeremy P. Tarcher, 1987.

Aldous Huxley. *The Perennial Philosophy.* New York: Harper & Row, 1944.

Robert Johnson. *Inner Work: Using Dreams and Active Imagination for Personal Growth.* New York: Harper & Row, 1986.

Carl Jung. *Psychology and Religion.* Princeton, NJ: Princeton University Press, 1958.

Carl Jung, ed. *Man and His Symbols.* New York: Doubleday, 1986.

Louise J. Kaplan. *Oneness and Separateness: From Infant to Individual.* New York: Touchstone, 1978.

Gershen Kauffman. *Shame.* Cambridge, MA: Schenkman Books, 1980.

Sam Keen. *Fire in the Belly.* New York: Bantam Books, 1991.

———. *The Passionate Life.* New York: Harper & Row, 1983.

Sam Keen and Anne Valley-Fox. *Your Mythic Journey.* Los Angeles: Jeremy P. Tarcher, 1978.

John Lee. *At My Father's Wedding.* New York: Bantam, 1991.

Albert B. Lord. *The Singer of Tales.* Cambridge: Harvard University Press, 1960.

Rollo May. *The Cry for Myth.* New York: Norton, 1989.

Alice Miller. *For Your Own Good.* New York: Farrar, Straus and Giroux, 1983.

Alexander Mitscherlich. *Society without the Father.* London: Tavistock, 1969.

Robert Moore. *King, Warrior, Magician, Lover: Rediscovering Masculine Potentials.* Audiotapes. Wilmette, IL: Chiron, 1988.

Robert Moore and Douglas Gillette. *King, Warrior, Magician, Lover.* San Francisco: HarperSanFrancisco, 1990.

Augustus Napier with Carl Whitaker. *The Family Crucible.* New York: Harper & Row, 1978.

Shirley Nicholson, ed. *Shamanism: An Expanded View of Reality.* Wheaton, IL: Quest, 1987.

Samuel Osherson. *Finding Our Fathers.* New York: Fawcett Columbine, 1986.

Carol S. Pearson. *The Hero Within.* New York: Harper & Row, 1989.

John Weir Perry. *Lord of the Four Quarters: Myths of the Royal Father.* New York: Braziller, 1966.

Alix Pirani. *The Absent Father.* London: Arkana Books, 1988.

Gabriele Rico. *Pain and Possibility.* Los Angeles: Jeremy P. Tarcher, 1991.

W. H. D. Rouse, trans. *The Odyssey.* New York: Mentor Books, 1937.

Lillian B. Rubin. *Intimate Strangers.* New York: Harper & Row, 1983.

Maggy Scarf. *Intimate Partners.* New York: Random House, 1987.

Idries Shah. *Tales of the Dervishes.* New York: E. P. Dutton, 1970.

_____. *World Tales.* New York: Harcourt Brace Jovanovich, 1979.

Harry Slochower. *Mythopoesis.* Detroit: Wayne State University Press, 1970.

Elizabeth Stone. *Black Sheep and Kissing Cousins.* New York: Times Books, 1988.

Hyemeyohsts Storm. *Seven Arrows.* New York: Ballantine, 1972.

Victor Turner. *The Forest of Symbols: Aspects of Ndembu Ritual.* Ithaca, NY: Cornell University Press, 1967.

————. *Ritual Process.* Ithaca, NY: Cornell University Press, 1977.

A. E. Uysal, ed. *Selections from Living Turkish Folktales.* Ankara: Ataturk Kultur, Dil Ve Tarih Yuksek Kurumu, 1989.

Marie-Louise Von Franz. *Interpretation of Fairy Tales.* Dallas, TX: Spring Publications, 1970.

————. *Puer Aeternus.* Boston: Sigo Press, 1981.

Lee Wallas. *Stories for the Third Ear.* New York: Norton, 1985.

David B. Wexler. *The Adolescent Self.* New York: Norton, 1991.

D. W. Winnicott. *Human Nature.* New York: Schocken Books, 1988.

Marion Woodman. *The Ravaged Bridegroom.* Toronto: Inner City Books, 1990.

Jane Yolen, ed. *Favorite Folktales from around the World.* New York: Pantheon Books, 1986.

Among selected readings for this book were pertinent issues of *Utne Reader, Mentor, Wingspan, The Sun, Boulder Men's Council Journal, The Men's Journal, MAN, Seattle M.E.N., The Family Networker, Journal of Marriage and Family Therapy, The Spokesman-Review,* and *The Spokane Chronicle.*

ABOUT THE AUTHOR
AND THE MYTHOS INSTITUTE

Michael Gurian, co-founder of the Mythos Institute, has been working with mythology and gender issues for over ten years. A counselor, poet, and storyteller, Michael has led men's groups in various settings, from churches to prisons, since the mid-1980s. He leads men's wilderness events and gender-reconciliation workshops for men and women throughout the United States and Canada. Adjunct Professor at Gonzaga University, Michael is also Director of the Inland Northwest Men's Evolvement Network. *The Prince and the King* is his third book.

Mr. Gurian and his colleagues offer workshops, seminars, and individual and organizational consultation. Their work is designed to help men and women better understand and achieve healthy male spiritual growth and healing in their private lives, work, and relationships. For more information, write to the Mythos Institute, P.O. Box 8714, Spokane, Washington 99203, or phone 509/624-0623.

A two-tape audio set entitled *The Prince and the King: Guided Imagery for Confronting Your Father and Discovering Your Masculine Potentials* is available from The Sounds True Catalog. The tape features all of the book's guided imagery, set to meditative background music:

- Meeting Your Inner Mentor
- A Visit with the Old Men
- Meeting Your Inner Lover
- Meeting Your Inner Warrior
- Meeting Your Father Again
- Becoming Your Father
- Bidding Your Mentors Goodbye
- Activating Your Inner King

The tapes are available for $16.95 plus $3.00 for shipping and handling. To order please call 1-800-333-9185 or send check or money order to:

The Sounds True Catalog
Dept. MG
735 Walnut St.
Boulder, CO 80302